VICTORIOUS
WHO CHANGED THE WORLD

Peter Hammond

Reformation Society
Cape Town

VICTORIOUS CHRISTIANS
WHO CHANGED THE WORLD

by Peter Hammond

*Typesetting: Colin and Marion Newman
Cover Design: Riaan Rhode and Colin Newman*

Christian Liberty Books

P.O. Box 358 Howard Place Pinelands 7450
Cape Town South Africa
Tel & Fax: (021) 689-7478
Email: admin@christianlibertybooks.co.za
Website: www.christianlibertybooks.co.za

Dedication

This book is dedicated to my daughter
Daniela Christine Hammond
May you continue to stand steadfast in the Faith
and be courageous like the Daniel you are named after.
May God bless, guide and strengthen you to be a victorious Christian.

Victorious Christians
Who Changed the World
by Peter Hammond

CONTENTS

Foreword
by Dr. Joel R. Beeke

"Remember them which have the rule over you,
who have spoken unto you the Word of God:
whose faith follow, considering the end of their conversation.
Jesus Christ the same yesterday, and to day, and for ever."
Hebrews 13:7–8

Christians today have short memories. They sometimes feel rootless, for they have forgotten their heritage. But it was not always so. When the Reformers and Puritans wrote, they quoted godly leaders from a thousand years before them as still relevant for their day. Today we have an even richer treasury of Christian biography. We are surrounded by a great cloud of witnesses indeed—at least six thousand years of Covenant-keepers. And the Bible says, *"Remember them."* Get to know the men of God who adorn the pages of church history. For in remembering them you will see Jesus Christ, and He remains ever the same.

This book will help you to do that. Written in language ordinary people can understand, and beautifully illustrated, it is a welcome introduction to remembering our spiritual fathers and mothers. Here you will find ministers, musicians, missionaries, and martyrs. The table is spread with many dishes—thirty-two biographies ranging from the second century to the twentieth century. Yet each comes in a bite-sized portion which you can read in a single sitting. When the meal is done, you will be satisfied. You will know that you have roots, an identity, and a legacy from godly ancestors. The Christian has a family tree that is older than any nation on earth. And your appetite will be whetted to learn more about your spiritual family through the ages.

May God graciously add His blessing to Dr. Hammond's book, grant it a wide circulation, and continue to bless his courageous and multifaceted ministry to the building up of His Kingdom and the breaking down of the strongholds of satan.

Dr. Joel R. Beeke
Puritan Reformed Theological Seminary   Grand Rapids, Michigan

Introduction
by Dr. Ian Paisley

The title of this book – ***Victorious Christians – Who Changed the World*** is a title that well describes those who hungered and thirsted for Righteousness. They tasted and saw that God was good but their Salvation experience did not stop there. Taking up the name of Christian, they went on to lead victorious lives, which still inspire the Church of Christ on earth today!

In reading of these saints I am reminded of the words of John Bunyan:
"Who would true Valour see
  let him come hither;
  One here will constant be,
  come wind, come weather.
  there's no discouragement,
  shall make him once relent,
  his first avow'd intent,
  to be a Pilgrim."

The characters who fill these pages are men and women of differing natures and abilities, diverse in their talents and individual in their contribution to history, but they all have the common mark of the Cross upon them.

From age to age, from century to century, from decade to decade, God has His peculiar people set aside for His glory. That glory is diligently recorded in these pages. This work is not only a book which will encourage the believer, but it is a book which will help the scholar. Dr Peter Hammond has done the donkey work – you and I are indebted to him for his labour.

More importantly, he has recorded for another generation these 'Pilgrims of Valour' who 'come wind, come weather', were faithful unto death.

As you begin your journey through their lives I would encourage you to take time to ask their God to instil in you the same fruit of the Spirit that turned their human weakness into Christian victory!

Dr. Ian R K Paisley,
(Lord Bannside)   Belfast, Northern Ireland

Chapter 1

PERPETUA
Courageous Christian Martyr
(182 - 203)

Perpetua was a Christian noblewoman who, at the end of the second century, lived in Carthage (North Africa). Her Christian courage and steadfastness so impressed the famous theologian Augustine that he preached four sermons about her witness for Christ.

Persecution
In AD 202 when the Roman Emperor Septimius Severus determined to eradicate the vibrant Christian community in North Africa, Perpetua, a 22-year-old mother, was among the first to be arrested.

Parental Pressure
From her diary, and that of another prisoner, we have some insights as to her witness in prison. Her pagan father visited her and pleaded with her to deny that she was a Christian. Perpetua responded that it was impossible that she *"be called anything than what I am, a Christian."*

"I am a Christian!" Those who refused to worship the emperor were condemned to death.

Some days later, when her father again visited her, Perpetua was nursing her young son. The father pleaded with her: *"Have pity on my grey head. Have pity on me, your father...do not abandon me to be the reproach of men. Think of your brothers; think of your mother and your aunt; think of your child, who will not be able to live once you are gone. Give up your pride!"*

Steadfast

Perpetua remained steadfast. *"It will all happen in the prisoner's dock as God wills, for you may be sure that we are not left to ourselves but are all in His power."*

On Trial

On the day of her trial, Perpetua and her friends were marched before the governor Hilarianus. The friends of Perpetua were questioned first. Each of them readily admitted to being a Christian and each refused to make an act of Emperor worship.

As the governor turned to question Perpetua, her father, carrying Perpetua's son in his arms, dramatically rushed to Perpetua and, grabbing hold of her arm, pleaded: *"Perform the sacrifice. Have pity on your baby!"*

The governor, Hilarianus, added: *"Have pity on your father's grey head; have pity on your infant son. Offer the sacrifice for the welfare of the Emperor."*

The response of Perpetua was straightforward: *"I will not."*

"Are you a Christian then?" asked the governor.

"Yes, I am," Perpetua responded decisively.

The Roman governor then condemned Perpetua and her friends to be thrown to the wild beasts and to die in the arena.

The blood of the martyrs was the seed of the Church. For every Christian martyred in the arena many spectators in the stands were converted.

When Perpetua and her friends entered the stadium they were dressed in belted tunics and they were singing Psalms. The amphitheatre was filled with nobles, ladies, senators and ambassadors, and tens of thousands shouted their insults and derisions as she was led to her death. Wild beasts and gladiators circled them on the arena floor and the crowds in the stands roared, demanding to see blood. Because of their joyful demeanour the crowd demanded that the Christians be scourged first. This was done.

As the mob screamed abuse, Perpetua was heard to say: *"You have condemned us, but God will condemn you."*

Courage

A wild heifer charged and tossed Perpetua into the air. As she fell on her back she sat up and adjusted her ripped tunic, *"thinking more of her modesty than of her pain."* She then walked over to help Felicitas, her servant to her feet. Perpetua encouraged the other Christians: *"You must all stand fast in the Faith and not be weakened by what we have gone through."*

Then a starved leopard, which had been goaded, was let loose, but it would not harm Perpetua. The impatient crowd began to scream for the death of the Christians. Perpetua, Felicitas and their Christian friends were lined up and one by one they were slain with the sword by gladiators.

Perpetual Faithfulness

Perpetua was only 22 years old when she died in the arena in Carthage. Her bold testimony: *"I am a Christian and cannot deny Christ"* was repeated throughout the empire. Those in the amphitheatre who had witnessed her martyrdom reported that Perpetua and Felicitas came into the arena *"joyfully as though they were on their way to Heaven."* Witnesses described Perpetua in the arena as *"young and beautiful"*, *"a pure and modest Christian lady"*, *"with shining countenance and calm step, as the beloved of God, as a bride of Christ, putting down everyone's stare by her own intense gaze."* As Perpetua means perpetual and Felicitas means faithful, their courageous martyrdom together spelled out what is today the motto of the Marines: *Always Faithful.*

The Most Famous Female Martyr in the Roman Empire

Perpetua became the most famous Christian lady to die a martyr's death in the Roman Empire. Her example of Christian resolve and courage, choosing to suffer and die with a clear conscience, rather than deny her Saviour, inspired generations of Roman Christians to stand firm in the face of relentless persecution. Her published diary also made her the first female Christian author.

"In this you greatly rejoice, though now for a little while, if need be, you have been grieved by various trials, that the genuiness of your faith, being much more precious than of gold that perishes, though it is tested by fire, may be found to praise, honour and glory at the Revelation of Jesus Christ."   1 Peter 1:6-7

"With shining countenance and calm steps" the *"young and beautiful Perpetua met her death with joyful courage."*

"Be faithful unto death and I will give you the crown of life."
Revelation 2:10

Chapter 2
ST. PATRICK
Missionary to Ireland
(389 – 461)

Patrick was only 16 years old when he saw a fleet of 50 longboats heading for the shore. As the Roman Legions had long since departed Britain, Patrick's home town was vulnerable to attack. As the Irish raiders leapt from their boats onto the pebbled beach, sounding their war-horns, the population fled in terror. The attackers looted and burned the village and carried away captives, including young Patrick.

A stained glass window of Patrick at Downpatrick Cathedral.

Enslaved

The year was AD 405. Patrick's name in Latin was *Patricius*, meaning "*Noble*". He was the son of a Civil Magistrate, but now he had become a slave in Ireland. Patrick was sold to a cruel warrior chief whose stockade in Northern Ireland was surrounded by sharp poles with the heads of his opponents impaled on them. Patrick was put to work as shepherd to care for his master's pigs and sheep. He lived a lonely existence in the nearby hills, enduring long bouts of hunger and thirst, isolated from human company for months at a time. Patrick witnessed the superstitions of the druid priests who sacrificed prisoners of war to their war gods and newborns to the harvest gods. Skulls were used as drinking bowls; heads of decapitated enemies were used as footballs.

Conversion

In this strange place at "the ends of the earth" amongst these fierce people, Patrick remembered the faith of his father and grandfather, and the prayers of his mother and turned to Christ. Kneeling on the slopes of the Slemish Mountain, near what is now the town of Ballymena, Patrick prayed, sometimes a hundred times a day.

Escape

After six years of slavery, Patrick was led of the Lord to escape and run nearly 200 miles to a coastal port where he was able to persuade a captain to take him along with a shipment of Irish wolfhounds. A storm blew them off course to land on the coast of Gaul (France). Attacks by Vandals had devastated the area and there was no food to be found in the once fertile area. Here Patrick was able to repay the kindness of the ship's captain by praying for the Lord's provision and seeing a herd of pigs appear.

Patrick returned to the land where he had been enslaved to win the Irish to Christ.

Called

Patrick received a Macedonian call. In a vision, an Irishman named Victoricius presented him with letters entitled *"The Voice of the Irish"*: *"We appeal to you, holy servant boy, to come and walk among us again."* Patrick was *"pierced to my very heart"* and he returned to the land where he had suffered as a slave many years before.

Opposition

Patrick was over 40 years old when he arrived as a missionary to Ireland in AD 432. He faced fierce opposition from the Druids. Patrick survived numerous attempts on his life and confronted the idolatry, immorality, slavery and human sacrifices of the savage tribes.

"Daily I expect murder, fraud or captivity, but I fear none of these things because of the promises of Heaven. I have cast myself into the hands of God Almighty who rules everywhere."

The Missionary who won Ireland for Christ.

Patrick delighted in taking risks for the Gospel. *"I must take this decision disregarding risks involved and make known the gifts of God and His everlasting consolation. Neither must I fear any such risk in faithfully preaching God's Name boldly in every place, so that even after my death, a spiritual legacy may be left for my brethren and my children."*

Confrontation

At Tara, Patrick challenged the Druids to a contest. The Druids invoked demons and brought a dark fog over the land. Patrick prayed and suddenly the fog cleared and the sun shone brightly. The king ordered 27 chariots to go and seize Patrick. He prayed aloud: *"May God come up to scatter His enemies and may those who hate Him flee from His face."* The charioteers fell dead.

Patrick rebuked the king: *"If you do not believe now, you will die on the spot, for the wrath of God descends on your head."* The king fell on his knees before the missionary and pledged his realm to Christ. Many turned to Christ on that day.

Tara, where Patrick challenged the Druids and demonstrated that they were powerless before Christ.

One of Patrick's writings was a letter excommunicating a tyrant Coroticus who had carried off some of Patrick's converts into slavery. Within his lifetime Patrick ended the slave trade in Ireland. The legend that Patrick drove all the snakes out of Ireland has to do with his spiritual warfare in driving the demons from the land.

The famous *Lorica* "Patrick's Breastplate" prayer of protection expresses Patrick's confidence in God to protect him from *"every fierce, merciless force that may come upon my body and soul, incantations of false prophets, black laws of paganism, deceit of idolatry, spells of druids…"*

Fire on the Hill of Tara

Mission Strategy

Patrick was one of the first great missionaries who brought the Gospel beyond the boundaries of the old Roman civilisation. Patrick's missionary strategy was to concentrate on converting the tribal kings. As the kings converted, they gave their sons to Patrick to be trained as missionaries. From kingdom to kingdom, Patrick converted pagans, built churches, trained disciples, ordained deacons and ministers and built mission stations. Patrick provided pastors with written doctrinal standards with which to teach their people.

Faithful and Fruitful

For 30 years Patrick evangelised Ireland, converting many chiefs and kings, establishing over 300 congregations and baptising 120,000 people.

Inspiring Example

Patrick became an inspiring example for Celtic Christians. His life of continuous prayer, his love for the Scriptures, his love of God's Creation and his missionary vision inspired many hundreds of Celts to take the Gospel to Scotland, England and throughout the continent of Europe.

Saint

Although Patrick is commonly called Saint, he described himself as a sinner. Although Patrick is the Patron Saint of the Irish, he was not actually born in Ireland, but in Britain. It may also surprise people to know that Patrick was never canonized by the Roman Catholic church, but has been considered the Patron Saint of Ireland as a result of popular devotion and long-standing tradition.

On the last Sunday of every July, up to 30,000 pilgrims pass Saint Patrick's statue and climb to the top of Croagh Patrick, commemorating Patrick's 40 day fast on that 2,710 foot summit. 17 March is celebrated as St. Patrick's Day worldwide.

The greatest legacy of Patrick was the tremendous spiritual movement he launched in Ireland and his followers who sent out missionaries to evangelise not only the rest of the British Isles, but much of the continent of Europe.

"In mighty signs and wonders, by the power of the Spirit of God, …I have fully preached the Gospel of Christ. And so I have made it my aim to preach the Gospel, not where Christ was named, lest I should build on another man's foundation."　　　　Romans 15:19 – 20

Ireland for Christ.

The Grave of Patrick.

Chapter 3

COLUMBA
Missionary to Scotland
(521 - 597)

From an Illustrious Family

The handsome and hot-headed Columba was one of the most successful missionaries in history. In A.D 521 in Ulster, Northern Ireland, he was christened Colum (from the Latin word for Dove). Columba's grandfather, Conarl, had been baptised by the great missionary to Ireland, Patrick. Columba's parents were both Christians; his father was a member of the royal O' Neill family, from which the High King of the Irish was chosen at Tara. His mother, Ethme, was a descendant of a king of the Irish province of Leinster.

Intelligent and Energetic

Columba was described as a robust child, full of mischief and energy and combative. He was described as a *"fine figure, his splendid colour and his noble manliness made him beloved by all."* Tall and strong, his first rate mind and zeal for learning, combined with a powerful voice and a well developed sense of humour, made him very popular.

Evangelistic Zeal and Missionary Vision

Columba loved reading and praying the Psalms and, as his relationship to Christ developed, he began a systematic study of the Scriptures and entered monastic life. Columba was ordained to the priesthood and

Columba preached, practised and lived missions. He instilled a love for poetry and for music in his converts.

studied further. Columba developed a fervent calling to missionary outreach and began to conduct evangelistic campaigns. He established monasteries throughout Ireland. His reputation as a Godly and scholarly Christian increased.

Conflict

However, in the year of 561, a traumatic incident occurred that altered the direction of Columba's life. Eager for Scriptural knowledge and for the best Bible texts, he copied (without permission) a manuscript of Jerome's translation of the Psalms and Gospels. When the authorities learned of this, they demanded that his copy of the rare text be destroyed. When Columba refused to do this, a judgment was sought from the High King, Ataru, who decided against Columba. When he still refused to surrender his precious copy of the Psalms and Gospels, a civil war erupted between Columba and his cousin the High King.

Celtic Christianity was dynamic and quite independent of the Roman church.

The Battle of Culdrevmey

Columba and his allies were victorious at the Battle of Culdrevmey in which more than 3,000 men were killed.

Missionary Restitution

Columba felt such remorse over the carnage he had caused that he left Ireland determined to convert the same number of souls in Scotland as those whose deaths he felt responsible for in Ireland. Selecting 12 companions from among his old and trusted friends, Columba set out and established a mission station on the island of Iona, about half a mile off the Scottish mainland. From this missionary base camp, Columba and his co-workers launched missionary outreaches amongst the war-like Picts and Scots.

Iona Mission Base

Columba himself lived a Spartan lifestyle in austerity, sleeping on a bare rock, with a stone pillow. Under his leadership the Iona community was a place of constant activity where the monks engaged in agricultural work, carpentry, prayer and study – with evangelistic preaching and missionary work in nearby Scotland.

From the island of Iona, Columba mobilised the Evangelisation of Scotland.

Missions to Europe

From A.D 563 – 597, Iona was the centre for the evangelisation of Scotland and Northern England. Using the political contacts of his royal lineage, Columba developed relationships with the chiefs and kings to aid in the conversion of their subjects. Columba and his monks founded possibly more than 100 monasteries throughout Europe. Columba and his men undertook missionary outreaches as far afield as France, Germany, Switzerland and Italy.

Confrontations

He feuded with popes, kings, bishops and even his own followers. At one point, he had a conflict with the polygamous king, Theuderic, and his mother, Brunhilde, and was expelled from Gaul.

Winning Scotland for Christ

From Iona, Columba and his missionary monks spread out to make an immeasurable impact for the Gospel on Scotland and the entire Celtic Christian world.

Psalms and Prayer

On his last day, at age 75, after a day spent transcribing a Psalter, he rose from his stone bed to join his brethren at their traditional midnight service. He collapsed while kneeling in prayer at the altar, revived briefly to give his beloved monks a farewell blessing and died peacefully in the early hours of Sunday 9 June A.D. 597.

Work, Prayer and Study

Columba's life served as a model of devotion and dedication for future generations of Christians. To Columba his ideal of the Christian life consisted of *"Work, prayer and reading."* This was the heart of his monastic code and central for his converts.

Living the Bible

Columba's emphasis was living the Bible. His preaching was direct, simple and Biblical. He called on his hearers to submit to Christ as Saviour and Lord, living the rest of their lives in devotion and service for Him.

Work, prayer and reading were at the heart of the mission bases established by Columba.

Celtic Christianity

Columba left an indelible mark on Irish and Scottish Christianity, bequeathing to his converts a love for books, especially for the Bible. Columba's emphasis on bold evangelism and missionary vision inspired thousands of missionary volunteers from Scotland and Ireland through the centuries.

Discipling Nations

Columba had a passion for missions. He preached, practised and lived missions. He wrote poetry and instilled his love of poetry and music into his converts. He emphasised the evangelistic impulse in Christianity and promoted it in every way he could throughout his productive life.

"And so I have made it my aim to preach the Gospel, not where Christ was named, lest I should build on another man's foundation"

Romans 15:20

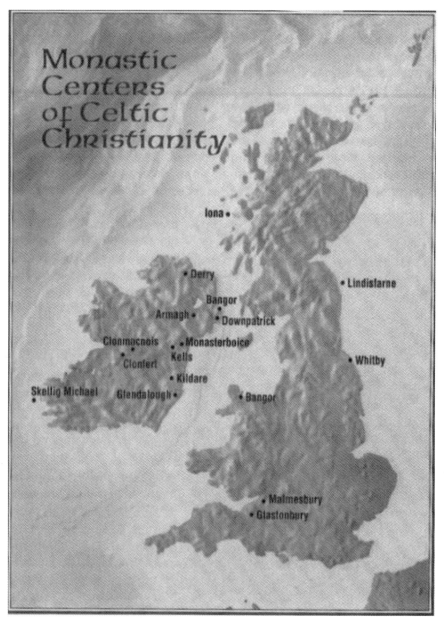

Monastic
Centers
of Celtic
Christianity

Iona

Derry

Bangor
Armagh
Downpatrick

Clonmacnois
Monasterboice
Clonfert   Kells

Skellig Michael   Kildare

Glendalough

Bangor

Lindisfarne

Whitby

Malmesbury
Glastonbury

The main missionary sending bases in Britain.

Chapter 4
THE VENERABLE BEDE
The Father of English History
(672 – 735)

Bede was one of the most influential Bible teachers and historians, and it is from his practice of dating events from the incarnation of Christ – *Anno Domini* – that our present dating method of separating events before Christ (B.C.) and after Christ (A.D.) came into general use.

Disciplined Study

Bede was born to Saxon parents in Jarrow, Northumbria, in Northern England. He entered the monastery at age 7 and devoted all of his time to the study of the Scriptures and absorbtion in monastic disciplines: daily singing, working, worshipping, learning, teaching and writing. In his 19th year he was admitted to the diaconate and in his 30th year to the priesthood.

Bede dedicated his life to prayerful study and writing for the strengthening and edifying of the Church of Christ.

The First English Author

Bede was a prodigious writer, he wrote 45 books, including commentaries, textbooks, translations and histories. His knowledge was encyclopaedic. He wrote grammatical and chronological works, geography, hymns, poems, sermons, Biblical exegeses and the first Martyrology with historical notes. Although most of his works were in Latin, Bede was also the first known writer of English prose.

The Teacher of the Middle Ages

His didactic and ethical works were so widely spread throughout Europe, and so highly esteemed, that he was described as the Teacher of the Middle Ages. He engaged in lengthy research concerning seasons, cycles, times and events. In 703 he wrote *On Times* and twenty years later, *On the Reckoning of Time*. His chronological research and calculations profoundly affected the way we continue to date events – to this day.

The Most Learned Man of His Time

Bede led a life of simplicity and devotion, always occupied with learning, teaching and writing. He was zealous in the performance of his duties. He was known as the most learned man of his time. Proficient in Patristic literature, he mastered the classics and studied in Greek, Hebrew and Latin. Bede was described as kind and generous with a tremendous love for truth and fairness. Many expressed admiration for his devotion to the Lord and service to God's people.

Faith in Action

Bede wrote that *"the door of the Kingdom of Heaven"* was not opened to *"those who only know in their learned minds the mysteries of faith and the commandments of their Creator, but to those who have progressed far enough to live by them."*

The First English Historian

One of his greatest achievements was the invaluable *Ecclesiastical History of the English Nation* completed in 731 A.D. His authoritative history of the Christian origins in Britain speak of the Celtic people who were converted to Christianity during the first three centuries after Christ, and details the coming of the Anglo-Saxons, and their subsequent conversion by Celtic missionaries. Bede's devotion to truth and accuracy set an unprecedented standard for future historians. His *History* remains the major source of information on life in early England.

History is His Story
Bede described the importance of history: *"For if history records good things of good men, the thoughtful hearer is encouraged to imitate what is good; or if it records evil*

The Celtic and Anglo Saxon churches evidenced a vibrant faith and missionary vision.

of wicked men, the good religious reader or listener is encouraged to avoid all that is sinful and perverse, and to follow what he is in God." Bede emphasised the Evangelical and civilizing mission of the church. The history of nations has moral meaning.

Christ Centred
The prayer with which Bede closed his *Ecclesiastical History* gives an insight as to the motives of this dedicated disciple of Christ: *"I pray You,*

noble Jesus, that as You graciously granted me joyfully to abide in the Words of Your Knowledge, so You will also of Your bounty grant me to come at length to Yourself, the Light of all wisdom, and to dwell in Your presence forever."

Bible Translation
At the end of Bede's long and productive life, as illness and weakness overcame him, he insisted on completing his translation of John's Gospel into English. Despite sleepless nights and days of weariness, he continued his task, taking every care in comparing the text and preserving its accuracy. He told his scribe: *"I don't want my boys to read a lie, or to work to no purpose after I have gone."*

Productive to the End
On his last day, Bede called his scribe, Wilbert, and told him to write with all possible speed: *"There is still a chapter wanting, be quick with the writing, for I shall not hold out much longer."*

Finishing the Race
He worked till nightfall and when his young scribe had completed the task, Bede rejoiced: *"It is finished!"* He sang the *Gloria Patria*, then breathed his last and entered into the joy of the Lord's presence.

Influencing all of Europe
The Teacher of the Middle Ages continued to influence all of Christendom, not only through his writings, but through one of his star pupils, Egbert, who established schools throughout Europe and became master of Charlemagne's palace school at Aachen.

Tumultuous Times
Bede lived and ministered during tumultuous times with theological, political and geographical conflicts between the Greek Orthodox church in the East and the Western Roman Catholic church, and the rise of Islam which spread through the sword, conquering most of the

The Venerable Bede

Through his writings Bede became *"the Teacher of Europe."*

Byzantine Empire and massacring Christian communities across the whole of North Africa and Spain.

BC and AD

However, instead of becoming entangled in the controversies of his day, Bede dedicated himself to serving God in obscurity, and using his gifts to produce some of the most important works of ecclesiastical literature in history. Every time we write the date, we are using the dating method that Bede established.

"If you instruct the brethren in these things, you will be a good minister of Jesus Christ, nourished in the Words of Faith and of the good doctrine which you have carefully followed." 1 Timothy 4:6

A prayer of the Venerable Bede

I implore you, good Jesus, that as in your mercy you have given me to drink in with delight the words of your knowledge, so of your loving kindness you will also grant me one day to come to you, the fountain of all wisdom, and to stand for ever before your face. Amen

Chapter 5
BONIFACE
The Apostle to the Germans
(672 - 754)

The Founder of the West

Boniface (originally called Winfrith) has been described as *"The Founder of the West"* and *"The Apostle to the Germans."* Boniface was undoubtedly one of the most successful missionaries of the first millennium. He not only converted many individuals, but he discipled an entire nation.

Diligent and Disciplined

Boniface was born to Christian parents in the Saxon kingdom of Wessex in England. At an early age he became preoccupied with spiritual matters. Boniface proved to be a zealous student of the Bible and was devoted to disciplined prayer. He was a gifted scholar who excelled in his studies, and served as a noted teacher, poet and grammarian in a Saxon monastery. Boniface grew in purposeful holiness and became a powerful Gospel preacher.

Frustration and Failure

In 716, at the age of 43, Boniface set out on a mission to Europe. He had learned that the pagan Friesian king, Radbod, had wiped out the evangelistic work of Saxon missionary Willibrord in Friesland (what is today the Netherlands). This first missionary journey of Boniface was frustrating and unsuccessful. Radbod

Boniface – the pioneer missionary who won Germany to Christ.

was involved in a war with Charles Martel, the king of the Franks, and the conflict undermined all attempts at missionary work in Friesland.

Determined to Avoid Distractions and Deviations
When he returned home to England, he was offered the prestigious position of being head of the monastery. Boniface had written the first Latin grammar produced in England, several poems and a treatise on metrics. However, Boniface's heart was set on missions, and he turned down this appointment. Boniface was determined to be a missionary.

Missionary to Europe
In 722 he sailed away from England for the last time and worked with Willibrord in Friesia. When King Radbod died, the work in Friesland was able to advance. This freed Boniface to go further south to the pagans of what are now the German states of Hesse and Thuringia. Under the protection of Charles Martel, Boniface *"more than any other individual became God's instrument to carry Christianity into Germany."*

Fearless Perseverance
A contemporary described Winifrith as: *"he seemed to glow with the salvation bringing fire which our Lord came to send upon the earth."* He *"surpassed all his predecessors in the extent and results of his ministry."* With fearless ardour and indomitable perseverance he sought to evangelise the pagans.

Bold Evangelism
Boniface was zealous in evangelism and in suppressing heresy. He established churches and monasteries, destroyed idols, baptized heathens and opposed corrupt and immoral clerics. He dealt decisively with heresy and made many enemies, being described as *"difficult, prickly and tactless."*

Boniface

Boniface boldly confronted the Druids and proved that Christ was more powerful than the idols they feared.

Confronting Paganism

In a dramatic confrontation with the pagans of Hesse, Boniface hacked down the Sacred Oak of Donar in Geismar. The huge oak was a shrine to the pagan god, Thor. As the tree fell to the ground it broke into four pieces and revealed itself to be rotten from within. Thor's lack of response in the eyes of the pagans established the authority of the Christian God. This led to thousands of conversions.

Destroying Idols

The historian, Willibald, described the scene: *"A great throng of pagans who were there cursed him bitterly among themselves because he was the enemy of their gods."* However, when they saw the rottenness of the felled oak, *"they stopped cursing and believing, blessed God."* Boniface used the wood from this felled oak to build a chapel in Fritzlar, which became the centre of his new mission station.

Working for Reformation

As Boniface continued to clash with pagans, heretics and fellow Christians, he became convinced that the church needed to be reformed. No church councils had been held in the Frankish realm for decades before his arrival. Boniface convened 5 councils between 742 and 747.

Boniface took the lead in removing corruption from the existing churches, causing much friction with the Frankish clergy. Most of the Frankish clergy resisted Boniface's work of reform and evangelism and he had to send word to England to recruit more Saxon missionaries to support his dynamic mission. Having thoroughly evangelised Thuringia and Hesse he now turned his attention to Bavaria.

Germany is Won to Christ

Fulda became the spiritual hub of Christianity in Germany. Boniface and his followers travelled throughout the land destroying pagan shrines, building churches and baptizing many thousands. He established a vast network of schools and mission stations.

Faithful to the End

In 754, Boniface prepared a new missionary campaign to the pagans in the North. Already an old man, Boniface took not only his books, but also a burial shroud, anticipating that this could be his last mission. On the Wednesday of Pentecost Week, at Dorkum on the River Borne, while Boniface was teaching 52 new converts, they were surprised and massacred by a horde of unconverted barbarians. Boniface died as he had lived, a solider of Christ. In seeking to destroy pagan worship and save pagan souls, he incurred the wrath of those whom he had come to seek and help.

Converting his Enemies

Next to the martyred missionary was found a copy of Ambrose's book: *"The Advantage of Death"* with two deep slashes in it. This book is still on display in Fulda, Germany. Many of the pagans who had been part of this attack were so struck by his courage that they repented and were converted to Christ.

A Martyr for Christ

By suffering martyrdom at the end of his long and productive life, Boniface sealed his ministry in a unique way. He left a legacy of

Boniface chopped down the sacred oak worshipped by the pagans and built a chapel with its wood.

dedication, hard work and Christian courage in defence of the Christian faith that would live long after him. Boniface gave German Christianity a distinctively militant character, reflected in the Christian chivalry and military orders of the Middles Ages.

A Challenge

As Boniface had declared: *"Let us die for the holy laws of our fathers. Let us not be dumb dogs, silent spectators, hirelings who flee from the wolf, but faithful shepherds, watchful for the flock of Christ. Let us preach the whole counsel of God to the high and to the low, to the rich and to the poor, to every rank and age, whether in season or out of season, as far as God gives us strength."*

Pentecostal Power

Throughout his ministry, Boniface hungered and thirsted for the Pentecostal power of the Holy Spirit. He consciously disciplined his life to follow faithfully the example and teaching of Christ and he eagerly embraced the suffering that comes from preaching and living the Gospel. He proved to be an effective missionary, an exceptional organiser, a superb administrator and a courageous Reformer.

An Inspiration and Example

Through his extensive, dynamic missionary outreaches, his reform of the Frankish churches, his uniting of the churches in Southern and Central Germany, and the revitalizing of nominal Christians throughout Northern Europe, Boniface became one of the most prominent role models for later missionaries, and a key figure in the creation of medieval Christian Europe.

Apostolic Impact

In bringing the light of the Gospel to a Europe darkened by barbarianism, Boniface earned the titles: *"Apostle to the Germans"* and *"The Founder of the West."*

"Whoever desires to come after Me, let him deny himself and take up his cross, and follow Me. For whoever desires to save his life will lose it, but whoever loses his life for My sake and the Gospel's will save it." Mark 8:34 – 35

Boniface inspired generations of bold missionaries who won all Europe for Christ.

Chapter 6
KING ALFRED THE GREAT
The Reformer King
(849 – 901)

King Alfred of Wessex spent most of his life fighting against the invading Danes and he is the only king in English history to be known as *"The Great."* His reign has been recognised as one of the most important turning points in English political and ecclesiastical history. He lived through tumultuous times and is recognised as one of the most intelligent, devout, industrious and effective of all medieval monarchs.

Gifted and Productive
Alfred was both soldier and scholar, lawmaker and educator, author and Reformer.

A Love for Literature
Alfred was born the fourth son of Aethelwulf and Osburh at Wantage in 849. His mother taught him a love for knowledge, and at a young age he responded to her challenge that

King Alfred laid the foundations for a truly Christian Kingdom.

whichever one of her children first learned to read a beautifully illuminated Saxon book of poetry should have it for his own. Alfred dedicated himself to the task and won the prize. This was characteristic of his entire life's love for literature, hunger for knowledge and passion for advancing English literature.

Propelled to the Throne

As the fourth son of the king, it was not expected that Alfred would ever come to rule. However, the death of his brothers in battle against the Danes, propelled Alfred to the throne.

A Soldier King

For most of Alfred's 30 years reign he was a soldier king who led his people in a desperate war for survival. Alfred personally commanded in 54 pitched battles, frequently fighting against overwhelming odds. In just the first five months of 870 Alfred fought 9 pitched battles against the Danish Vikings.

The Battle of Ashdown

Alfred was defeated at Reading, and a few days later turned this defeat into victory at Ashdown. The Battle of Ashdown in January 874 was critically important. As Winston Churchill described it: *"If the West Saxons had been beaten all England would have sunk into heathen anarchy. Since they were victorious the hope still burned for a civilized Christian existence in this Island. This was the first time the invaders had been beaten in the field."*

Fighting for Survival

There was an inconclusive battle at Basing, followed by a defeat at Marton. It was at this battle that his brother, Aethelred, died and Alfred succeeded to the throne. Shortly after this he fought the Danes to a standstill at Wilton,

All of England was threatened by the Viking raids.

Almost all of England was overrun by the invading Danes.

but the result of the battle was indecisive. Alfred and the men of Wessex had proven too stubborn a foe for easy subjugation so their resistance secured five uneasy years of peace in which to consolidate.

Rebuilding and Reorganising Resistance
In the uneasy peace that followed, Alfred reorganised his army and started to rebuild his realm which had suffered under the merciless ravages of the Danish Vikings. Many towns and villages were raided and plundered, London had fallen to the Danes, and Northumbria and East Anglia were firmly under Danish control.

The Father of the English Navy
Alfred realised that it was vital to create a navy to defend England effectively from the seafaring Danes. To be safe in an island it was necessary to command the sea. Alfred contracted Friesian seamen to build a fleet superior to any that had previously been seen. For building up the English Navy from very small beginnings, Alfred has justly been called: *"The Father of the English Navy."*

Law and Order
Alfred also instilled a great respect for law and order in his kingdom
and it was said that a traveller might hang a valuable jewel on a bush by
the roadside and nobody would dare touch it. Alfred brought scholars
from Europe in order to help educate his people. He was determined to
give his nation a stable system of laws based upon God's Law. He
blended Mosaic law with the Sermon on the Mount and Germanic
customs. Alfred's *Dooms* began with The Ten Commandments, the
Laws of Moses, the Golden Rule of Christ, and other Biblical
principles.

A New Danish Offensive
In 876 the Danes launched a surprise offensive, seized Wareham,
besieged and took Exeter, and rounding by sea, landed in Devon; then
besieged Kenwith Castle. When they captured Kenwith they put all the
inhabitants to the sword. Alfred was defeated at the battle of
Chippenham, and forced to retreat.

Under the Shadow of Odin
Wessex seemed to be in danger of falling under the shadow of Odin's
bird (the great raven which the Danes took as their symbol).

In Defeat and Retreat
Alfred's defeated forces withdrew to the Isle of Athelney, amidst the
forests and marshes of Somerset. It was here that the well-known event
of Alfred burning the housewife's cakes took place. Seeking shelter
while on the move, Alfred was asked by his host to watch her cakes
which were being baked. Absorbed in thought, planning his strategies
to counter attack the Danes, Alfred failed to notice the blackened cakes
he was meant to be watching and was berated by the irate housewife
when she returned. The woman did not know that he was the king!

The Battle of Edington
After reorganising his forces, Alfred surprised the Danes after force-
marching his soldiers at up to 40 miles a day.The Battle of Edington, in
Wiltshire, was a decisive victory for Alfred. The area is still known as

Slaughterford. On the hillside above this decisive battlefield is a great white horse, which Alfred had cut out to commemorate this major victory.

The First Vikings Converted to Christianity
Alfred also forced King Guthrum of the Danes, along with 30 of his earls, to be baptized as Christians. These were the first Viking converts to Christianity.

The First King of England
The Danes withdrew from Alfred's territory until 884 when they attempted another invasion. This time Alfred gained a swift victory, seizing London in 885 and fortifying it strongly. Thereafter, Alfred received the submission of the leaders of the Angles and the Saxons and from several princes of Wales. At this point, Alfred became in fact the first king over all of England.

Victory on Land and Sea
In 892 a large invasion of Danes was met in battle. Alfred defeated the invaders at Farnham in 893. Again at Thorney and Benfleet, he out-maneuvered and out-fought them. Then, hearing of a second Danish army besieging Exeter, he force-marched his army and drove out the besiegers. At this point, his newly formed English Navy attacked the galleys of the invading Danes at sea and defeated them.

As a large army of Danes marched up the Thames valley, numerous fierce battles ensued. The Danish garrison at Chester was besieged and forced to retreat in 894. To prevent the Danes re-supplying their forces, Alfred obstructed the Thames River, forcing them to withdraw. By 896 he had driven the invaders out of his kingdom.

Virtue and Valour
Through virtue and valour, tactics and tenacity, Alfred had fought the Viking invaders to a standstill and turned them back out of his country. He succeeded in uniting the fragmented dominions of England against a common foe. His Christian courage was an inspiration to all.

A Family Man
Alfred enjoyed over 32 years in marriage to Ealhswith – of the royal family of Mercia. They raised three daughters and two sons. His son Edward and daughter Elhelfleda, *"The Lady of the Mercians"*, together defeated the Danes and liberated all England.

Reforming the Nation
Now, having rescued his country from invasion, he set to work reforming the laws, customs and culture of his people. He personally translated many Latin works into Anglo-Saxon so that the English people could read them. Amongst his many translation projects were *Bede's Ecclesiastical History*, *Orosius' Universal History*, *Gregory's Pastoral Theology*, *Aesop's Fables*, *Boethius' Consolation of Philosophy*, and the Psalms of David. Alfred was also the author of many original titles, including a book against unjust judges.

Educating the Nation
Alfred desired that every Englishman should learn to read, and so he devised a plan for the general education of the people. He donated half of his personal income to church schools. Alfred taught that for a kingdom to be effective, it needed men of prayer, men of war and men of work. Alfred insisted that his nobles learn to read, and learn the great history and heritage of Christendom.

God and Government
King Alfred wrote: *"Local government ought to be synonymous with local Christian virtue, otherwise it becomes local tyranny, local corruption and local iniquity."*

King Alfred pioneered education for all his subjects and sponsored many church schools throughout the kingdom.

Caring for the Poor and Needy

Alfred founded two monasteries and numerous schools. His charities were numerous. He received and cared for foreigners and strangers in his court and allocated $1/8^{th}$ of his revenue to the poor and needy.

The Defence of the Realm

He instituted a system of fortified posts (burgs) and established a national militia (the *fyrd*) ensuring that the common people were armed, trained and organised for local defence. He enlarged and improved the English fleet. He also entrenched and enforced the Law of God as the Common Law of England.

An Example of Excellence

Historians have noted that while the world has had other examples of kings who have been great generals or great magistrates, no other sovereign did more in battle, in rule making, in forming and developing the literature and education of their people, as well as working for the spiritual benefit of both subjects and enemies.

Converting His Enemies

Winston Churchill marveled that Alfred should have wished *"to convert these savage foes...This sublime power to rise above the whole force of circumstances, to remain unbiased by the extremes of victory or defeat, to persevere in the teeth of disaster, to greet returning fortune with a cool eye, to have faith in men after repeated betrayals, raises Alfred far above the turmoil of barbaric wars to his pinnacle of deathless victory."*

An Amazing Life

Edmund Burke wrote of Alfred: *"One cannot help being amazed that a prince who lived in such turbulent times, who commanded personally in 54 pitched battles, who had so disordered a province to regulate, who was not only a legislator but a judge, and who was continually superintending his armies, his navies, the traffic of his kingdom, his revenues and the conduct of all his officers, could have bestowed so much of his time on religious exercises and speculative knowledge, but the exertion of all his faculties and virtues seems to have given mutual strength to all of them."*

A Heritage of Faith and Freedom

King Alfred stands out as the model king, the perfect knight, a dedicated Christian, a Protestant before Protestantism, soldier and scholar, law maker and educator, author and Reformer. He successfully fought against spiritual decay within the English church as well as against the Viking invaders, creating the first English Navy, authored English literature, ensured the survival of Christianity in England, and began the great process of converting the bloodthirsty Viking invaders to Christianity.

"Blessed be the Lord my Rock, who trains my hands for war, and my fingers for battle – my loving-kindness and my fortress, my high tower and my Deliverer, my shield and the One in whom I take refuge, Who subdues the people under me... Stretch out Your hand from above; rescue me and deliver me out of great waters, from the hand of foreigners... the One who gives salvation to kings, who delivers David His servant from the deadly sword... Happy are the people whose God is the Lord!" Psalm 144

The Church in England flourished under the inspiring leadership of King Alfred.

Soldier and Scholar, Law maker and Educator, Author and Reformer, King Alfred was the model Christian Knight.

Chapter 7
JOHN WYCLIFFE
The Morning Star of the Reformation
(1320 - 1384)

In the 14th Century, Oxford was the most outstanding university in the world, and John Wycliffe was its leading theologian and philosopher.

The Black Death (the Bubonic Plague), which killed a third of the population of Europe, led Wycliffe to search the Scriptures and find salvation in Christ.

The King's Champion
As a professor at Oxford University, Wycliffe represented England in a controversy with the Pope. Wycliffe championed the independence of England from Papal control. He supported King Edward III's refusal to pay taxes to the Pope. (It was only one step away from denying the political supremacy of the Pope over nations to questioning his spiritual supremacy over churches). The royal favour which Wycliffe earned from this confrontation protected him later in life.

As Professor Wycliffe had defended the Throne, so the Crown frequently intervened to protect their professor from the Catholic bishops.

Wycliffe's patron and protector was John of Gaunt. This English prince was the most powerful political figure in late 14th Century England. Gaunt, known in his day as the Duke of Lancaster, was effectively the Prime Minister of England during the last years of the 50-year reign of his then senile father, King Edward III. Gaunt was *"a wise diplomat, a bold soldier, the epitome of chivalry, hard on his enemies and always faithful to what he believed was best for England."* In 1399 Gaunt's son ascended the throne as King Henry IV.

All Authority is Under God

In Wycliffe's book *Civil Dominion*, he maintains that the ungodly have no right to rule. All authority is granted by God, but God does not grant any authority to those who are in rebellion against Him. Those who rule unjustly are in breach of the terms under which God delegates authority. So wicked rulers have forfeited their right to rule. In fact, all of those who lead blatantly sinful lives forfeit their rights in this world.

Corruption Disqualifies Leaders

Wycliffe also taught that the clergy of his time were so corrupt that the secular authorities had the right to confiscate their properties. The Roman church at that time owned about one third of all land in England and claimed exemption from taxation, yet the Pope claimed the right to tax the English – to finance his own wars!

Wycliffe maintained that the English government had the God-given responsibility to correct the abuses of the church within its realm and to remove from office those churchmen who persisted in their corruption and immorality.

Servant Leadership and Sacrifice

Wycliffe taught that our personal relationship with God is everything. Character is the fundamental basis of any leadership. He emphasised apostolic poverty, insisting that those who claimed to sit on Saint Peter's chair should, like the Apostle, be without silver or gold. To Wycliffe, those who claimed to follow the Apostles should live poor and humble lives spent in the service of the Church, setting an example of holiness. Therefore the Pope of Rome should be a shepherd of the flock and a preacher who brings men to Christ. Wycliffe denounced the worldliness and luxury of the Popes and the spiritual bankruptcy of the office of pope. The papacy had departed from the simple Faith and practice of Christ and His disciples. Wycliffe wrote: *"Christ is truth, the Pope is the principle of falsehood. Christ lived in poverty, the Pope labours for worldly magnificence. Christ refused temporal dominion, the Pope seeks it."*

Bible translator and Reformer, Professor John Wycliffe challenged the papacy.

Christ Alone is the Head of the Church

In his book *"The Power of the Papacy"* published in 1379, Wycliffe argues that the papacy is an office instituted by man, not God. No pope's authority could extend to secular government. The only authority that any pope might have would depend upon him having the moral character of the Apostle Peter. Any pope who does not follow Jesus Christ is the anti-Christ.

Wycliffe proclaimed that *"Christ alone is the Head of the Church."*

Unbiblical Practices Condemned

The Church on earth Wycliffe defined as the whole company of the elect, those chosen by God. The Church is the body of Christ, a unity that knows nothing of popes, hierarchies, monks, friars, priests or nuns. Nor can the salvation of the elect be effected by masses, indulgences, penance, or any other devices of priestcraft. There is nothing in the

Bible about transubstantiation, pardons, absolutions, worship of images, the adoration of saints, the treasury of merits laid up at the reserve of the Pope, the distinction between venial and mortal sins or confession to a priest. Compulsory confession Wycliffe considered *"the bondage of the anti-Christ."*

Wycliffe declared that **the reading and preaching of God's Word** *"is of more value than the administration of any sacrament."*

God's Law is Supreme
In a letter written by Wycliffe to Pope Urban VI he maintained: *"The Gospel of Christ is the body of the Law of God, Christ is true God and true man...the Roman pontiff is most bound to this Law of the Gospel...Christ's disciples are judged...according to their imitation of Christ in their moral life...Christ was the poorest of men during the time of His pilgrimage...He eschewed all worldly dominion...never should any of the faithful imitate the Pope himself nor any of the saints except in so far as he may have imitated the Lord Jesus Christ...the*

"God alone can forgive sins." **Wycliffe stood firm before the church councils.**

46

Pope should leave temporal dominion to the secular arm…God…has always taught me to obey God rather than men."

In this letter Wycliffe also refers to the *"deceitful counsel…malicious counsel…anything contrary to the Law of the Lord"* as *"anti Christ."*

Scripture Alone is our Authority

In 1378 Wycliffe completed the book *"The Truth of Holy Scripture."* In it he wrote: *"Holy Scripture is the pre-eminent authority for every Christian and the rule of faith and of all human perfection…it is necessary for all men, not for priests alone…Christ and His Apostles taught the people in the language best known to them…therefore the doctrine should not only be in Latin, but in the vulgar tongue…the more these are known the better…believers should have the Scriptures in a language which they fully understand."* Wycliffe taught that Scripture contains everything that is necessary for our salvation. All other authorities must be tested by the Scripture. *"Christ's Law is best and enough, and other laws men should not take, but as branches of God's Law."*

From Lutterworth, John Wycliffe mobilised the Lollards to evangelise England.

Translating the Scriptures

Therefore Wycliffe supervised a handful of scholars at Oxford in the translation of the Latin Bible into the English language. This was the very first translation of the entire Bible into the English language. The only source that Wycliffe's translators had to work with was a Latin hand-written manuscript of a translation made 1000 years previously.

Wycliffe is called *"the father of English prose"* because of the clarity and effectiveness of his writings and sermons which did much to unify and shape the English language.

The Lollards Evangelise England

From Oxford, Wycliffe trained and sent out *"poor priests"* (the Lollards) into the fields, villages and churches, to preach in the marketplaces, to read and sing the Scriptures in English and to win people for Christ. These itinerant evangelists became a tremendous power in the land as they spread the knowledge of the Scriptures throughout England.

Persecution from Papal Pharisees

As a result of these activities and teachings, one Pope issued five bulls against John Wycliffe for *"heresy"*. The Catholic Church tried him

Prince John of Gaunt, the Duke of Lancaster, defended Professor Wycliffe from the papal powers that sought to destroy him.

John Wycliffe

Professor Wycliffe turned the tables on his inquisitors by rebuking them for being *"priests of Baal, selling blasphemy and idolatry in the mass and indulgences."* **Then he walked out and refused a summons.**

three times, and two popes summoned him to Rome. However, Wycliffe wisely refused each summons and the political protection of the Duke of Lancaster kept Wycliffe alive and free. He was never imprisoned.

However, his followers were hunted down, expelled from Oxford and mercilessly persecuted. To get an idea of the scandal and controversy engendered by Wycliffe's Reformation, we should note what was written by Henry Knighton, a Catholic chronicler: *"Christ gave His Gospel to the clergy...but this master John Wycliffe translated the Gospel from Latin into the English...common to all and more open to the laity and even to women...and so the pearl of the Gospel is thrown before swine and trodden under foot...the jewel of the clergy has been turned into the jest of the laity...has become common."*

The Archbishop of Canterbury, Arundel, said: that *"pestilent and most wretched John Wycliffe, of damnable memory, a child of the old devil, and himself a child or pupil of anti-Christ...crowned his wickedness by translating the Scriptures into the mother tongue!"*

The Bible in English – Banned

A synod of clergy in 1408 decreed: *"It is dangerous...to translate the text of Holy Scripture...we decree and ordain that no-one shall in future translate on his authority any text of Scripture into the English tongue or into any other tongue, by way of book, booklet or treatise. Nor shall any man read, in public or in private, this kind of book, booklet or treatise, now recently composed in the time of the said John Wycliffe...on the penalty of the greater excommunication."*

Earthquake Interrupts Anathemas

In 1382, at a church council called by Archbishop Courtenay, 24 of Wycliffe's teachings were condemned. During that council there was an earthquake. Wycliffe and the Lollards interpreted the earthquake as a sign of God's displeasure with the corrupt and un-Biblical Roman clergy.

Rome vs Jerusalem

Wycliffe scorned the idea that because Peter died in Rome therefore every Bishop of Rome is to be set above all of Christendom. By the same reasoning, he noted, the Muslim Turk might conclude that because they controlled Jerusalem, where Christ died, their Mullah has power over the Pope!

Who Can Forgive Sins?

Wycliffe attacked the corruptions, superstitions and abuses of the friars and monks. He exposed their supposed powers to forgive sins as fraudulent. ***"Who can forgive sins?"*** Wycliffe taught: ***"God alone!"*** **Christ alone is the Head of the Church and God alone can forgive sins.**

Preparation for Reformation

Wycliffe's field workers (the Lollards) helped to prepare the way for the English Reformation (in the 16th Century) by reading, preaching and singing the Scriptures in English in marketplaces, fields and homes throughout the land.

The Catholic bishops condemned the writings of Professor Wycliffe to be burned.

Turning the Tables

Summoned to appear before a church council Wycliffe rebuked the bishops for being *"priests of Baal, selling blasphemy and idolatry in the mass and indulgences."* He then walked out of the assembly and refused a summons from the Pope. When Wycliffe was excluded from teaching in Oxford, he withdrew to the congregation at Lutterworth, in Leicestershire, where he devoted himself to writing during his few remaining years.

Wycliffe's Ashes and Doctrine

In 1428, 44 years after Wycliffe's death, by order of the Pope, the bones of Wycliffe were dug up and burned. As one historian commented: *"They burned his bones to ashes and cast them into the Swift, a neighbouring brook running close by. Thus the brook conveyed his ashes to the Avon, the Avon into the Severn, the Severn into the narrow seas and they into the main ocean. And so the ashes of Wycliffe are symbolic of his doctrine, which is now spread throughout the world."*

Wycliffe was the father of the Reformation – its morning star. Wycliffe's writings and example inspired John Hus and Martin Luther.

"The fear of the Lord is the beginning of wisdom, and the knowledge of the Holy One is understanding."   Proverbs 9:10

The Morning Star of the Reformation.

Chapter 8
ANNE OF BOHEMIA
The Reformers Friend
(1366 - 1394)

Anne of Bohemia, was the eldest daughter of Emperor Charles IV of the Holy Roman Empire. Her brother was King Wenceslaus of Bohemia (who was named after the subject of a famous Christmas carol).

A Great Love for The Scriptures
Anne was taught the truths of the Scripture from her youth. There were

a number of faithful Gospel preachers in Bohemia at that time including Conrad Strichna, Johan Melice and Matthias Janovius. Anne asked many probing questions concerning Scriptural truth.

An Inquiring Mind
Anne was described as a godly, intelligent young girl with an inquiring mind. She was renowned for her love of reading and for her possession of the Scriptures in three languages. Her favourite books of the Bible were the four Gospels, which she constantly studied.

Anne became Queen of England.

A Hunger for Reformation
Anne came to recognise the many errors prevailing in the Roman church and she persisted in praying for a return to Biblical faithfulness to the Doctrine of the Apostles and to the purity of the early Church.

Crecy Changes Bohemia's Allegiance
The traditional alliance of Bohemia with France was shattered by their joint defeat at the hands of the English King Edward III and his son, The Black Prince, at the Battle of Crecy in 1346. Richard II's Father, Edward, was called the Black Prince because of his dark coloured armour. Then the Papal Schism further divided the Bohemians from their traditional allies, the French. As France supported pope Clement VII of Avignon, King Wenceslaus chose to support pope Urban VI in Rome. As the English also allied against the French pope, the Bohemians came into alliance with the English.

The father of Richard II was the famous Black Prince who defeated the French at Crecy.

A New Alliance with England
As King Richard II's father, The Black Prince, died in 1376 and his grandfather, King Edward III, the following year, Richard II became King of England at age 10. Negotiations began to solidify the alliance

between Bohemia and England by the marriage of Princess Anne to King Richard.

A Courageous Young King
At age 14, King Richard II showed remarkable courage during the Peasants Revolt of 1381. At Smithfield, at great personal risk, Richard II rode out to meet the violent mob and calmed them into ending the revolt.

Marriage at Westminster
In January 1382, when Richard II was 15 years old and Anne was 16 years old, they were married in St. Stephens Chapel, at Westminster. Although their marriage had been arranged by diplomats, it appears to have been a good, loving and positive partnership. Anne was undoubtedly an excellent influence on Richard during their 12 years together.

A Friend of The Reformation
Reportedly Anne had been persuaded to accept the proposal because of positive reports that she had received of the Reformation work of Professor John Wycliffe of Oxford University.

The Archbishop of York, Arundel, one of the most vitriolic enemies of Wycliffe's Reformation work, was horrified to hear that the Queen owned copies of the Gospels, which she avidly studied.

Anne protected Professor Wycliffe and supported his Reformation work.

Professor John Wycliffe was delighted to learn of Anne's love for the Scriptures, and he publically compared her to the Biblical Mary who sat at Jesus' feet listening to what the Master had to say.

Protecting the Professor
For her part, Queen Anne protected Wycliffe from his many enemies and intervened on numerous occasions to protect him from prosecution and to save his life.

Students of Reformation
At the encouragement of Queen Anne, Bohemian students came to Oxford to study under John Wycliffe. Many of these students carried back the Reformation writings and teachings of Wycliffe to Prague, Bohemia and throughout central Europe. Students sponsored by Queen Anne were soon taking the Reformation writings and teachings as far afield as Lithuania.

Evangelistic
Many of Queen Anne's friends and servants became dedicated Christian believers.

Generosity
The common people of England came to love the Queen. Her kindness and generosity to the poor was legendary. It is said that as many as six thousand people were fed daily through her benevolence.

Deeply Mourned
Tragically, this bright and shining light was cut short on the 7 June 1394 as Anne died at age 27 from the plague. Her husband, King Richard II, was devastated and the people of England deeply mourned her.

The Reformation comes to Bohemia
Many of her Christian friends and servants returned to Bohemia with the translations of the Gospels and writings of John Wycliffe that had been so highly treasured by Queen Anne. These led to the conversion of Professor Jan Hus of Bohemia, the Hussite movement and later the Moravians. From them missionaries went out, literally, to the ends of the earth.

"These things command and teach. Let no one despise your youth, but be an example to the believers in word, in conduct, in love, in spirit, in faith, in purity. Till I come, give attention to reading, to exhortation, to doctrine. Do not neglect the gift that is in you, which was given to you by prophecy with the laying on of the hands of the eldership. Meditate on these things; give yourself entirely to them, that your progress may be evident to all. Take heed to yourself and to the doctrine. Continue in them, for in doing this you will save both yourself and those who hear you." 1 Timothy 4:11-16

Queen Anne's Shield.

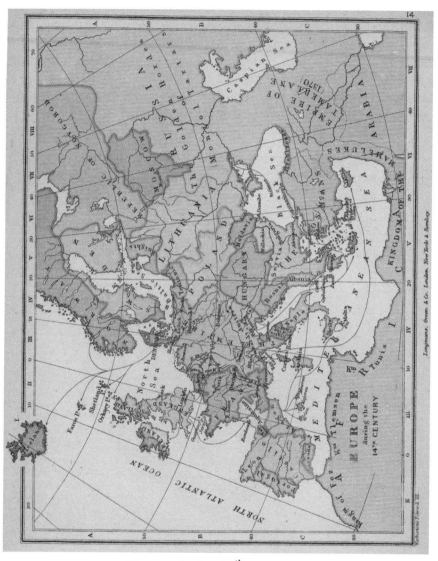

Europe in the 14th Century.

Chapter 9
JOHN HUS
The Reformer of Prague
(1372 - 1415)

The Reformation movement launched by Wycliffe and his Lollards in England was intensely opposed and fiercely persecuted by the Roman Church. The Reformation movement was largely driven underground in the British Isles. But Wycliffe's teachings spread to Bohemia where they resulted in a dynamic revival.

The two nations of England and Bohemia were linked in 1383 by the marriage of Anne of Bohemia to King Richard II of England. Czech students went to Oxford and English students went to Prague.

Preparation for Reformation
Scripture translations from the persecuted Waldensian refugees had begun entering Bohemia in the 13th Century. When Anne of Bohemia married King Richard II she sent copies of Wycliffe's writings back to her homeland. Queen Anne's love for the Bible was shared by many of

Professor John Hus proclaimed Reformation doctrines at the Chapel of Bethlehem and at the University of Prague.

her countrymen. Soon, Conrad Stickna was preaching the Gospel in the open air to large crowds. Matthew of Janov travelled throughout Bohemia preaching against the abuses of the church. His followers were imprisoned and burned at the stake. John Milic, Archdeacon of the cathedral in Prague, preached fearlessly against the abuses of the church and wrote *"Anti-Christ Has Come"* over a cardinal's doorway. He was imprisoned.

Courageous Czech Confronts Corruption
Born in the village of Husinec, John Hus studied for the priesthood and received a Master's degree in 1396. In 1402 he was appointed preacher in Bethlehem Chapel. John Hus, when appointed Rector of Prague University at age 34, also began to preach Reformation principles (in the common Language) in the Chapel of Bethlehem in Prague. Hus translated Wycliffe's works into Czech, exposed the superstitions, fraudulent *"miracles"* and the sale of indulgences. In 1405, Hus denounced the alleged appearances of *"Christ's blood"* on communion wafer as an elaborate hoax. He condemned the sins of the clergy as *"fornicators"*, *"parasites"*, *"money misers"*, *"fat swine"*, *"drunks"* and *"gluttons"*. He condemned the practice of simony (buying spiritual offices), and the taking of multiple paid positions without faithfully serving any. He described churches that sold indulgences as *"brothels"*.

Hus adopted Wycliffe's view of the Church as an elect community with Christ – not the Pope – as its true Head. Hus's fiery sermons in the Bohemian language received widespread enthusiastic support. Hus believed pastors should be examples of God-fearing integrity. He preached vivid, accessible sermons, which captured the people's imaginations. Hus was described by his supporters as *"a passionate Reformer."*

On the walls of the Chapel of Bethlehem were paintings contrasting the behaviour of the Popes and Christ. The Pope rode a horse; Christ walked bare-foot. Jesus washed the disciples' feet; the Pope preferred having his feet kissed. Hus insisted that no human institution – including the church - can be ultimate in authority. Only God has ultimate authority.

In 1410 the Archbishop obtained from the Pope a ban on teaching in chapels, including specifically the Bethlehem Chapel. This ban Hus refused to obey. In that same year the Archbishop burned over 200 volumes of Wycliffe's works. Hus responded: *"Fire does not consume truth. It is always the mark of a little mind that it vents its anger on inanimate objects."* Hus defended Wycliffe's orthodoxy. Hus was summoned to Rome, but wisely refused to go.

The Papacy Strikes Back

Archbishop Zbynek excommunicated Hus. (Hus was actually excommunicated 5 times) Hus was described as *"radical"* and *"dangerous."* Hus then openly attacked the Pope's sale of indulgences in support of his war against Naples. The Pope thereupon placed the City of Prague under a papal interdict. This meant that the entire city was placed under an ecclesiastical ban (all churches were closed, no masses were allowed, no confessions received, no marriages or burials permitted). Until this time Hus had been protected by the king, university and nobility from the wrath of the Pope. But with the entire city in

John Hus was treacherously arrested, the guarantee of his safe conduct was violated and he was condemned without the opportunity to defend himself.

turmoil, the Reformer chose to go into exile. During this time Hus wrote: *"On the Church."* And he preached in the villages and countryside.

Treachery at Constance

A General Church Council was called at Constance in 1414 to heal 'The Great Schism' (that had raged from 1378). Hus lived during The Great Schism when Europe was divided between two and then three rival popes who bitterly anathematized one another. It was this Council of Constance, which aimed to bring the Schism to an end, that summoned Hus. The Emperor Sigismund guaranteed Hus safe conduct in both directions, whatever the outcome of the case against him might be.

However, upon arriving, Hus was imprisoned on orders of Pope John XXII. Despite the Imperial guarantee of safe conduct, Hus was taken through a mockery of a trial in which he was allowed no defence. Hus had hoped to present his views to the assembled authorities, but instead he found himself a victim of a cruel Inquisition, which condemned him for heresies, which he had neither believed nor taught (including that he had claimed to be the fourth member of the Trinity!) Hus prayed aloud that Christ might forgive his judges and accusers.

Steadfast to the End

Under pressure to recant Hus declared: *"I would not, for a chapel full of gold, recede from the truth…the truth stands and is mighty forever."* Hus stated that he would prefer to be burned in public than to be silenced in private *"in order that all Christendom might know what I said in the end."*

On 6 July 1415 Hus was condemned to death and taken to the outskirts of the city of Constance to be burned. Hus prayed: *"O most holy Christ…strengthen my spirit…give me a fearless heart, a right faith, a firm hope, a perfect love, that for Thy sake I may lay down my life with patience and joy."*

Condemned to death for his Reformation teaching, Professor Hus declared: *"In the truth of the Gospel I have written, taught and preached, today I will gladly die."*

On arriving at the execution ground, Hus knelt and prayed: *"God is my witness that the evidence against me is false. I've never thought nor preached except with the one intention of winning men, if possible, from their sins.* **In the truth of the Gospel I have written, taught and preached; today I will gladly die."**

Hus died singing *"Jesus, Son of the Living God, have mercy on me."* He was 43 years old.

Resistance to Rome Spreads

After Hus's martyrdom his followers organised military resistance to the Holy Roman Empire. Remarkably, these vastly outnumbered Hussites repelled six crusades against them. These Hussites fought under Hus's motto: ***"Truth conquers."*** They proved that you could take on the Holy Roman Empire – and survive!

"Be faithful unto death, and I will give you the crown of life." Revelation 2:10

A Spiritual Heritage

His followers, *The Unity of the Brotherhood*, survived as an independent church, co-operating with the Waldensians, and later with the Lutherans and the Calvinists. The Hussites became known as the Moravians. Under Count Nicholas Van Zinzendorf the Moravians started a prayer chain that lasted 150 years! During that extended prayer meeting, 2,400 Moravian missionaries were sent throughout the world. Moravians were instrumental in the conversion of John Wesley.

The Goose and the Swan

One interesting anecdote is that Hus is accredited with making a prophecy at his death. *"My goose is cooked!"* he said. (Hus is the Bohemian word for goose!) *"But a hundred years from now a swan will arise whose voice you will not be able to silence."* Many saw Luther as that voice, hence the prevalence of swans in Lutheran art and architecture.

Hussites gather to receive both the bread and the cup of Communion.

Hussites organised military resistance to the papacy and defeated six crusades launched against them.

"Truth Conquers."

Chapter 10
JOHANNES GUTENBERG
The Inventor of the Printing Press
(1400 – 1468)

Man of the Millenium
At the end of the 20th Century, numerous publications discussed who they believed were the most important people of the millennium. Johannes Gutenberg, the inventor of the Printing Press, was in everybody's top 10, and many voted him as The Most Important Man of the Millennium!

An Insatiable Appetite for Knowledge
Johannes Gutenberg was born in the city of Mainz near the shores of the Rhine River.   His father, Friel Gensfleisch, married Else Von Gutenberg, who gave her name to her second son, Johannes.   As a young boy, Johannes developed an insatiable appetite for knowledge, reading every book he came across.

An Itinerant Student
During his teen years, Johannes and his family were forced into exile twice due to political in-fighting and conflicts.   Johannes travelled from town to town, studying monuments and visiting men who were renowned for their knowledge in science, art or the trades.   He travelled alone, on foot, carrying a knapsack with his precious books and clothes.   As an itinerant   student,   he   travelled throughout   Italy,   Switzerland, Germany and Holland.

"The Most Important Man of the Millenium"

A Deepening Love and Growing Vision

His love for God grew and deepened the more he read and studied. And the further he travelled, the greater his vision developed of spreading the Word of God to all people.

Inspiration

One day, in Haarlem, his friend, Lawrence Koster, handed him a piece of wood that had letters carved on it, wrapped in a piece of parchment. Some of the sap from the greenwood had hardened into the relief shape of the letters on the parchment. As Johannes saw this simple plaque of wood an inspiration flashed into his heart and mind with the force of lightening. The possibility of producing a machine that could print the Word of God welled up inside him. Gutenberg travelled up the Rhine to Strassburg and closeted himself in his workroom.

Tools and Testing

He fashioned his own tools, developed plans, tested and tried, reorganized and attempted again and again to produce an effective printing machine. Starting with moveable wooden types, he bored through the side of each with a small hole to string together the letters of the alphabet cut in relief on one side.

Movable type printing presses revolutionised communication and laid the foundations for the Reformation, the Industrial Revolution, the Scientific Age and the Age of Information.

An Immense Vision

Johannes Gutenberg seemed to understand something of the immense importance of this invention upon industry, society and civilisation itself. When he contracted a skillful craftsman, Conrad Saspach, to create a full size version of his scale model, the craftsman responded: *"But it is just a simple press you are asking from me Master Hans."*

"Yes," replied Gutenberg, *"It is a press, certainly, but a press from which shall soon flow in inexhaustible streams the most abundant and most marvellous liquor that has ever flowed to relieve the thirst of man! Through it God will spread His Word. A spring of pure truth shall flow from it! Like a new star, it shall scatter the darkness of ignorance, and cause a light heretofore unknown to shine among men."*

Limitations and Secrecy

Despite his great vision, Johannes was acutely aware of his limitations. He was just one man, with very limited resources. He was concerned about his work being discovered and possibly pirated for lesser goals. He worked on the mechanics of printing secretly, moving his workshop into the ruins of an old deserted monastery.

Dedication and Discipline

He spent sleepless nights wearing himself out in pursuit of his invention. He engraved his movable types in wood and projected casting them in metal. He studied hard to find the means of enclosing them in forms, whether of wood or of iron, to make the types into words, phrases, lines and to leave spaces on the paper. He invented coloured mediums, oily and yet able to dry, to reproduce the characters, brushes and dabbers that spread the ink on the letters, boards to hold them, and screws and weights to compress them. He invested months and years, and his entire fortune in these experiments. There were many disappointments, failures and frustrations before he developed a model press, which combined all elements for an efficient printing press.

Johannes Gutenberg examines the first printed pages of the Bible.

The First Book Ever Printed

The first book to be printed had to be the Holy Bible; the second was the *Psalter* (the first book to ever bear a date: 1457). The Gutenberg Bible, completed in 1455, was the first book ever published with movable type. Less than 200 copies were originally printed and only about 50 have survived to this day. Today, the original Gutenberg Bible is considered one of the finest works of art. In 1978 a two-volume edition of the Gutenberg Bible was sold for over $2 million. Since then a Gutenberg Bible was sold for over $4 million, the highest price ever paid for a book.

Overcoming Opposition

At first the Roman Catholic church opposed the Printing Press. For political reasons, and for the survival of his invention, Gutenberg wrote a dedication to pope Paul II on behalf of the Printing Press: *"Among the number of blessings which we ought to praise God is this invention, which enables the poorest to procure libraries at a low price. Is it not a great glory that volumes that used to cost 100 pieces of gold, are now to be bought for four, or even less, and that the fruits of genius... multiply over all the earth!"*

Hijacked

Soon Gutenberg could not sustain the demand for printing in his small workshop. He was forced to

The Printing press made possible the information revolution.

develop partnerships with successful businessmen, who unfortunately did not have the integrity of the inventor. These businessmen hijacked his invention and stole everything from Gutenberg. But, despite these trials and betrayals, Gutenberg maintained his integrity and honour, maintaining a faithful Christian witness to the end.

One of the Greatest Inventions in History

Gutenberg's invention of the Printing Press is rightly classified as one of the greatest events in the history of the world. The Printing Press prepared the way for the Reformation and the progress of modern science and literature. The Printing Press became an indispensible tool in the fulfillment of the Great Commission and the development of universal education. Gutenberg's invention enabled multiplied millions to discover for themselves great literature and, most importantly, the Word of God.

The Printing Press – The Reformer's Friend, the Tyrant's Foe
This one invention made possible the greatest Revival of faith and freedom ever experienced. The inventing of the Printing Press played a key role in mobilising the Reformation. Without printing, it is questionable whether there would have been a Protestant Reformation. A century before Luther, Wycliffe and Hus had inspired dedicated movements for Bible study and Reform, but the absence of adequate printing technology severely limited the distribution of their writings. As a result their ideas did not spread as rapidly, or as far, as they could have done. By God's grace, the Printing Press provided the Reformers, Martin Luther, Ulrich Zwingli, William Tyndale, John Calvin and others, with the spiritual weapons they needed to make the Reformation succeed.

"Making disciples of all the nations, teaching obedience to all things…" Matthew 28:19

**The Printing Press:
the Reformer's Friend, the Tyrant's Foe.**

Chapter 11

GIROLAMO SAVONAROLA
Italian Reformer and Martyr
(1452 – 1498)

Serious and Intelligent
Born of Italian nobility in the city of Ferrara in 1452, Savonarola was described as a serious and intelligent boy who at an early age gravitated to the writings of some of the most learned men in history. He received instruction in philosophy, logic and medicine from his father and grandfather. From studying the writings of Plato and Dante, he came to develop a deep spiritual hunger. The pictorial illustrations of hell in Dante's *Inferno* tormented him.

The Centre of the Renaissance
In 1475, he decided to become a monk and joined the Dominicans. After an intense time of study, he was sent to the city of Florence. In the 15th Century, the centre of the Renaissance was Florence, Italy. From this centre of science and art, masters such as Michelangelo, Leonardo Da Vinci and Raphael produced exquisite and timeless art.

Girolamo Savonarola denounced the corruption and immorality under Roman Catholicism.

Fearless Preaching
In studying the writings of Augustine of Hippo, Savonarola came to see how far the church had fallen from its Apostolic calling. Girolamo Savonarola began fearlessly to preach Christ amidst the moral decay, irreligious lifestyles, superstitious beliefs and unbiblical practices of the clergy and community. He was 38 years old when he began his work of Reformation in Florence.

Confronting Corruption
Vast crowds gathered to hear his denunciations of the prevalent corruption and immorality. The majestic cathedral was filled to over-flowing by citizens of Florence eager to hear this celebrated orator expose the corruptions of the ruling Medici family and the idolatry and corruptions of the Roman church. Savonarola preached repentance from sin with a growing earnestness. Many hardened sinners surrendered their lives to Christ and forsook their evil ways of life.

Incorruptible
The ruler of Florence, Lorenzo Medici, tried to silence the Reformer with gifts and attempted bribes. However, Savonarola was relentless and incorruptible. When Lorenzo was dying, at age 44, he sent for Savonarola, but when the Reformer found that Lorenzo had no intention of repenting of his sins, he refused him the blessing which was customary to grant to the dying.

Florence was swept by a dynamic revival under the preaching of Savonarola.

Reformation in Florence

The people ousted Lorenzo's son and unanimously chose Savonarola as ruler of Florence. For three years Savonarola governed Florence with justice and efficiency. Savonarola intended the city to become an example of a Christian commonwealth in which God is the Ruler, and His Gospel the Sovereign Law. Dens of iniquity and vice were closed down. Gambling was outlawed; licentious books and pictures were destroyed in a *"bonfire of vanities."*

"I do not desire any other crown than the crown of a martyr."

Papal Power Play

Some people began to resent the strictness of the new rule. Pope Alexander was one of the most notoriously immoral popes with five illegitimate children whom he openly promoted to high office. This pope engaged in the most unscrupulous conduct, including bribery and murder. Pope Alexander VI took the lead in attacking the Reformer of Florence. Firstly, Alexander VI tried to make Savonarola a cardinal and offered him great bribes. Savonarola rejected all these declaring: *"I do not desire any other crown than the crown of a martyr."*

Excommunication and Torture

Thereafter the pope attempted to spread slander to undermine the authority of Savonarola. Then the pope excommunicated and imprisoned him. People who had previously acclaimed and supported Savonarola now allowed him to be tortured and joined in a chorus of condemnation of the courageous Reformer.

On 23 May 1498 Savonarola was burned at the stake in Florence.

Steadfast

However, Savonarola remained steadfast. He refused to be shaken in his convictions even after the most unbearable tortures. On 23 May 1498, Savonarola was burned to death in the great square in the city of Florence. Before a huge crowd, a bishop declared to the condemned Savonarola: *"I separate thee from the church militant and triumphant."* Savonarola responded: *"Militant, not triumphant, for you have no power to separate me from the Church triumphant – to which I go."* Savonarola died at age 45.

Regeneration

"We must regenerate the church," taught Savonarola. *"None are saved by their own works. No man can boast of himself; and if, in the presence of God, we could ask all these justified of sins – have you been saved by your own strength? All would reply as with one voice: 'Not unto us O Lord! Not unto us; but to Him be the glory!'"*

Scripture Alone

Savonarola gave special emphasis to the authority of the Bible. *"I preach the regeneration of the church, taking the Scriptures as my sole guide."*

Christ Alone

As Savonarola was being severely tortured on the rack, he prayed: *"O Lord... I do not rely on my own justification, but on Thy mercy."* In between his tortures, he wrote meditations on Psalm 32 and 51, which Martin Luther later published, describing them as: *"a piece of Evangelical testimony and Christian truth"*

Courage and Faith

Savonarola met his martyrdom with courage and faith, declaring: *"Should I not willingly die for His sake Who willingly died for me, a sinful man?"*

"Do not be afraid of those who kill the body, and after that have no more that they can do.".
Luke 12:14

The Reformer and Martyr of Florence.

The Reformation Monument in Worms honours the pre-Reformers Peter Waldo, John Wycliffe, John Hus and Girolamo Savonarola as well as the greatest Reformer, Martin Luther.

Chapter 12

MARTIN LUTHER
Captive to the Word of God
(1483 - 1546)

The Reformation was one of the most momentous turning points in world history. It was led by men of strong faith, deep convictions, great intelligence, high moral standards and tremendous courage. Towering above all these great Reformers, Martin Luther stands out as the most courageous, controversial and influential Reformer of all time.

The Controversial
Luther has been alternatively described as the brilliant scholar who rediscovered the central message of the Bible, a prophet like Elijah and John the Baptist to reform God's people,

Martin Luther's earnest quest for peace with God and dedicated study of the Scriptures led to the Reformation.

the liberator who arose to free his people from the oppression of Rome, the last medieval man, and the first modern man. Zwingli described him as: *"the Hercules who defeated the tyranny of Rome."* Pope Leo X called Luther: *"A wild boar, ravaging his vineyard."* Emperor Charles V described him as: *"A demon in the habit of a monk!"*

The Son
Martin Luther was born 10 November 1483 in Eisleben, Saxony. His father, Hans Luder, had worked hard to climb the *"social ladder"* from his humble peasant origins to become a successful copper mining entrepeneur. Hans married Margaretha Lindemann, the daughter of a

prosperous and gifted family that included doctors, lawyers, university professors and politicians. Hans Luder owned several mines and smelters and he became a member of the City Council in Mansfield, where Martin was raised, under the strict discipline typical of that time.

The Student
From age 7, Martin began studying Latin at school. Hans intended his son to become a lawyer, so he was sent on to the University of Erfurt before his 14th birthday. Martin proved to be extraordinarily intelligent and he earned his BA and MA degrees in the shortest time allowed by the statutes of the University. Martin proved so effective in debating, that he earned the nickname: *"the philosopher."*

The Storm
As Martin excelled in his studies, he began to be concerned about the state of his soul and the suitability of the career his father had set before him. While travelling on foot, near the town of Stotternhein, a violent thunderstorm brought Martin to his knees. With lightning striking all around him, Luther cried out for protection to the patron saint of miners: *"St. Anne, help me, I will become a monk!"* The storm around him matched the conflict raging within his soul.

The Monk
Although his parents were pious people, they were shocked when he abandoned his legal studies at Erfurt and entered the Augustinian monastery. Martin was 21 years old when, in July 1505, he gave away all his possessions – including his lute, his many books and clothing – and entered the Black Cloister of the Augustinians.

Luther quickly adapted to monastic life, throwing himself wholeheartedly into the manual labour, spiritual disciplines and studies required. He went way beyond the fasts, prayers and ascetic practices required and forced himself to sleep on the cold stone floor without a blanket, whipped himself, and seriously damaged his health. He was described as: *"devout, earnest, relentlessly self-disciplined, unsparingly self-critical, intelligent..."* and *"impeccable."* Luther rigorously pursued the monastic ideal and devoted himself to study, prayer and the sacraments. He wearied his priest with his confessions and with his punishments of himself with fasting, sleepless nights, and flagellation.

The Professor

Luther's wise and godly superior, Johannes von Staupitz, recognised Martin's great intellectual talents, and to channel his energies away from excessive introspection ordered him to undertake further studies, including Hebrew, Greek and the Scriptures, to become a university lecturer for the order.

Extra-ordinarily gifted and intelligent, Martin Luther's studies sparked the Reformation.

Luther was ordained a priest in 1507 and studied and taught at the Universities of Wittenberg and Erfurt (1508 – 1511). In 1512, Martin Luther received his doctoral degree and took the traditional vow on becoming a professor at Wittenberg University to teach and defend the Scriptures faithfully. This vow would be a tremendous source of encouragement to him later. Luther never viewed himself as a rebel, but rather as a theologian seeking to be faithful to the vow required of him to teach and defend Holy Scripture. Luther committed most of the New Testament, much of the Old Testament and all of the Psalms to memory.

Wittenberg

The University of Wittenberg had been founded by Prince Frederick of Saxony in 1502. Luther's friend from his university days in Erfurt, George Spalatin, was now chaplain and secretary to the Prince, and closely involved in the Prince's pet project of his new university. Wittenberg at this time was a small river town with only about 2,000 residents. Prince Frederick wanted to build it up into his new capital of Saxony.

Studies That Shook the World

From 1513 to 1517, Luther lectured at the University on the Psalms, Romans and Galatians. Being a university professor would have been a full-time job; however, Luther had other responsibilities as well. He was the supervisor for 11 Augustinian monasteries, including the one at Wittenberg. Luther was also responsible for preaching regularly at the monastery chapel, the town church and the castle church. It was a combination of Luther's theological and pastoral concerns that led him to take the actions that sparked the Reformation.

Luther had long been troubled spiritually with the righteousness of God. God demanded absolute righteousness: *"Be perfect, even as your Father in Heaven is perfect." "Be holy, as I am Holy."* We are obligated to love God whole-heartedly, and our neighbours as ourselves.

It was because of his great concern for his eternal salvation that Luther had sought to flee the world. In spite of the bitter grief and anger of his father, he had buried himself in the cloister and devoted himself to a life of the strictest asceticism. Yet, despite devoting himself to earning salvation by good works, cheerfully performing the humblest tasks, praying, fasting, chastising himself even beyond the strictest monastic rules, he was still oppressed with a terrible sense of his utter sinfulness and lost condition.

"The Just Shall Live By Faith"

Then Luther found some comfort in the devotional writings of Bernard of Clairvoux, who stressed the free grace of Christ for salvation. The writings of Augustine provided further light. Then, as he begun to study the Scriptures, in the original Hebrew and Greek, joy unspeakable flooded his heart. It was 1512, as he began to study Paul's Epistle to the Romans, that the verse *"For in the Gospel a righteousness from God is revealed, a righteousness that is by faith from first to last, just as it is written: the righteous will live by faith"*   Romans 1:17

Luther later testified that as he began to understand that this righteousness of God is a free gift by God's grace through which we may live by faith, *"I felt entirely born again and was led through open gates into Paradise itself. Suddenly the whole of Scripture had a different appearance for me. I recounted the passages which I had memorised and realised that other passages, too, showed that the work of God is what God works in us... thus St. Paul's words that **the just shall live by faith**, did indeed become to me the gateway to Paradise."* The burden of his sin rolled away. Up until then, Luther had tried to earn salvation by his good works, although he never felt that he had been able to do enough. Now, God had spoken to him through the Scripture. Man is not saved by works, but by faith alone.

A Turning Point

As a doctor, Luther had taken an oath to serve the Church faithfully by the study and teaching of Holy Scripture. At the university, he was responsible to prepare pastors. Now, having experienced God's grace in Christ, studying God's Word, Luther began to see the emptiness, self-absorption, pious pretence and superstitious unbelief of his previous religious devotion. Nor could Luther fail to recognise the same pious fraud and pharisaical futility all around him.

In 1510, before being made a professor at Wittenberg, Luther had been sent to Rome for his monastic order. What he had seen there had shocked and disillusioned him. Rome was the pre-eminent symbol of ancient civilisation and *"the residence of*

Professor Martin Luther was required to vow to defend the Scriptures.

Christ's Vicar on earth" the pope. Luther was horrified by the blatant immorality and degeneracy prevalent in Rome at that time.

Understanding Catholicism

The centre of medieval Roman Catholic church life was the Mass, the Sacrament of the altar. The Roman Catholic institution placed much emphasis on the punishment of sin in Purgatory, as a place of cleansing by fire before the faithful were deemed fit to enter Heaven. They taught that there were four sacraments that dealt with the forgiveness, and the removal of sin, and the cancellation of its punishment: Baptism, The Mass, Penance and Extreme Unction. The heart of Penance was the priestly act of Absolution whereby the priest pardoned the sins and released the penitent from eternal punishment. Upon the words of Absolution, pronounced by the priest, the penitent sinner received the forgiveness of sins, release from eternal punishment and restoration to a state of grace. This would required the sinner making some satisfaction, by saying a prescribed number of prayers, by fasting, by giving alms, by going on a pilgrimage, or by taking part in a crusade.

During Luther's visit to Rome he was shocked and deeply disillusioned by the prevalent immorality.

Indulgences

In time, the medieval church had come to allow the penitent to substitute the payment of a sum of money for other forms of penalty or satisfaction. The priest could then issue an official statement, an indulgence, declaring the release from other penalties through the payment of money. In time, the Catholic church came to allow indulgences to be bought, not only for oneself, but also for relatives and friends who had died and passed into Purgatory. They claimed that these indulgences would shorten the time that would otherwise have to be spent suffering in Purgatory. This practice of granting indulgences was based upon the Catholic doctrine of *Works of Supererogation*. This unbiblical doctrine claimed that works done beyond the demands of God's Law earned a reward. As Christ and the saints had perfected Holiness and laid up a rich treasury of merits in Heaven, the Roman church claimed that it could draw upon this treasury of *"extra merits"* to provide satisfaction for those who paid a specified sum to the church.

The Indulgence Industry

This system of indulgences was very popular with the masses of people who preferred to pay a sum of money to saying many prayers and partaking in many masses to shorten the suffering in Purgatory of either themselves or a loved one. The industry of indulgences had also become a tremendous source of income for the Papacy.

In order to fund the building of the magnificent St. Peter's Cathedral in Rome, pope Leo X had authorised a plenary, or total indulgence. And so it was on this papal fundraising campaign to complete the construction of St. Peters *Basilica*, that the Dominican monk and indulgence salesman extraordinary, John Tetzel, arrived in Saxony. The shameless and scandalous manner in which Tetzel hawked the indulgences outraged Martin Luther. Sales jingles such as: *"As soon as the coin clinks in the chest, a soul flies up to Heavenly rest"* were deceiving gullible people about their eternal souls.

Luther's study of the Scripture had convinced him that salvation came by the grace of God alone, based upon the atonement of Christ on the cross alone, received by faith alone. Indulgences could not remove any guilt, and could only induce a false sense of security. People were being deceived for eternity.

The 95 Theses

Concerns that had been growing since his visit to Rome in 1510 led Luther now to make a formal objection to the abuses of indulgences.

On All Saint's Day (1 November), people would be coming from far and wide in order to view the more than 5,000 relics exhibited in the *Schlosskirche*, which had been built specifically for the purpose of housing this massive collection. So, on 31 October 1517, Martin Luther nailed his 95 Theses against indulgences on to the door of the castle church. He also posted a copy to the Archbishop of Mainz.

These Theses created such a sensation that within 2 weeks, they had been printed and read throughout Germany. Within the month, translations were being printed and sold all over Europe.

The 95 Theses begin with the words: *"Since our Lord and Master, Jesus Christ says: 'Repent, for the Kingdom of Heaven is near'(Matthew 4:17), He wants the whole life of a believer to be a life of Repentance."*

A declaration of War! When Luther publically burned the Papal bull outside the walls of Wittenberg it marked the final break with Rome.

Luther maintained that no sacrament can take away our responsibility to respond to Christ's command by an inner repentance evidenced by an outward change, a transformation and renewal of our entire life. Luther emphasised that it is God alone who can forgive sins, and that indulgences are a fraud. It would be far better to give to the poor, than to waste one's money on indulgences. If the Pope really had power over the souls suffering in Purgatory, why would he not release them out of pure Christian charity?

Martin Luther

The Empire Strikes Back

Luther's 95 Theses radically undermined Tetzel's business, almost bringing the sale of indulgences to a standstill. Tetzel, Mazzolini, and John Eck published attacks on Luther, defending the sale of indulgences. When none of Luther's friends rose to his defence, Luther felt deserted. Many of his closest friends believed that he had been too rash in his criticism of this established church practice.

Luther's *95 Theses* created a sensation throughout Europe.

With the pope's power challenged and papal profits eroded, church officials mobilised their forces to bring this rebellious professor into line. First the Augustinians at their regular meeting in Heidelberg sought to silence Luther. Then he underwent three excruciating interviews with Cardinal Cajetan in Augsburg. Then in June 1519, John Eck debated Luther in Leipzig.

Some close friends of Luther tried to persuade him to settle things peacefully by giving in, but to Luther this was now a matter of principle. Scriptural truth and eternal souls were at stake.

In preparation of the Leipzig debate, Luther had plunged into the study of church history and canon law. His studies convinced Luther that many of the decretals, such as the donation of Constantine, were forgeries.

The Leipzig Debate

On 4 July 1519, Eck and Luther faced one another in Leipzig. The issue being debated was the supremacy of the Pope. Luther pointed out that the Eastern Greek Church was part of the Church of Christ, even though it had never acknowledged the supremacy of the Bishop in Rome. The great Church Councils of Nicea, Chalcedon and Ephesus knew nothing of papal supremacy. But Eck maneuvered Luther into a corner and provoked him to defend some of the teachings of (condemned heretic) John Hus. By making Luther openly take a stand on the side of a man official condemned by the church as a heretic, Eck was convinced that he had won the debate. However, Luther greatly strengthened his cause amongst his followers, winning many new supporters, including Martin Bucer, (who became a crucial leader of the Reformation, even helping to disciple John Calvin).

Luther published an account of the Leipzig debate and followed this up with an abundance of teaching pamphlets. *"On Good Works"* had a far-reaching effect teaching that man is saved by faith alone. *"The noblest of all good works is to believe in Jesus Christ."* Luther maintained: that shoemakers, housekeepers, farmers and businessmen, if they do their work to the glory of God, are more pleasing to God than monks and nuns.

Papist officials mobilised every ecclesiastical force to bring the rebellious Professor Luther back in line.

88

On 4 July 1510 Luther debated Eck at the University of Leipzig.

Excommunication

On 15 June 1520, Pope Leo X signed the Bull excommunicating Luther. Describing Luther's teaching as: *"heretical," "scandalous," "false," "offensive"* and *"seducing,"* the Bull called upon all Christians to burn Luther's books and forbid Luther to preach. All towns or districts that sheltered him would be placed under an interdict.

In response, Luther wrote: *"Against the Execrable Bull of AntiChrist."* On 10 December 1520, surrounded by a large crowd of students and lecturers, he burned the Papal bull, along with books of canon law, outside the walls of Wittenberg.

Having exhausted all ecclesiastical means to bring Luther to heel, Pope Leo now appealed to the Emperor to deal with Luther.

Summoned to Worms

Previously, in 1518, when the Pope had summoned Luther to Rome, Prince Frederick had brought all his influence to have this Papal summons cancelled. When Luther had been summoned to Augsburg and

10 December 1520 Dr. Luther burned the papal bull excommunicating him.

Leipzig, Prince Fredrick had arranged for safe conduct guarantees. But now that the Emperor Maximilian had died, Charles V of Spain had been elected Emperor of the Holy Roman Empire. Prince Frederick himself had been a serious contender for this position, and still held tremendous influence. So he prevailed upon Charles V to guarantee safe conduct for Luther as he was summoned to Worms for a Council of German rulers.

The State

In the year before his summons to the Diet of Worms, Luther published some of his most powerful and influential treatises. In the *Address to the German Nobility* (August 1520) he called on the Princes to correct the abuses within the church, and to free the German church from the exploitation of Rome.

The Church

In *The Babylonian Captivity of the Church* (October 1520), Luther argued that Rome's sacramental system held Christians captive. He attacked the papacy for depriving individual Christians of their freedom to approach God directly by faith – without the mediation of unbiblical priests and sacraments. To be valid, a sacrament had to be instituted by Christ and be exclusively Christian. By these tests, he could find no justification for five of the Roman Catholic sacraments. Luther retained only Baptism and The Lord's Supper and placed these within the community of believers, rather than in the hands of a church hierarchy. Indeed, Luther dismissed the traditional view of the church as the sacred hierarchy headed by the Pope and presented the Biblical view of the Church as a community of the regenerate in which all believers are priests, having direct access to God through Christ.

The Christian Life

In *The Liberty of a Christian Man* (November 1520), Luther presented the essentials of Christian belief and behaviour. Luther removed the necessity of monasticism by stressing that the essence of Christian living lies in serving God in our calling, whether secular or ecclesiastical. In promoting this Protestant Work Ethic, Luther laid the foundation for free enterprise and the tremendous productivity it has inspired. He taught that good works do not make a man good, but a good man does good works. Fruit does not produce a tree, but a tree does produce fruit. We are not saved by doing good works, but by grace alone. However, once saved, we should expect good works to flow as the fruit of true faith.

Facing Certain Death

Summoned to Worms, Luther believed that he was going to his death. He insisted that his co-worker, Philip Melanchthon, remain in Wittenberg. *"My dear brother, if I do not come back, if my enemies put me to death, you will go on teaching and standing fast in the truth; if you live, my death will matter little."* Luther at Worms was 37 years old. He had been excommunicated by the Pope. Luther would have remembered that the Martyr, John Hus, a century before had travelled to Constance with an imperial safe conduct, which was not honoured. Luther declared: *"Though Hus was burned, the truth was not burned, and Christ still lives... I shall go to Worms, though there be as many devils there as tiles on the roofs."*

Luther's journey to Worms was like a victory parade. Crowds lined the roads cheering the man who had dared to stand up for Germany against the Pope.

Before the Emperor

At 4 o' clock on Wednesday 17 April, Luther stood before the rulers of the Holy Roman Empire. Charles V, Emperor of the Holy Roman Empire, ruled all the Austrian domains, Spain, Netherlands, a large part of Italy and the Americas. At 21 years old, Charles V ruled over a territory larger than any man since Charlemagne.

Amidst the pomp and splendor of this imperial gathering stood the throne of the Emperor on a raised platform. It was flanked by Spanish knights in gleaming armour, 6 Princes, 24 Dukes, 30 Archbishops and Bishops, and 7 Ambassadors.

Luther was asked to identify whether the books on the table were his writings. Upon Luther's confirmation that they were, an official asked Luther: *"Do you wish to retract them, or do you adhere to them and continue to assert them?"* Luther had come expecting an opportunity to debate the issues, but it was made clear to him that no debate was to be tolerated. The Imperial Diet was ordering him to recant all his writings. Luther requested more time, so that he might answer the question without injury to the Word of God and without peril to his soul. The Emperor granted him 24 hours.

Confrontation

The next day, Thursday 18 April, as the sun was setting and torches were being lit, Luther was ushered into the august assembly. He was asked again whether he would recant what he had written. Luther responded that some of his books taught established Christian doctrine on faith and good works. He could not deny accepted Christian

18 April 1521, Dr. Martin Luther stood firm in the face of the assembled ecclesiatical and political might of the Roman Catholic church.

"My conscience is captive to the Word of God!"

doctrines. Other of his books attacked the papacy and to retract these would be to encourage tyranny and cover up evil. In the third category of books, he had responded to individuals who were defending popery and in these Luther admitted he had written too harshly.

The examiner was not satisfied: *"You must give a simple, clear and proper answer... will you recant or not?"*

"Here I Stand"

Luther's response, first given in Latin and then repeated in German, shook the world: ***"Unless I am convinced by Scripture or by clear reasoning that I am in error – for popes and councils have often erred and contradicted themselves – I cannot recant, for I am subject to the Scriptures I have quoted; my conscience is captive to the Word of God. It is unsafe and dangerous to do anything against one's conscience. Here I stand. I cannot do otherwise. So help me God. Amen."***

After the shocked silence, cheers rang out for this courageous man who had stood up to the Emperor and the Pope. Luther turned and left the tribunal. Numerous German nobles formed a circle around Luther and escorted him safely back to his lodgings.

Condemned

The Emperor was furious. However, Prince Frederick insisted that Charles V honour the guarantee of safe conduct for Luther. Charles V raged against *"this devil in the habit of a monk"* and issued the edict of Worms, which declared Luther an outlaw, ordering his arrest and death as a *"heretic."*

Kidnapped

As Luther travelled back to Wittenberg, preaching at towns along the route, armed horsemen plunged out of the forest, snatched Luther from his wagon and dragged him off to Wartburg Castle. This kidnapping had been arranged by Prince Frederick amidst great secrecy in order to preserve Luther's life. Despite the Emperor's decree that anyone helping Luther was subject to the loss of life and property, Frederick risked his throne and life to protect his pastor and professor.

Wartburg Castle

For the 10 months that Luther was hidden at Wartburg Castle, as Knight

George (*Junker Jorg*), he translated The New Testament into German and wrote such booklets as: *"On Confession Whether the Pope Has the Authority to Require It; On the Abolition of Private Masses"* and *"Monastic Vows."* By 1522, The New Testament in German was on sale for but a week's wages.

Revolution Rebuked

In Luther's absence, Professor Andreas Karlstadt instituted revolutionary changes, which led to growing social unrest. In March 1522, Luther returned to Wittenberg, and in 8 days of intensive preaching, renounced many of

Reformer Martin Luther kidnapped and led away to Wartburg Castle.

Karlstadt's innovations, declaring that he was placing too much emphasis on external reforms and introducing a new legalism that threatened to overshadow justification by faith and the spirituality of the Gospel. Luther feared that the new legalism being introduced would undermine the Reformed movement from within.

At Wartburg Castle, disguised as Knight George, Martin Luther translated the New Testament into German.

The Peasants' Revolt

When the peasants' revolt erupted, Luther was horrified at the anarchy, chaos and bloodshed. He repudiated the revolutionaries and wrote *"Against the Robbing and Murdering Hordes of Peasants."* Aghast at the devastation and massacres caused by the peasants' revolt, Luther taught that the princes had the duty to restore social order and crush the insurrection.

Marriage

Also in 1525, on 13 June, Luther married Katherine von Bora, a former nun from a noble family. Luther called home life: *"the school of character"* and he stressed the importance of the family as the basic building block of society. Luther and Katie were blessed with 6 children.

The Bondage of the Will

Also in 1525, Luther wrote one of his most important books: *"On the Bondage of the Will."* This was in response to Desiderius Erasmus's book on *The Freedom of The Will*, published in 1524. Luther responded scathingly to Erasmus's theories on free will, arguing that man's will is so utterly in bondage to sin, that only God's action could save. Luther

The Marriage of Dr. Martin Luther to Katherine Von Bora, 13 June 1525.

articulated the Augustinian view of predestination and declared that he much preferred that his salvation be in God's Hands, rather than in his own.

As a result of the exchange between Luther and Erasmus, many Renaissance Humanist scholars ceased to support Luther.

A Time of Change
The Reformation not only brought about sweeping changes in the church, but dramatic changes in all of society. First of all the Reformation focused on bringing doctrines, forms of church government, and of worship and daily life into conformity with the Word of God. This, of course, had tremendous implications for political, economic, social and cultural life as well.

God's Word Above All Things
Luther revised the Latin liturgy and translated it into German. Now the laity received the Communion in both bread and wine, as the Hussites had taught a Century earlier. The whole emphasis in church services

changed from the sacramental celebration of the Mass as a sacrifice to the preaching and teaching of God's Word. Luther maintained that every person has the right and duty to read and study the Bible in his own language. This became the foundation of the Reformation: a careful study of the Bible as the source of all truth and as the only legitimate authority, for all questions of faith and conduct.

The True Church
The Church is a community of believers, not a hierarchy of officials. The Church is an organism rather than an organisation, a living body of which each believer is a member.

Luther stressed the priesthood of all believers. We do not gain salvation through the church, but we become members of the Church when we become believers.

"Christ alone is the Head of the Church."
Luther preaching in the chapel of Wartburg Castle.

Scripture alone is our ultimate authority.

Reformation Basic Principles

Luther dealt with many primary issues, including:

1. **Authority** – the Bible alone is our authority and not the councils or leaders of the Church. *The Bible is above tradition.*

2. **Salvation** – is by the grace of God alone, accomplished by the atonement of Christ alone, received by faith alone. *Grace comes before sacraments.*

3. **The Church** – the true Church is composed of the elect, those regenerated by God's Holy Spirit. *Regenerate Church membership.*

4. **The Priesthood** – consists of all true believers. *The priesthood of all believers.*

The Battle Cries of The Reformation

The Protestant Reformation mobilised by Luther rallied around these great battle cries:

Sola Christus – Christ alone is the Head of the Church.

Sola Scriptura – Scripture alone is our ultimate authority.

Sola Gratia – Salvation is by the grace of God alone.

Sola Fide – Justification is received by faith alone.

Soli Deo Gloria – Everything is to be done for the glory of God alone.

Surviving as an Outlaw
Despite Luther being declared an outlaw by the Emperor, he survived to minister and write for 25 more years, and died of natural causes, 18 February 1546.

Translator, Author and Musician
In spite of many illnesses, Luther remained very active and productive as an advisor to princes, theologians and pastors, publishing major commentaries, and producing great quantities of books and pamphlets. He completed the translation of the Old Testament into German by 1534. Luther continued preaching and teaching to the end of his life. He frequently entertained students and guests in his home, and he produced beautiful poems and hymns, including one hymn that will live forever: *"Ein Feste Burg Ist Unser Gott"*(A Mighty Fortress Is Our God).

Teacher
Luther also did a great deal to promote education. He laboured tirelessly for the establishment of schools everywhere. Luther wrote his *Shorter Catechism* in order to train up children in the essential doctrines of the faith.

Martin and Katherine Luther had six children and provided the Church with its first example of a pastoral family.

An Exceptional Professor
It has been common to portray Luther as a simple and obscure monk, who challenged the pope and emperor. Actually Luther was anything but simple or obscure. He was learned, experienced and accomplished far beyond most men of his age. He had lived in Magdeburg and Eisenach and was one of the most distinguished graduates of the University of Erfurt. Luther travelled to Cologne, to Leipzig, and he had crossed the Alps, and travelled to Rome. Luther was a great student, with a tremendous breadth of reading, who had excelled in his studies, and achieved a Master of Arts and Doctorate in Theology in record time. He was an accomplished bestselling author, one of the greatest preachers of all time, a highly respected Theological professor, and one of the first professors to lecture in the German language, instead of in Latin.

Productive and Influencial
Far from being a simple monk, Luther was the Prior of his monastery and the district vicar over 11 other monasteries. Luther was a monk, a priest, a preacher, a professor, a writer, and a Reformer. He was one of most courageous and influential people in all of history. The Lutheran Faith was adopted not only in Northern Germany, but also throughout Denmark, Norway, Sweden, Finland and Iceland.

Luther Changed the World
Luther was a controversial figure in his day and has continued to be considered controversial to this very day. There is no doubt that Luther's search for peace with God changed the whole course of human history. He challenged the power of Rome over the Christian Church, smashed the chains of superstition and tyranny and restored the Christian liberty to worship God in spirit and in truth.

"For I am not ashamed of the Gospel of Christ, for it is the power of God to salvation for everyone who believes ...For in it the righteousness of God is revealed from faith to faith; as it is written, the just shall live by faith." Romans 1:16 – 23

Chapter 13
ULRICH ZWINGLI
The Reformer of Zürich
(1484 - 1531)

Ulrich Zwingli was the father of the Reformation in Switzerland. Born and raised in the Alps, Zwingli was one of the most colourful and audacious characters in Swiss history. A devout student of Scripture, Zwingli was transformed and shaped by the Word of God. He has been described as *"an amazing combination of intellect, passion and wit."*

Man of the Mountains
Born at an altitude of 3,600 feet (1,100 metres), the son of the Mayor of Wildhaus, Zwingli studied in Bern, Basel, and Vienna. In 1506, he received his MA degree. As a pastor in Glarus, Zwingli served as a chaplain with Swiss mercenary soldiers in Italy. The Swiss regularly hired out their men to fight for foreign powers. At that time, the Swiss generally believed that their national economy depended on this war industry.

"Selling Blood for Gold"
During the Italian campaign, Zwingli saw 6,000 Swiss youth die, in the service of the pope, at Marignon. He returned home convinced that *"selling blood for gold"* not only was a waste of young manhood through senseless violence, but also it was corrupting the men's souls through avarice, pride and greed. He observed that the entire country was deteriorating spiritually and morally under the lure of gold from foreign princes. Zwingli spoke out boldly: *"The*

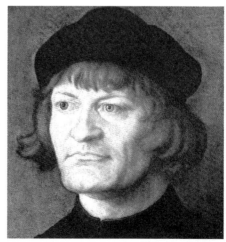

The dynamic Reformer who transformed Switzerland.

situation is very serious, we are already contaminated. Religion is in danger of ceasing amongst us. We despise God..." Zwingli's outspoken preaching against this lucrative profession cost him his pulpit in Glarus.

Forced out of Glarus, he was able to secure a pastoral position at Einsiedeln - where he continued to preach against mercenary service.

Won by the Word
When Erasmus's New Testament in Greek appeared in 1516, Zwingli immediately purchased a copy. Zwingli taught himself Hebrew and Greek and wrote out and memorized Paul's Epistles in the Greek New Testament. He carried around his little pocket edition with him, memorizing much of the New Testament. Zwingli was shocked to find that there was a world of difference between the teachings of the Bible and the teachings and practices of the Roman Catholic Church.

Launching a Reformation
When Zwingli was appointed pastor at *Grossmünster*, (the Great Cathedral) in Zürich, he began his duties, on 1 January 1519, by preaching through the Gospel of Matthew. This bold action of replacing the mass with the preaching of the Word as the central focus of church services marked the beginning of expository preaching.

Facing Death
Shortly after he became pastor in Zürich, the city was hit by the plague. Zwingli showed his courage by giving no thought to his own safety, but staying in Zürich and ministering selflessly to the highly contagious victims. He himself was soon struck down with the plague, and nearly died.

While in the grip of this debilitating illness, Zwingli wrote *"The Song of the Plague"* in which he shows a vibrant faith in the all sufficiency of God's grace in Christ Jesus:

"Help me, O Lord, my strength and rock; lo at the door I hear death's knock.

Ulrich Zwingli

1 January 1519, Ulrich Zwingli began preaching through the New Testament, verse by verse, expositionally, in Grossmünster, Zürich.

"Uplift Thine arm once pierced for me; that conquered death and set me free.

" Yet if Thy voice in life's midday, Recalls my soul, then I obey.

" In faith and hope earth I resign, secure of Heaven, for I am Thine.

"My pains increase; haste to console; for fear and woe seize body and soul.

"Death is at hand, my senses fail, my tongue is dumb; Now, Christ, prevail.

"Lo! Satan strains to snatch his prey; I feel his grasp; must I give way?

"He harms me not, I feel no loss, for here I lie beneath Thy cross.

"My God! My Lord! Here by Thy hand, upon the earth once more I stand.

"Let sin no more rule over me; my mouth shall sing alone to Thee."

Revival Sweeps Zürich

Zwingli recovered from this ordeal, his faith deepened and matured, his mind resolute. He called the people to return to the Bible as the sole standard of faith and practice, to recognise Christ as the only true Head of the Church. Zwingli attacked one Roman doctrine after another. He attacked unbelief, superstition and hypocrisy. Eagerly he strove after repentance, applying Christ's Lordship to all areas of life, in Christian love and faith. He emphasized the need to care for and protect widows and orphans, to maintain law and uphold justice. Zwingli was concerned that our personal Christian faith and love also result in justice established by the laws of the community.

At the heart of the Swiss Reformation was a dynamic sense of Christian community. The Church is a genuine community, one in body and spirit, having the grace of Christ in common and bearing the fruits of the Spirit, the fruits of Christ and the Spirit of God. This unity must extend beyond matters of the spirit to social concern for the entire community, taught Zwingli.

The Alpine Reformer and Bible Translator, Ulrich Zwingli.

Zürich Transformed

As Zwingli systematically preached through the New Testament, he laid the foundations for the Reformation in Switzerland. In 1523, the City Council of Zürich voted to become Protestant.

At the First Zürich Disputation, in 1523, the City Council and 600 citizens, convened in the City Hall to observe the debate between Ulrich Zwingli and four delegates from the Bishop of Constance. At this gathering the city formerly adopted the Reformation and encouraged Zwingli to continue with his Reforms.

At the First Zürich Disputation, in 1523, Ulrich Zwingli convinced the City Council to adopt the Reformation doctrines.

In Zwingli's *67 Theses*, which he made public at The First Zürich Disputation (29 January 1523), he stated: *"3. Christ is the only way to salvation for all who ever were, are and shall be."*

"19. Christ is the only mediator between God and ourselves.

"42. But if ministers are unfaithful and transgress the Laws of Christ, they may be deposed in accordance with God's Will.

"56. Whoever remits any sin only for the sake of money is the companion of Simon (Magus) and Balaam, and a real messenger of the devil."

Diethelm Roist, the Mayor of Zürich from 1524 to 1544, became the chief supporter of Zwingli's Reformation in Zürich. Without Roist's support and protection, it was unlikely that Zwingli's Reformation would have succeeded.

Zwingli was a patriotic Swiss Republican. He was able to create an entirely new Switzerland without any compromise with old unbiblical customs, and free from all foreign bondage and interference.

With the support of the City Council, Zwingli launched a comprehensive programme of Reform. The City Council of Zürich put an end to mercenary service. All images, statues and relics were removed from the church buildings. The mass was abolished. Altars, processions and other trappings and superstitions were discarded. The school system was reformed. Monastery buildings were turned into hospitals and orphanages. The Bible became the basis for all law. All Zürich clergymen were ordered to preach only from Scripture. Priests, monks and nuns were permitted to marry.

Removing idols from Grossmünster.

Work Ethic Restored
Zwingli worked hard to shift the Swiss economy from dependence on mercenary service to agriculture and trade. He urged the people to productive labour: *"You are a tool in the Hands of God. He demands your service... how fortunate you are that He lets you take part in His work."*

From Death to Life
Zwingli compared the moral sickness and spiritual death of sin to the plague, which had killed one out of every three people in Zürich, and he compared their physical recovery to health to the need for spiritual Reformation of the church and society.

Ulrich Zwingli

The Bible Translated

Zwingli began to translate the Scriptures into Schweizer-Deutsch (*Swiss-German*). His lively and dynamic translation reflects his upbringing amidst the towering mountains and lush valleys of Switzerland's Alps. For example in Psalm 23 he wrote: *"In schoner Alp weidet Er mich"(In the beautiful Alps He tends me).*

The Zürich Bible translated into Swiss-German by Ulrich Zwingli.

Zwingli compared the Word of God to the mighty Rhine river that flowed out of the Alps: *"For God's sake, do not put yourself at odds with the Word of God. For truly, it will persist as surely as the Rhine follows its course. One can possibly dam it up for a while, but it is impossible to stop it."*

A Solemn Duty

Zwingli took his pastoral duties most seriously, writing that they *"inspired in me more fear than joy, because I knew, and I remain convinced, that I would give an account of the blood of the sheep which would perish as a consequence of my carelessness."*

Marriage

Earlier, on behalf of 11 other priests, Zwingli had written to the Bishop of Constance seeking permission for priests to marry. This the Bishop had refused. Now, after 2 years of secret marriage, Ulrich married Anna Reinhart, a young widow with 3 children. Ulrich and Anna Zwingli were blessed with another 3 children in their marriage.

Evangelising in the Market Place

Zwingli preached in the market place on Fridays that the crowds from surrounding villages might hear the Word of God. He proclaimed the sufficiency of faith in Christ, the deficiency of superstition and indulgences, and the necessity of true repentance and holy living. He also emphasized the importance of caring for the poor and needy, the widow and the orphan.

Grace could not be bought or sold. Zwingli confessed his own sins publically, including an affair with a nun while a priest in Einsiedeln, and declared Christ's saving grace to be sufficient for the salvation of all who truly repent. Zürich's freedom-loving city, known for its efficient army and love of political independence, found itself drawn to this dynamic preacher and Reformer.

The Disaster of Disunity
It is unfortunate that attempts to bring about a unity between the Swiss and the German Reformations failed. Prince Philip of Hesse, in his attempt to bring about a political alliance of Protestant states, sponsored the Marburg Colloquy between Martin Luther and Ulrich Zwingli. This historic meeting was held at Prince Philip's castle at Marburg. Although Zwingli and Luther agreed quickly on 14 Articles of Faith, there was sharp disagreement on the 15th Article - concerning the Lord's Supper.

Luther and Zwingli came from very different backgrounds and perspectives, and at several points the debate was harsh and acrimonious. At other points the parties appeared to seek each other's forgiveness for name-calling and for the break down in charity. Ultimately, however, their attempt to forge a theological union, that could be the basis of a political and military alliance failed.

As Reformers, Zwingli and Luther had so much in common. They both rejected the authority of the Pope and held to the authority of Scripture alone. They both agreed to the principle of justification by faith alone and rejected the concept of the mass as a sacrifice.

Zwingli had been very complimentary of Luther, describing him in classical allusions *"that one Hercules...who slew the Roman boar."* Zwingli also attributed Biblical titles to Luther: *"Here indeed you were*

Ulrich Zwingli

The Marburg Colloquy where Zwingli and Luther failed to reach full agreement on the Lord's Supper.

the only faith David anointed hereto by the Lord and furnished likewise with arms." But Zwingli did not think that Luther's Reformation went far enough. While Luther taught that whatever is not condemned in Scripture is permitted. Zwingli taught that whatever is not specifically commanded in Scripture should be prohibited.

Luther regarded Zwingli as a *Schwarmer* (a fanatic). Luther insisted that they had to take the Lord's Word's *"This is My body"* literally. Zwingli maintained that this has to be understood as a metaphor (as in *"I am the Vine"* and *"I am the Bread of Life"*). After the resurrection, Christ ascended bodily into Heaven and sits at the right hand of God. Christ is omnipresent only in His Divinity, not in His humanity. *"The Spirit gives life, the flesh is of no avail."*

The Lord's Supper

To Zwingli, the chief significance of the Lord's Supper was that it was a meal eaten in celebration, in remembrance, and in thanksgiving, for what God has done in Christ, but also to exhibit the transformed fellowship of believers. Zwingli had limited the number of Eucharistic services to 4 times a year, while Luther's Eucharist services were held every Sunday. Zwingli maintained: *"I believe that the real Body of Christ is eaten in the Lord's Supper, sacramentally and spiritually by the religious, faithful and pure mind, as also St. Chrysostom held."*

While the Enemy Mobilised

It was one of Zwingli's greatest regrets that he and Luther could not come to any point of agreement on this 15th doctrinal point. Zwingli urged toleration for the different views. Luther regarded Zwingli's plea for toleration as an indication that the Zürich pastor did not take his own views seriously enough.

With the forces of Charles V of the Holy Roman Empire mobilising against them, Philip of Hesse was frustrated in his attempts to bring about a union between the Protestants in Switzerland and Germany.

The Battle of Kappel

From the time that Zwingli began his expository preaching on the Gospel of Matthew, 1 January 1519, he only had 12 years to establish the

Zwingli's Swords and Helmet.

Reformation in Switzerland. He died in battle, fighting to defend Zürich from attack, in 1531. In 1529, a Protestant missionary from Zürich was burned at the stake for preaching the Gospel in the Catholic Canton of Schwyz. Zürich stopped trading with Schwyz in protest. The Catholic Cantons declared war. In October 1531, 8,000 Catholic soldiers met 1,500 Protestant soldiers in battle at Kappel. Historian Myconius described Zwingli's death at the Battle of Kappel: *"Three times Zwingli was thrown to the ground by the advancing forces, but in each case he stood up again. On the fourth*

"They can kill the body, but they cannot kill the soul."

occasion, a spear reached his chin and he fell to his knees saying: 'They can kill the body, but they cannot kill the soul'."

Steadfast to the Last

Zwingli's successor, Heinrich Bullinger, added these details: *"While the Catholic forces were looting the bodies of the dead and dying, they found Zwingli still alive, lying on his back, with his hands together as if he was praying,and his eyes looking upward to Heaven... He was stricken with a mortal wound, so they asked whether a priest should be fetched to hear his confession. At this, Zwingli shook his head... They encouraged him to call upon Mary, the Mother of God and upon the Saints."* When Zwingli again shook his head, the Catholics cursed him, and said that he was one of the obstinate, cantankerous heretics and should get what he deserved. One of the Catholic captains then drew his sword and thrust Zwingli through. When his body was identified, there were tremendous shouts of joy throughout the Catholic camp. It was decided to quarter his body and burn the portions, throwing into the fire the entrails of some

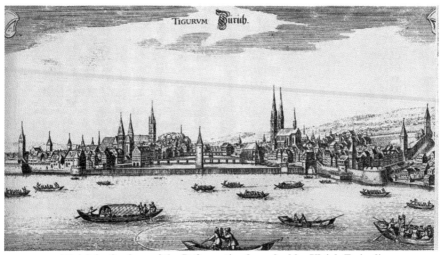

Zürich in the days of the Reformation launched by Ulrich Zwingli.

pigs and mixing the pig offal with Zwingli's ashes, scattering it to prevent a burial of the great Reformer.

An Enduring Legacy
Although Zwingli's career had been cut down at the Battle of Kappel, he laid firm foundations, which were later built upon by Heinrich Bullinger and John Calvin.

Zwingli succeeded in establishing a thoroughly Reformed Church in Zürich, which served as a model for the Swiss National Protestant Church. Zwingli's model of Reform was adopted in Bern, Basel, Schaffhausen, Zürich and later Geneva. His courageous preaching was successful in putting an end to the Swiss custom of selling its soldiers for mercenary service to the French and to the Papacy.

The deep internal divisions between the various Protestant cantons were healed shortly after Zwingli's death by a military alliance (The Christian Civic Union), which succeeded in securing the independence of Switzerland. Zwingli's dream of establishing a European-wide alliance against the Hapsburgs was not fully realized, but Bern did make an alliance with Hesse, Strassburg and Constance. Without Bern's military support, Geneva could never have become the international centre of Protestantism, which it achieved under the leadership of John Calvin.

Zwingli's successes and sacrifices were effectively built upon by his successor Heinrich Bullinger, who from 1531 to 1575 served as pastor in *Grossmünster*. Until the founding of the Geneva Academy by Calvin in 1559, the Carolinum in Zürich was the only Theological college in Europe where students could study Reformed Theology. The Academy in Geneva, and universities of Heidelburg and Holland, built upon the good foundations laid in Zürich.

The English Prayer Book, The 39 Articles, and the Puritan emphasis on Head and Heart, Doctrine and Devotion, as well as the Reformed Episcopacy, adopted by the Church of England, were all built upon the teachings of Ulrich Zwingli and Heinrich Bullinger - which English exiles learned during their time in Zürich. Bullinger, Farel, Viret, Calvin and Beza all consolidated and continued the Reformation begun by Ulrich Zwingli.

"For to me, to live is Christ, and to die is gain."
Philippians 1:21

The Zürich Bible in Zwingli's pulpit in Grossmünster.

Ulrich Zwingli was not only the Father of the Reformation in Switzerland, but also of the Puritan tradition which had such a dramatic impact on England.

Chapter 14

WILLIAM FAREL
Fiery Debater and Evangelist
(1489 - 1565)

A Man of Action

Guillaume Farel (1489 – 1565) was a dynamic man of action who gave his whole life to spreading the Gospel of Christ. Farel was one of the most important leaders of the French Reformation from its beginnings.

By Grace Alone

While studying under Professor Jacques Lefevre at Sorbonne University in Paris, Farel came to faith in Christ. Professor Lefevre had published a Latin translation of, and commentary on, *The Epistles of St. Paul*. As he taught that it is God who saves by grace alone, Farel said his eyes were opened and his heart believed.

"The scourge of the priests," William Farel won whole cities to Christ with his fiery preaching and debates.

Leader of the French Reformation
When Luther's Reformation writings came to France, Farel was one of the most prominent leaders in the French Reformed movement. When persecution forced him to flee from France in 1523, he became the leader of a group of evangelists who preached in French speaking Switzerland.

Winning Switzerland to Christ
Farel's energetic efforts were central in opposing Catholicism and promoting the Protestant Reformation in Basel, Bern, Lausanne and Geneva. Everywhere he proclaimed the supremacy of the Scriptures and the need to return to a purified faith, which was based on the Bible alone. With great skill in debating and evangelistic zeal, Farel succeeded in winning most of French speaking Switzerland to the Protestant Faith.

The Scourge of the Priests
Farel's powerful preaching was described as full of fire and fury. The pope was antichrist. The Mass idolatry. His sermons were cannon blasts. His oratory gripped whole cities. Farel was called *"The scourge of the priests."*

Fearless under Fire
Several priests attempted to assassinate Farel. After one attempt on his life failed, Farel whirled around and declared to the priest who had fired the bullet: *"I am not afraid of your shots!"*

A Church Planter and Author
Many new churches were established and organised under his energetic leadership. Although more of an orator than a writer, and a man of action rather than a theologian, Farel did provide the newly created churches with discipleship books in French. In his *"Summary"* Farel showed how Christian doctrine should be

Farel's unique preaching style in the market places always created controversy and led to public debate with the local bishop. Farel always won the debates.

practically applied to everyday life, and he drew up the first liturgy for French-speaking Reformed churches.

The Waldensians
Farel crossed the Alps to participated in a Synod of the Waldensians. He recruited these believers to the Reformation movement, and convinced them to have the Scriptures translated and printed. This was the first French translation of the Holy Scriptures and was published in 1535.

Neuchatel
After winning Neuchatel to the Reformation, he introduced the book publisher, Pierre de Vingle, to Neuchatel who, just between 1533 and 1535, published 20 Protestant books, which spread the Faith far and wide.

Practical Faith
Farel was a man of deep devotion, personal piety and a very practical faith. He taught that true Christianity functions through charity.

Winning Towns through Debates
Farel's practice was to go into the market places of Catholic towns and preach the Gospel. When attempts were made to arrest him, he challenged the local priests, or bishop, to a public debate. Inevitably, Farel won these debates. He then would appeal directly to the masses to vote on whether they were in favour of converting to the Protestant Faith, or whether they wanted to remain with Roman superstitions.

Confrontational
On such mission trips, Farel's confrontational style and tactics provoked violent reactions. In one town, the bishop tried to have him drowned in the fountain! On occasion, Farel resorted to his fists to eject the papists and seize their pulpits. It is significant that in the Reformation Wall monument, in Geneva, Farel is the only one of the Reformers depicted with a Bible in his left hand (not his right) and his right hand in a fist. Farel was ridiculed, beaten, shot at and abused, but he never gave up. Farel was a fighter.

Ready to Dispute
In the summer of 1535, Farel seized the church of La Madeleine and the Cathedral of St. Peter (in Geneva). Farel declared: *"I have been baptized in the Name of the Father, the Son and the Holy Ghost...I go about preaching Christ - why He died for our sins and rose again for our justification. Whoever believes in Him will be saved; unbelievers will be lost. I am bound to preach to all who will hear. I am ready to dispute with you..."*

William Farel

21 May 1536, the City of Geneva voted to join the Reformation, making the
Protestant Faith their official religion.

Destroying Idols

In response to his vehement sermon against idolatry, there was a
wave of destroying superstitious religious images, statues and idols
throughout Geneva.   Altars were demolished, the mass was
abolished, and images were removed from churches.

Geneva Chooses for Reformation

On 21 May 1536, a General Assembly of the citizens of Geneva
voted in favour of the Reformation and made the Protestant Faith the
official religion of the city.

Revolt against Savoy

With Geneva in revolt against the Duke of Savoy and its bishop,
waves of political and religious turmoil swept the city and emotions
were high.   Surrounded by mountains in the control of Catholic
France and the Duke of Savoy, the Reformation in Geneva was very

21 May 1536, the people of Geneva voted for the Reformation.

vulnerable. Farel knew his limitations, and he prayed for a man who would be capable of discipling this distracted and debauched city.

A Decisive Detour

It was at this decisive point that 27-year-old, French Reformer, John Calvin was forced by a local war to detour through Geneva. He expected to be in the city for only one night. But Farel heard of this famous scholar and author of *"The Institutes"* and he rushed over to recruit him.

A Contest of Wills

But Calvin was not interested. The more Farel explained his plans and described the situation in Geneva, the less Calvin felt inclined to stay. He realized that to accept Farel's challenge would involve him in controversies and conflict, and his timid nature shrank from such un-scholarly activities. Calvin's mind was set on studying in Strassburg, but Farel insisted that he stay in Geneva. Others observing this escalating argument could not have appreciated what a dramatic impact the result of this contest of wills would have on world history.

Confronting Calvin

When, at last, Calvin pleaded his inexperience, general unsuitability for the pastorate, and his need for further study, Farel rose from his chair, and stretched himself out to his full height. As his long beard swept his chest, Farel directed his piercing eyes at the young man seated before him. He thundered: *"May God curse your studies if now, in her time of need, you refuse to lend your aid to His Church!"*

"May God curse your studies if now, in her time of need, you refuse to lend your aid to His Church!" Farel, with Pierre Viret behind him, challenged John Calvin.

Called to Geneva

Calvin was visibly shaken, and, as he said later, he was struck with terror. In Farel's voice of thunder, Calvin had heard the call of God. There and then he yielded and consented to stay in Geneva. Just as Barnabas was used to mobilise Saul for ministry, so Farel recruited Calvin.

Calvin's Closest Friend

Farel probably was Calvin's closest friend through the years. They endured much together, including being expelled from Geneva in 1538. Again it was the persuasions of Farel that convinced Calvin to accept Geneva's requests for him to return in 1541.

Pioneer Pastor

For the last 27 years of his life, Farel pastored the church in Neuchatel, one of the first towns that he had won to Christ. Farel's dynamic faith, missionary vision and evangelistic campaigns had in large measure been used of God to win much of French speaking Switzerland to Christ. And it was he who ensured that Calvin became the pastor, educator and Reformer of Geneva.

"Whoever confesses Me before men, him the Son of Man also will confess before the Angels of God." Luke 12:8

St Pierre in Geneva where Farel defeated the bishop in a marathon debate. The Reformation Museum to the left is built on the very place where the citizens of Geneva voted for the Reformation, 21 May 1536.

Chapter 15
MARTIN BUCER
The Reformer of Strassburg
(1491 - 1551)

Martin Bucer was converted to the Protestant Faith when he heard Martin Luther's arguments at the Leipzig debate with John Eck, in 1519. Bucer became the leader of the Reformation in Strassburg.

Reconciler
Bucer tried hard to reconcile the differences between the Swiss Reformer, Ulrich Zwingli, and German Reformer, Martin Luther, on their different interpretations of the Lord's Supper. Bucer's tolerance of the doctrinal differences earned Luther's scorn. Luther declared: *"It is better for you to have your enemies, than to set up a fictitious fellowship."*

However, although Bucer failed to reconcile Zwingli and Luther, he continued trying throughout his life to unite the Lutheran and Reformed branches of the Protestant Faith.

Calvin's Mentor
When John Calvin was exiled from Geneva, Bucer welcomed him to Strassburg. Calvin pastored the French speaking congregation in Strassburg and developed a firm friendship with Martin Bucer. In some ways, Bucer was Calvin's mentor. During the formative years, between 1538 and 1541, Calvin benefitted from Bucer's teaching and organizational skills.

Martin Bucer, the Reformer of Strassburg and mentor of John Calvin.

Heartache

In 1541, after playing a key role in the Regensburg Colloquy, Martin Bucer saw four of his five sons and his wife die in the plague.

Reformation in England

When Bucer was exiled from Strassburg in 1548 (this was a key condition of a peace treaty dictated by Emperor Charles V), he travelled to England to assist Archbishop Cranmer with the Reformation in England. Bucer was appointed Regius Professor at Cambridge University and assisted in the production of the 1549 edition of *The Book of Common Prayer*.

Archbishop Thomas Cranmer was assisted by Professor Martin Bucer with the Reformation of the Church in England.

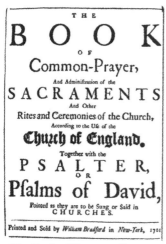

The Book of Common Prayer.

"For God is not unjust to forget your work and labour of love which you have shown toward His Name, in that you have ministered to the saints, and do minister." Hebrews 6:10

124

Chapter 16
WILLIAM TYNDALE
And the Battle for the Bible
(1494 - 1536)

Bishop Stephen Bradley observed: *"We are in danger of forgetting truths for which previous generations gave their lives."*

That our churches are in danger of forgetting the great Reformation truths, for which previous generations of martyrs willingly laid down their lives, was forcefully impressed upon me during a recent ministry trip to Europe. I had the opportunity to visit Oxford and see the Martyrs Memorial. It drew my attention to an event that occurred 450 years before.

The Oxford Martyrs

On 16 October 1555, just outside the walls of Balliol College, Oxford, a stout stake had been driven into the ground with faggots of firewood piled high at its base. Two men were led out and fastened to the stake by a single chain bound around both their waists.

The older man was Hugh Latimer, the Bishop of Worcester, one of the most powerful preachers of his day, and the other Nicolas Ridley, the Bishop of London, respected as one of the finest theologians in England.

More wood was carried and piled up around their feet. Then it was set alight. As the wood kindled and the flames began to rise, Bishop Latimer

Hugh Latimer and Nicholas Ridley were burned at the stake in Oxford, 16 October 1555.

encouraged his companion: *"Be of good cheer, Master Ridley, and play the man! We shall this day light such a candle, by God's grace, in England, as I trust shall never be put out."*

Hundreds in the crowd watching the burning of these bishops wept openly.

The place of their execution is marked today by a small stone cross set in the ground in Broad Street, while nearby in St. Giles stands the imposing Martyrs Memorial, erected 300 years later in memory of these two men and of Thomas Cranmer, the Archbishop of Canterbury, who 4 months after their execution suffered the same torturous death by burning, in the same place, and for the same reason.

In his trial, Bishop Ridley was urged to reject the Protestant Faith. His reply: *"As for the doctrine which I have taught, my conscience assureth me that it is sound, and according to God's Word...**in confirmation thereof I seal the same with my blood."***

After much further pressure and torment, Bishop Ridley responded: *"So long as the breath is in my body, I will never deny my Lord Christ, and His known truth:* ***God's will be done in me!"***

Bishop Latimer declared: *"I thank God most heartily, that He hath prolonged my life to this end, that I may in this case glorify God by that kind of death."*

Faith and Freedom
On one day, in 1519, seven men and women in Coventry were burned alive for teaching their children the Lord's Prayer, the Ten Commandments and the Apostles Creed – in English!

The Illegal English Bible
It may surprise most English-speaking Christians that the first Bible printed in English was illegal and that the Bible translator was burned alive for the crime of translating God's Word into English.

William Tyndale

New Testaments translated into English by William Tyndale were publically burned by the bishop of London at St Paul's Cathedral, where previously Luther's books had been burned.

William Tyndale is known as the father of the English Bible, because he produced the first English translation from the original Hebrew and Greek Scriptures. 150 Years earlier Wycliffe had overseen a hand written translation of the Bible, but this had been translated from the Latin Vulgate. Because of the persecution and determined campaign to uncover and burn these Bibles, few copies remain. It would take an average of 8 months to produce a single copy of the Wycliffe Bible, as they had to be written out by hand. William Tyndale's translation was the first copy of the Scriptures to be printed in the English language.

The official Roman Catholic and Holy Roman Empire abhorrence for Bibles translated into the vernacular can be seen from these historic quotes: The Archbishop of Canterbury Arundel declared: *"That pestilent and most wretched John Wycliffe, of damnable memory, a child of the old devil, and himself a child and pupil of the anti-Christ...crowned his wickedness by translating the Scriptures into the mother tongue."*

Catholic historian Henry Knighton wrote: *"John Wycliffe translated the Gospel from Latin into the English...made it the property of the masses and common to all and...even to women...and so the pearl of the Gospel is thrown before swine and trodden under foot and what is meant to be the jewel of the clergy has been turned into the jest of the laity...has become common..."*

A synod of clergy in 1408 decreed: *"It is dangerous...to translate the text of Holy Scripture from one language into another...we decree and ordain that no-one shall in future translate on his authority any text of Scripture into the English tongue or into any other tongue, by way of book, booklet or treatise. Nor shall any man read, in public or in private, this kind of book, booklet or treatise, now recently composed in the time of the said John Wycliffe...under penalty of the greater excommunication."*

God's Outlaw

William Tyndale was a gifted scholar, a graduate of both Oxford and Cambridge Universities. It was at Cambridge that Tyndale was introduced to the writings of Luther and Zwingli. Tyndale earned his M.A. at Oxford, then he was ordained into the ministry, served as a chaplain and tutor and dedicated his life to the translation of the Scriptures from the original Hebrew and Greek languages.

Tyndale was shocked by the ignorance of the Bible prevalent amongst the clergy. To one such cleric he declared: *"I defy the Pope and all his laws. If God spares my life, before many years pass I will make it possible for the boy who drives the plough to know more of the Scriptures than you do."*

Failing to obtain any ecclesiastical approval for his proposed translation, Tyndale went into exile to Germany. As he described it *"not only was there no room in my lord of London's palace to translate the New Testament, but also that there was no place to do it in all England."*

William Tyndale

Supported by some London merchants, Tyndale sailed in 1524 for Germany, never to return to his homeland. In Hamburg he worked on the New Testament, which was ready for printing by the following year. As the pages began to roll off the press in Cologne, soldiers of the Holy Roman Empire raided the printing press. Tyndale fled with as many of the pages as had so far been printed. Only one incomplete copy of this Cologne New Testament edition survives.

Outlawed for his translation work, William Tyndale produced the English Bible in Germany.

Tyndale moved to Worms where the complete New Testament was published the following year (1526). Of the 6000 copies printed, only 2 of this edition have survived.

Not only did the first printed edition of the English New Testament need to be produced in Germany, but they had to be smuggled into England. There the bishops did all they could to seek them out and destroy them. The Bishop of London, Cuthbert Tunstall, preached against the translation of the New Testament into English and had copies of Tyndale's New Testaments ceremonially burned at St. Paul's. The Archbishop of Canterbury began a campaign of buying up these contraband copies of the New Testament in order to burn them. As Tyndale remarked, his purchases helped provide the finance for the new improved editions.

In 1530 Tyndale's translation of the first five books of the Bible, the Pentateuch (the books of Moses), were printed in Antwerp, Holland. Tyndale continually worked on further revisions and editions of the

New Testament. He also wrote *The Parable of Wicked Mammon* and *The Obedience of a Christian Man.*

This book, *The Obedience of a Christian Man*, was studied by Queen Anne Boleyn and even found its way to King Henry VIII who was most impressed: *"This book is for me and all kings to read!"* King Henry VIII sent out his agents to offer Tyndale a high position in his court, a safe return to England and a great salary to oversee his communications.

However, Tyndale was not willing to surrender his work as a Bible translator, theologian and preacher merely to become a propagandist for the king! In his book *The Practice of Prelates* Tyndale argued against divorce and specifically dared to assert that the king should remain faithful to his first wife! Tyndale maintained that Christians always

have the duty to obey civil authority, except where loyalty to God is concerned. Henry's initial enthusiasm for Tyndale turned to rage and so now Tyndale was an outlaw both to the Roman Catholic Church and its Holy Roman Empire, and to the English kingdom.

Tyndale also carried out a literary battle with Sir Thomas More, who attacked him in print with *Dialogue Concerning Heresies* in 1529. Tyndale responded with *Answer to More.* More responded with *Confutation* in 1533, and so on.

Betrayed by Henry Phillips in Antwerp.

Betrayal and Burning

In 1535 Tyndale was betrayed by a fellow Englishman, Henry Phillips, who gained his confidence only to arrange treacherously for his arrest. Tyndale was taken to the state prison in the castle of Vilvorde, near Brussels. For 500 days, Tyndale suffered in a cold, dark and damp dungeon and then on 6 October, 1536, he was taken to a stake where he was garrotted and burned. His last reported words were: *"Lord, open the king of England's eyes."*

William Tyndale

For 500 days Tyndale suffered in a cold, dark and damp dungeon in Vilvorde.

Tyndale's Dying Prayer Answered

The Lord did indeed answer the dying prayer of Tyndale in the most remarkable way. By this time there was an Archbishop of Canterbury (Thomas Cranmer) and a Vicar General (Thomas Cromwell) both of whom were committed to the Protestant cause. They persuaded King Henry to approve the publication of the **Coverdale** translation. By 1539 every parish church in England was required to make a copy of this English Bible available to all of its parishioners.

Miles Coverdale was a friend of Tyndale's, a fellow Cambridge graduate and Reformer. His edition was the first complete translation of the Bible in English. It consisted mainly of Tyndale's work

"Lord open the king of England's eyes!" Tyndale's dying prayer was
dramatically answered.

supplemented with those portions of the Old Testament which Tyndale
had not been able to translate before his death.

Then, a year after Tyndale's death, the **Matthews Bible** appeared. This
was the work of another friend and fellow English Reformer, John
Rogers. Because of the danger of producing Bible translations, he used
the pen-name Thomas Matthews, which was an inversion of William

Tyndale's initials (WT), 'TM'. In fact at the end of the Old Testament
he had William Tyndale's initials 'WT' printed big and bold.

At Archbishop Thomas Cranmer's request, Henry VIII authorised that
this Bible be further revised by Coverdale and be called **The Great
Bible.**

And so in this way Tyndale's dying prayer was spectacularly answered. The sudden, unprecedented countrywide access to the Scriptures created widespread excitement. Just in the lifetime of William Shakespeare, 2 million Bibles were sold throughout the British Isles. About 90% of Tyndale's wording passed on into the **King James Version** of the Bible.

The Most Influential Englishman

William Tyndale can be described not only as the father of the English Bible, but in a real sense the foremost influence on the shaping of the English language itself. Because Tyndale's translation was the very first from the original Hebrew and Greek into the English language, he had no previous translations to help in his choice of language. While Latin is noun-rich, Greek and Hebrew are verb-rich. At that time the English language had been heavily influenced by French and Latin. Tyndale went back to the original Saxon and found that Saxon English was more compatible with Greek and Hebrew than with Latin and French.

The clarity, simplicity and poetic beauty which Tyndale brought to the English language through his Bible translation served as a linguistic rallying point for the development of the English language. At the time of his translation there were many variations and dialects of English and in many sections of the country the English language was being swamped with French words and Latin concepts. Tyndale's translation rescued English from these Latin trends and established English as an extension of the Biblical Hebrew and Greek worldview.

Thus, every person in the world who writes, speaks, or even thinks, in English, is to a large extent indebted to William Tyndale. It is also extraordinary that while English was one of the minor languages of Europe in the early 16th Century, today it has become a truly worldwide language with over 2 billion people communicating in English.

133

Pioneers for Freedom

The Reformation in the 16th Century was one of the most important epochs in the history of the world. The Reformation gave us the Bible – now freely available in our own languages. The now almost universally acknowledged principles of religious freedom, liberty of conscience, the rule of law, the separation of powers and constitutionally limited republics were unthinkable before the Reformation. The Reformers fought for the principles that Scripture

Within two years of Tyndale's martyrdom, English Bibles were being read in every church in England - by order of the King.

alone is our final authority, that Christ alone is the Head of the Church, that salvation is by the grace of God alone, received by faith alone on the basis of the finished work of Christ alone.

The Power of the Gospel

The Gospel of Christ is life-changing, culture-shaping, history-making and nation-transforming. If it doesn't change your life, and the lives of those around you, then it's not the Biblical Gospel.

"All Scripture is given by inspiration of God, and is profitable for doctrine, for reproof, for correction, for instruction in righteousness, that the man of God may be complete, thoroughly equipped for every good work."　2 Timothy 3: 16-17

Chapter 17
JOHN CALVIN
A Heart Aflame and a Mind Renewed
(1509 - 1564)

The exiled French Reformer, John Calvin, became the most influential man of his age and his teachings have proven to be some of the most influential in the shaping of Great Britain and the United States of America.

Prominent Calvinists
Some of the greatest philosophers, writers, Reformers and Christian leaders in history have described themselves as Calvinists. Some of Calvin's influential disciples include: John Knox, William the Silent, Oliver Cromwell, John Owen, John Milton, Richard Baxter, Jonathan Edwards, David Brainerd, George Whitefield, William Carey, William Wilberforce, Sir Isaac Newton, Lord Shaftesbury, Charles Spurgeon, David Livingstone, The Covenanters in Scotland, The Hugenots of France, and the Pilgrim Fathers who emigrated to New England.

A Heritage of Freedom
The Reformation teachings of John Calvin were foundational in the development of modern Europe and North America. Calvin's concept of the separation of church and civil government – where each stand independent of each other yet recognise each other's Divine authority, supporting each other within their own spheres – transformed Western Civilisation. Calvin's ideals of religious toleration, representative government, constitutionalising the

Calvin's motto was: *"Promptly and sincerely in the service of my God."*

monarchy, establishing the rights and liberties of citizens and the Christian Work ethic – in which secular society is seen as sacred (whereby the arts, crafts, sciences and industries are all developed for the glory of God) led to the industrial and scientific revolutions developing the most productive and prosperous societies in history.

A Strong Doctrine for Tough Times

Calvin's Reformation teachings dominated European and American history for the rest of the 16th and 17th centuries – setting the agendas and inspiring most of the greatest social reformers. The record of history is that in every fight for freedom, whether the Puritans in England, or the Dutch fighting for freedom from Catholic Spain in the Netherlands, the Calvinists were in the forefront of political and military resistance to tyranny.

Resilience

It is an interesting historical observation that one of the most enduring characteristics of Calvinism was that it thrived in those countries where opposition was the greatest.

Following Luther

John Calvin was a second-generation Reformer. He carefully and consciously built upon the solid foundations laid by Martin Luther and Ulrich Zwingli. Calvin looked to Luther as his father in the Faith, with great respect. Luther was very aware of the up and coming distinguished scholar and author, John Calvin, and praised his Institutes.

However, while their foundations were the same, Luther's central focus was justification by faith, whereas Calvin's focus was primarily the sovereignty of God. These Reformers shared an overwhelming sense of the majesty of God. Luther focused on the miracle of forgiveness, while Calvin went on to give the assurance of the impregnability of God's purpose. If Luther's central Biblical text was: *"the just shall live by faith,"* Calvin's was: *"Thy will be done on earth as it is in Heaven."*

Skilled in Logic and Law

John Calvin was born at Noyon, Picardy, on 10 July 1509. (He was 25 years younger than Martin Luther). Calvin entered the University of Paris at age 14, studied Law, and graduated at age 19 with a Master of Arts degree. He was described as having a brilliant writing style and a remarkable skill in logical argument. In later years, it

John Calvin

By age 26 John Calvin was already an author of note, having produced the monumental *"Institutes."*

was said that while people may not have liked what Calvin said, they could not have misunderstood what he meant!

From Law to Outlaw

While Calvin was engaged in further studies at Orleans University he experienced what he described as a *"sudden conversion"* from papal prejudice to Protestant conviction. With this spiritual quickening, Calvin launched into preaching, teaching and counselling amongst his peers. This in turn drew the attention of the state and soon Calvin was on the run as an outlaw, living under aliases and having to move frequently to avoid arrest.

The Institutes

In Basel, Calvin produced the first edition of his Institutes. *The Institutes of the Christian Religion* has been described as *"the clearest, most logical and most readable exposition of Protestant doctrines that the Reformation age produced."*

The full title of this 1536 edition of the Institutes reads: *"Basic Instruction in the Christian Religion comprising almost the whole sum of Godliness and all that it is needful to know of the doctrine of*

Despite frequent bad health Calvin was incredibly productive.

salvation. A newly published work very well worth reading by all who aspire to Godliness. The preface is to the most Christian King of France, offering to him this book as a Confession of Faith by the author, Jean Calvin of Noyon."

This first edition was 516 pages long – divided into 6 chapters on The Ten Commandments, The Apostle's Creed, The Lord's Prayer, The Sacraments (true and false) and Christian Liberty. The Institutes was an immediate success and catapulted Calvin into international prominence. To the French Protestants no one had spoken so effectively on their behalf, and so with the publication of the Institutes, Calvin assumed a position of leadership in the Protestant cause in the French-speaking world.

An Accidental Detour

And so it was as a respected young author that Calvin arrived in Geneva a mere 5 months later. Calvin never intended to spend more than one night in Geneva. He was heading for Strassburg, and was compelled to take a deviation to avoid a local war. The Protestants in Geneva recognised him, and William Farel (the redheaded evangelist and Reformer who had won Geneva over to the Protestant Cause after a marathon debate with the papists just 2 months previously) rushed over to persuade Calvin to stay.

But Calvin had other plans, as he later observed: *"Being by nature a bit antisocial and shy, I always loved retirement and peace..."*

Calvin planned a life of seclusion, study and *"literary ease."*

Challenged, Convicted and Called

Farel would have none of this. He threatened Calvin with a curse: *"You are following only your own wishes, and I tell you, in the Name of God Almighty, that if you do not help us in*

John Calvin

William Farel (with Pierre Viret behind him) threatened to pray for God to curse Calvin's studies if he refused to help disciple the newly converted City of Geneva

this work of the Lord, the Lord will punish you for seeking your own interests rather than His."

Convicted by Farel's serious threat of imprecations, gripped by the fear of God, and ashamed by his selfish plans to avoid controversy and conflict, Calvin agreed to stay.

The Reformer of Geneva

For the next 28 years, apart from 3 years of banishment, Calvin devoted himself to evangelising, discipling, teaching and nurturing the churches in Geneva. Calvin's dedication to duty and intense drive set the highest standards of Christian work ethic. During those two and a half decades in Geneva, Calvin lectured to theological students and preached an average of 5 sermons a week, in addition to writing commentaries on almost every book in the Bible, as well as various other theological books. His correspondence alone fills 11 volumes.

Productivity Despite Ill Health

Calvin was never physically strong, and by the age of 30 he had broken his health. He would not sleep more than 4 hours a night, and even when ill, he kept four secretaries busy with his French and Latin dictation. He ate little, only one meal a day, suffered from intense migraine headaches, was frequently ill with fever, gallstones, chronic asthma and tuberculosis – yet he maintained a steady discipline of study, preaching, producing a river of Theological treatises, a massive amount of correspondence and sustained constant counselling, labour in the courts and received a stream of visitors. How Calvin managed to remain so productive while suffering from such chronic bad health is one of the mysteries of history.

Discipling a City
Calvin's goal in Geneva was a well-taught, faithful church, dedicated to honouring God by orthodox praise and obedient holiness. He prepared a Confession of Faith to be accepted by everyone who wished to be a citizen, planned an educational programme for all, and insisted on effective church discipline, including excommunication for those whose lives did not conform to Biblical standards. His was the most strenuous programme of moral discipline in the Protestant world. And quite a lot more than the City Fathers of Geneva had bargained for. In April 1538, the City Council expelled Calvin and Farel.

Exile and Return
For the next 3 years Calvin pastored a church of French refugees in the German city of Strassburg. These were the happiest years in Calvin's life. He married a widow, Idelette, was honoured by the City of Strassburg as a respected teacher of Theology and was made the City's representative to important religious conferences in Germany. However, the city of Geneva urged His return. In September 1541, with great reluctance, he once again took up the burden of discipling Geneva. Calvin succeeded in turning Geneva into a model example of a disciplined Christian community, a refuge for persecuted Protestants from all over Europe, and a centre for ministerial training.

Predestination and Perseverence of the Saints
Calvin considered Divine election to eternal life the deepest source of confidence, humility and moral power. While Calvin taught that one could not know with a certainty who were God's elect, he believed that

John Knox described Geneva under John Calvin's influence as *"the most perfect school of Christ since the Apostles."*

three tests could be adequate for effective church discipline. A true Christian, John Calvin taught, could be recognised by his or her public profession of faith, active participation in church life, including participation in the two sacraments of Baptism and the Lord's Supper, and by an upright moral life.

Law and Grace

Calvin taught that though Christians were no longer condemned by the Law of God, the true Christian finds in the Law God's pattern for moral behaviour. Man is not justified by works, but no man who is justified is without works. No one can be a true Christian without aspiring to holiness in his or her life. Calvin set justification by faith in a God-centred, sanctification orientated covenantal frame.

Life Changing and Liberating

This rigorous pursuit of moral righteousness, both personally and in society, was one of the primary features of Calvinism. It made character a fundamental test of genuine Christianity and explains Calvinism's dynamic, social activism. God calls His elect for His own purposes. To Calvin, the consequence of Faith is strenuous effort to build God's Kingdom on earth.

Faith and Freedom

Calvin taught that no man – whether pope or king – has any claim to absolute power. Calvin encouraged the development of representative governments, and stressed the right to resist the tyranny of unbelievers. Calvinist resistance to totalitarianism and absolutism (the arbitary abuse of power by leaders) was a key factor in the development of modern limited and constitutional governments. The Church has the obligation, under Almighty God, to guide the secular authorities on spiritual and ethical matters. As a result, Calvinism rapidly assumed international dimensions.

Holland

In Holland, Calvinism provided the rallying point for opposition to the

Street preaching in the City of Geneva.

142

oppression of Catholic Spain, which was occupying their country at that time.

Scotland
In Scotland, Calvin's disciple, John Knox, taught that Protestants had the right and duty to resist, by force if necessary, any leader who tried to prevent their worship and mission.

England
The Puritans in England established the supremacy of Parliament and constitutionally limited the power of the throne.

America
In North America, England's 13 colonies established the United States of America on Calvin's principles of representative government and the rule of Law, *Lex Rex*.

Evaluating Calvin
John Calvin stands out as one of the finest Bible scholars, one of the greatest systematic Theologians and one of the most profound religious thinkers in history. John Calvin was Bible-centred in his teaching, God-centred in his living and Christ-centred in his Faith. He integrated the confessional principles of the Reformation – Scripture alone is our authority, salvation is by the grace of God alone, received by faith alone. Christ alone is the head of the Church, everything should be done for the Glory of God alone – with supreme clarity and conviction.

Bible Based
The Institutes shows that Calvin was a Biblical Theologian. Nothing was in the *Institutes* which Scripture was not shown to support. As Calvin made clear in his Preface to the second edition, the *Institutes* is meant to be a general preparation for Bible study.

Calvin was a systematic theologian who interpreted Scripture with Scripture. As a second-generation Reformer he laboured consciously to confirm and conserve what those who preceded him, Luther, Zwingli,

Calvin's Auditoire where he trained ministers, evangelists and missionaries
who took the Gospel throughout Europe and as far as Brazil.

Melancthon, Bucer and others, had established. He spoke as a mainstream spokesman for the true universal Church.

A Monumental Masterpiece

The final edition of the *Institutes*, published in 1559, contained 80 chapters and more than 1000 pages. The *Institutes* stands as the finest textbook of Theology, apology for the Protestant Faith, manifesto for the Reformation, handbook for Catechism, weapon against heresy, and guide to Christian discipleship. It is a systematic masterpiece, which has earned itself a permanent place amongst the greatest Christian books in all of history.

The First Bible Commentaries

In addition to writing the *Institutes*, John Calvin produced the first Bible commentaries. He wrote commentaries on every book in the Bible, except for Revelation. A theme that binds all of Calvin's works together is to know God and to make Him known.

To Know God

He deals with what can be known about God (Theology) and how to know God personally (devotion). Calvin's motto was *Prompte et sincere in opere Dei* (promptly and sincerely in the service of God). His emblem was of a heart aflame in the hand of God. This is what Calvin wished to be, and this, in fact, was what he was: a heart aflame for God who sought to be faithful in the service of God, renewing his mind according to the Word of God. To him it was not enough to know about God, but essential that one knew Him personally, whole-heartedly, with a heart aflame for God. Not for Calvin the dry-as-dust, cold-hearted, external and empty religion, which epitomises so many of those who claim to follow him. Calvin's faith was intense, passionate and wholehearted.

William Farel, Theodore Beza, John Knox and John Calvin in Geneva.

To the question: What does it mean to know God? Calvin answered: To know God is to acknowledge Him as He has revealed Himself in Scripture and through Christ – worshipping Him and giving Him thanks, humbling ourselves before Him as foolish and depraved sinners, learning from His Word, loving God for His love in adopting and redeeming us, trusting in God's promises of pardon, glorifying what God has accomplished through Christ, living in obedience to God's Law and seeking to honour God in all our human relationships and in all connections with God's creatures.

To the question: From where comes our knowledge? Calvin answers: From the Holy Spirit, speaking in and through the written Word of God by uniting us to the Risen Christ for abundant life.

A Reason to Sing and a Message to Give
Calvin viewed music as a gift of God and encouraged congregational Psalm singing, even putting to music a number of the Psalms himself.

Calvin's Academy became a model and inspiration for countless other classical schools worldwide.

Calvin was an evangelist who worked diligently to bring the lost to repentance and faith in Christ.

A World to Win

Calvin's vision is attested to by the fact that during his ministry over 2,000 Reformed churches were established in France alone – with half a million church members in congregations led by pastors and evangelists he had trained and sent out. Calvin sent missionaries throughout Europe and even as far afield as Brazil.

The Reformation Monument in Geneva.

In his *Institutes*, Calvin wrote of *"the magnificence"* of Christ's reign prophesied in Daniel 2:32-35; Isaiah 11:4; Psalm 2:9 and Psalm 72 where Christ will rule the earth. *"Our doctrine must tower unvanquished above the glory and above all the might of the world, for it is not of us, but of the Living God and His Christ"* Who will *"rule from sea to sea and from the river even to the ends of the earth."*

Have You Read Calvin?

If you have never read Calvin's *Institutes* or benefited from his commentaries, perhaps this would be a good opportunity to invest the time in studying these treasures.

A Call to Suffer And Serve – Changing Cultures for Christ

Calvin's concept of the Christian life as a militant pilgrimage leading safely home by a predestined path of service and suffering – as we fulfill our cultural calling – has produced some of the most humble, hard-working heroes of the Faith. Has your mind been renewed by the Word of God? Is your heart aflame with devotion to Christ? And are you applying the Lordship of Christ to all areas of life, *promptly and sincerely in the service of God?*

"It is better to trust in the Lord than to put confidence in princes."
Psalm 118:9

St Pierre – The pulpit and cathedral in Geneva where Reformer John Calvin ministered for 26 momentous years.

Chapter 18
JOHN KNOX
The Reformer of Scotland
(1514 - 1572)

As the books of Martin Luther and Tyndale's translation of the New Testament entered Scotland, they were received with great interest. Students at St. Andrews University began to take their faith seriously. Patrick Hamilton, a student at St. Andrews, wrote a book that was condemned as heretical. He fled to Germany, met with Luther and soon returned to Scotland. Hamilton began preaching the Protestant Faith with great boldness.

The Betrayal of Hamilton
By an act of Parliament, 17 July 1525, the importation of Luther's books into Scotland was prohibited. In 1528, the Archbishop of St. Andrews summoned Hamilton for *"a debate."* However, he had no intention of debating Hamilton; it was a trap. Before any of his friends could come to Hamilton's defence, a church court hurriedly found him guilty of *"heresy."*

While most heresy trials took weeks, Hamilton's was rushed through in less than 12 hours. It took 6 long, excruciatingly painful hours for Hamilton to die by burning at the stake. Patrick Hamilton was Scotland's first Protestant martyr. He was just 24 years old. His death inspired widespread interest in the Reformation, and an intensified opposition to Catholicism.

The martyrdom of Patrick Hamilton intensified opposition to Catholicism.

Hamilton's last words were: *"How long, O Lord shall darkness cover this realm? How long will you suffer this tyranny of men? Lord Jesus, receive my spirit!"*

Conversion

In 1543, the Regent for the infant Mary Queen of Scots initiated a pro-English, therefore Protestant, policy. This was during the reign of King Henry VIII. The Regent encouraged Bible reading and promoted preaching by Reformers. It was through the preaching of Thomas Guilliame, a converted friar, that John Knox was converted in 1543. The exhilarating effect of this newfound faith and freedom, the joy of experiencing God's grace in Christ, transformed Knox forever.

Soon, however, the Scottish authorities reversed their initially pro-Reformation policies and began to threaten Protestants.

The Courage of Wishart

Tall, handsome and well-mannered George Wishart became the spokesman for Scotland's growing Protestant movement. Wishart travelled throughout the country proclaiming Reformation doctrines with skill and conviction.

Reformer George Wishart galvanised the movement for Reformation in Scotland.

Cardinal David Beaton, Archbishop of St. Andrews, had 5 Protestants executed in 1544 and twice tried to have the popular Wishart murdered. After one failed attempt on his life, out of concern for his safety, the Protestants organised for Wishart to move his location daily to avoid capture. John Knox, armed with a large double handed, broadsword was part of the bodyguard appointed to travel with Wishart. Those who came to a service by George Wishart found, instead of the normal

John Knox is shown here, with a huge sword, as a bodyguard for Reformer George Wishart.

mass in Latin, congregational singing and a fiery, hour-long sermon in their own tongue.

In 1536, believing his arrest imminent and unavoidable, Wishart dismissed his bodyguard saying, *"one is sufficient for a sacrifice."* Wishart was condemned as a heretic, strangled and burned by order of Cardinal Beaton. As the fire was lit, Wishart declared: *"This flame hath scorched my body, yet hath it not daunted my spirit. But he who from yonder high place beholdest us with such pride, shall, within a few days, lie in the same as ignominiously as now he is seen proudly to rest himself."*

Revenge
Within 2 months of the execution of Wishart, 16 Scottish nobles assassinated Beaton in a most brutal way. Before being struck down Beaton was admonished: *"Repent thee of thy former wicked life, but especially of the shedding of the blood of that notable instrument of God, Master George Wishart, which... cries for vengeance... We from God are sent to avenge it... Thou hast been, and remain an obstinate enemy against Jesus Christ and His holy Evangel."* Then a group of

The brutal Cardinal David Beaton was killed in revenge for his murder of Wishart.

ardent Protestants, the Castilians, took over the city of St. Andrews and garrisoned themselves in the castle there.

The Call

Although Knox was not part of either the assassination or this conspiracy, he decided to join the men to minister to them. Impressed by Knox's teaching abilities, they asked him to become the castle's chaplain. (Although, Knox had studied law and theology at the University of St. Andrews and had been ordained, because of the excess of priests in Scotland, he had ended up becoming a tutor and had not previously served as a parish priest.) Knox was overwhelmed, reduced to tears and declined the offer, not feeling worthy.

Over the next few days, the congregation persisted in extending to him the call. Then, while attending a local church service in St. Andrews, Knox heard Dean John Annand affirming Catholicism, claiming that it was *"the Bride of Christ."* Knox stood up in his pew and interrupted him, declaring that the Roman Church was no bride of Christ, but a prostitute. The Roman papacy had degenerated further from the Faith of the Apostles than the Jews had from Moses when they had crucified Christ.

At this, the congregation loudly demanded that Knox justify his remarks in a sermon the following Sunday – which he did. Knox declared that the Roman church had become the synagogue of Satan. He pulled no punches and one observer noted that while others snipped at the outer branches of the papacy, Knox *"struck at the root to destroy the whole!"* This was the beginning of the public career of one of the most powerful preachers of the Reformation era.

Captured and Condemned

The French fleet laid siege to St. Andrews Castle, which surrendered in July 1547. The rebels were taken to Rouen, in France. Knox and most of the Protestants were condemned for life to serve as galley slaves. A life sentence in the galleys was considered the next most severe punishment after execution. Knox said little about his time in the galleys, but two words that he used to described it were: *"torment"* and *"affliction."* During his time in the galleys he contracted kidney infection and stomach ulcers, which afflicted him for the rest of his life.

About 150 galley slaves, or *forsairs*, rode 6 to the oar. The 25 oars were each about 45 feet long. The rowers were kept chained to the oar, when not doing other duties. The *comites* on the ships carried whips to ensure that the convicts and prisoners of war pulled their weight. Galley slaves were considered a cheap and expendable form of fuel for ships.

Knox was about 33 years of age when he was condemned to the galleys. His strong character, which was evidenced throughout the rest his life and ministry served him well throughout this ordeal. On one occasion, while mass was being celebrated on the galley, and the *Salve Regina* (O, Holy Queen) was sung, a statue of the Virgin Mary (*Nostre Dame*) was handed around for all on board to kiss. He refused: *"Trouble me not; such an idol is accursed!"* When this statue was again thrust before Knox's face to kiss, he grasped it and threw the idol overboard declaring: *"Now, let our lady*

Knox struck at the root of Catholicism *"to destroy the whole!"*

save herself. She is light enough, let her learn to swim!"
Knox admitted that the prisoners on these galleys were *"miserably treated."* They were also placed under pressure to renounce Protestantism and embrace Catholicism.

Release and Freedom

The English Protestant government of King Edward VI took a direct interest in the plight of these prisoners and in February 1549, after 18 months as a galley slave, Knox was released. This was probably at the direct intervention of King Edward VI, as part of a prisoner exchange.

Knox the Puritan

Knox spent the next 5 years in England as an honoured guest. He was granted preaching opportunities in Berwick and Newcastle. In 1551, Knox was appointed a royal chaplain of King Edward VI. As a chaplain, he had the opportunity to preach before the king, and contributed to the preparation of the second *"Book of Common Prayer"* (BCP). Knox, for example, insisted that the statement be included that *"kneeling at the Lord's Supper does not imply any adoration of the bread and wine, nor is such adoration intended or permitted. On the contrary, it is stated explicitly, firstly that the natural body and blood of Christ are in Heaven, not on earth, and, secondly, that at the Lord's Supper both the bread and the wine stay the same as they are. To adore them is idolatry."*

When Knox was invited to become Bishop of Rochester, he declined.

Bloody Mary and Exile

When King Edward VI died, 6 July 1553, the future of Protestants in England looked bleak. Mary Tudor made clear her intention to reinstate Catholicism as the national religion. Knox described Mary as the *"wicked English Jezebel."* Knox, along with thousands of other English Protestants, sought refuge in Protestant Germany and Switzerland.

Switzerland
Early in 1554 Knox travelled to Geneva, where he met John Calvin. Knox described Calvin's Geneva as *"the most perfect school of Christ that ever was on earth since the days of the Apostles."* Knox also met Heinrich Bullinger in Zürich.

The Chapel in Geneva where John Knox preached to English Protestants who had fled the Catholic persecution of "Bloody Mary." This was also where the Geneva Bible was translated.

Frankfurt
Knox settled in Frankfurt where a group of English and Scottish exiles asked Knox to be their pastor. This plunged Knox into distressing quarrels and controversies over what liturgy should be used. Knox had become critical of the *"Book of Common Prayer"* (BCP) and even about Calvin's *"Genevan Order of Service"* (GOS), so he drew up a new Order of Service, which became known as the *"Book of Common Order"* (BCO). However, this was rejected by a large majority of the congregation. By March 1555, the congregation was split and the majority proposed Knox's dismissal. Some members of the congregation convinced the city authorities to prohibit Knox from preaching and to expel him from the city.

It is interesting to note that although his *"Book of Common Order"* was rejected by the exiles in Frankfurt, in 1560 it became the official worship book of the Church of Scotland.

The Lords of the Congregation
While Knox was in exile in Europe, Protestant congregations were forming back in Edinburgh, Dundee, St. Andrews, Perth and Brechin. Most of these were clandestine meetings, and many used the English *"Book of Common Prayer."*

In December 1557, a group of Scottish nobles drew up a covenant to *"set forward and establish the most blessed Word of God and His Congregation,"* to renounce Catholicism and to establish the Protestant Faith as the official religion of Scotland. This group became known as the *"Lords of the Congregation."*

Geneva and Scotland

After being expelled from Frankfurt, Knox helped co-pastor an English congregation in Geneva. In August 1555 he returned to Scotland and spent 9 months preaching extensively throughout the land. The Catholic bishops summoned him to Edinburgh in May 1556 to face legal charges. Knox returned to Geneva where he assisted members of his congregation in a new translation of the Bible into English. This became known as the *"Geneva Bible."*

When is it Right to Fight?

Knox asked Calvin whether it was permissible to resist by force a monarch who was *"idolatrous."* Calvin maintained that individuals might refuse to obey commands contrary to God's Law, yet he could not accept revolt. However, Knox was coming to believe that Christians had the obligation to revolt against a tyrannical monarch. A ruler's highest obligation was to preserve pure faith and worship. In Knox's *"A Godly Letter"* (1554) he taught that the nation could incur corporate guilt for tolerating evil. If the people permitted Catholicism to remain, the nation would be subjected to Divine judgment and plagues. God punished the entire tribe of Benjamin, for example, not because all were adulterers, but because some were tolerated.

Idols for Destruction

In his 1549 leaflet: *"A Vindication That The Mass Is Idolatry"*, Knox taught that idolatry entails not only worshipping what is not God, but also in trusting anything besides God. To honour anything in religion contrary to God's Word is to lean on something other than God. That is idolatry. *"The mass...is an abomination."* The mass promoted a false atonement based on works.

Rebellion against God

Since the Law of God never changes, He must respond to sin in Scotland as He did in ancient Israel, e.g. raising up a Jehu to slay an idolatrous ruler. Knox demanded that God's Law be upheld in Scotland. If the people obeyed the unjust commandments of evil rulers, they would receive a far more terrible punishment from God than any ruler could inflict upon them for treason. Not to revolt against an idolatrous ruler was *"plain rebellion against God."*

From Separation to Victory

Knox maintained that, when in a minority, the faithful are only required to separate themselves from idolatry. However, when the believers are in a dominant position, and reasonably unified, they must not simply separate from idolatry, they must also abolish it. If exterminating idolatry meant overthrowing a tyrannical ruler, then that was necessary. Knox's sermons and writings on the subject were full of Scriptural examples: Abraham, Moses, Deborah, Samuel, Elisha, Hezekiah, Jehu, Elijah, Amos, Isaiah, Josiah, Jeremiah, and many other passages dealing with the Covenant, purifying national religion, resisting authorities who promoted idolatry, and the Sovereignty of God. *"If princes exceed their bounds...there is no doubt that they may be resisted with power."*

The Minister of Justice

Luther was protected by Prince Fredrick of Saxony, Zwingli by the mayor and council of Zürich, Calvin had the support of the Geneva City Council, the English Reformation at that time had King Edward VI. However, since no civil authority in Scotland was able to provide protection for Protestants, Knox believed that the abusive powers should be overthrown. In this Knox stands alone amongst the leading Reformers of the 16th Century. He openly challenged the standard interpretation of Romans 13 held by such Reformers as Luther, Zwingli, Tyndale and Calvin.

A Call for Resistance

In his 1555 *"Admonition to England",* Knox condemned those leaders who had connived to restore the nation to Catholicism under Queen Mary Tudor. *"Had she...been sent to hell before these days, then should not their iniquity and cruelty so manifestly have appeared to the world."*

In 1558, Knox published his most notorious *"The First Blast of the Trumpet Against the Monstrous Regiment of Women"* aimed directly at *"Bloody Mary"* – The Queen of England at that time.

Knox stated that no woman could be a legitimate ruler – certainly not one who persecuted true Christians. *"Bloody Mary"* was a rebel against God, *"a traitoress and rebel against God."*

Knox declared that it was against the Law of God and nature for such a woman to rule any kingdom, because it subverted both the Divine and natural order. He called for the faithful to *"remove from honour and authority that monster in nature."*

In his, *"Appellations To the Nobility and Commonality of Scotland"* he extended to the common people the right and duty to rebel against tyranny.

Controversy

John Calvin severely disapproved of Knox's *First Blast* and banned its circulation in Geneva. Within weeks of its publication, *"Bloody Mary"* died and the Protestant Queen Elizabeth ascended to the English throne. Some saw Knox's bold stand against the tyranny of *"Bloody Mary"* vindicated by her sudden removal and the accession of a Protestant Queen to the throne.

However, most saw it as a monumental political mistake and distanced themselves from Knox. Knox admitted: *"My First Blast has blown from me all my friends in England!"*

Knox's fiery sermon against papist idolatry was so effective that immediately after the service the congregation began to demolish altars, smash images and remove statues and crucifixes.

Queen Elizabeth I was appalled at Knox's tract. Knox's explanation that *"the monstrous regiment of women"* that he was referring to were *"Bloody Mary"* Tudor of England, Mary of Guise and Mary Queen of Scots, didn't seem to repair the breach. Nor did Knox's public statement of support for the new Queen Elizabeth I as the Protestant Queen of England repair the damage of his once strong links to the Church of England.

Reformation Sweeps Scotland

In May 1559, Knox arrived in Perth. His fiery sermon against Catholic idolatry was so effective that when the service was over, the congregation immediately began to demolish altars, smash images, statues, and crucifixes. They removed all the superstitious trappings of Romanism. Then the Lords of the Congregation militarily occupied Perth, Sterling, St. Andrews, and by the end of June, Edinburgh. There,

Knox was elected minister at St. Giles Kirk in High Street. His Reformation preaching reverberated throughout Scotland.

The French Outmanoeuvered
To counter Mary of Guise and her French troops, the Scottish Lords of the Congregation drew up the Treaty of Berwick, February 1560, with the English. The Treaty was so effective that on 6 July 1560 the French and English both agreed to leave Scottish soil. Without French interference, the future of the Reformation in Scotland was assured!

Thanksgiving and Confession
Later that month the Scottish Parliament met at St. Giles, in Edinburgh, for a great Thanksgiving service where Knox preached to them. The Parliament then ordered Knox and 5 of his colleagues to write a confession of faith. Hurriedly put to paper in 4 days, *The Scots Confession* is vibrant and spontaneous, filled with prophetic and militant language. It was adopted by Parliament, and remained for 90 years, the Scottish churches' official theology. (In 1647, it was superseded by the Westminster Confession.)

Faith in Action
The Scots Confession stands out in how it specifies practical Christian ethics. It urges good citizenship, honourable living and a commitment to social justice in these words: *"To have one God, to worship and honour Him, to call on Him in our troubles, to reverence His Holy Name, to hear His Word and believe it, to share in His Holy sacraments.*

"The second kind is: to honour father, mother, monarchs, rulers and superior powers; to love them, support them, obey their orders providing they are not contrary to God's Commandments, save the lives of the innocent, overthrow tyranny, defend the oppressed, keep our bodies clean and holy, live in soberness and temperance, deal justly with all men in word and deed, and finally, to subdue any desire to harm our neighbour...Contrary acts are sins." (Article 14)

John Knox declared: *"Dangerous times demand vigorous faith."* **This picture is of John Knox preaching at St Andrews, 11 June 1559. On this occasion Knox was threatened that he would be shot in the pulpit.**

A Higher Duty

The Scots Confession not only permits the overthrowing of tyrants, but makes such action mandatory. Tyrants are defined as the real rebels to the King of kings. Article 13 defines workers of iniquity as: *"filthy persons, idolaters, drunkards and thieves... murderers, oppressors and cruel persecutors."*

The Scots Confession makes clear that no civil power is absolute. Civil leaders are permanently on probation and no Christian should give unqualified and absolute allegiance to any government. Christians must reserve the right of just rebellion against tyrants.

No other Reformation Confession ventured so far into such dangerous waters, providing theological justification for rebellion against tyrants. As Knox declared: *"Dangerous times demand vigorous faith."*

On August 17, Parliament abolished the mass, repudiated papal jurisdiction over Scotland, and rescinded all laws at variance with the Reformed Faith.

Comprehensive Reform

Also in 1560, Knox's Treatise on *Predestination* was published in Geneva. The Geneva Bible was also published. This was the work of the English congregation that Knox had pastored. In December 1560 the *"First Book of Discipline"* drawn up by Knox and his colleagues was submitted to the general assembly. Knox laid out plans for the comprehensive application of the Gospel to every area of Scottish life. He wanted a school in every parish, a college in every town, a university in every city, and regular, organised provision for the poor.

Also in 1560, Knox's wife, Marjory, died.

Mary Queen of Scots

Although the Reformation Parliament of 1560 had worked with John Knox to mandate a Calvinist Scotland, the return of the Catholic Mary Queen of Scots in 1561 put that in jeopardy. As Queen, she refused to assent to the new order and Scotland remained officially Catholic. Mary Stuart was heir to England's throne if Elizabeth died. With her strong ties to Philip II in Spain, and the Guises in France, the Catholic threat to Scotland's emerging Reformation was serious.

The Scots were well aware that in the Netherlands Protestants were being tortured, beheaded, hanged, drowned, burned and buried alive by the Vatican's heavy hand. They had recently witnessed the wave of horrible executions under *"Bloody Mary"* in neighbouring England. As rumours circulated that Mary Stuart would marry Don Carlos, the son of Philip II of Spain (the arch persecutor of Protestants), Knox preached a withering sermon declaring that: *"all papists are infidels!"*

Philip II was well aware that Mary Stuart was the Vatican's best hope of restoring Catholicism to England: *"She is the one gate through which religion can be restored in England. All the rest are closed."*

Immorality and Intrigue

Mary Stuart married Lord Darnley of England, hoping to unite the Catholics of England and Scotland. When the Queen became pregnant, her young husband accused the Queen of adultery with her private secretary, David Rizzio. Lord Darnley (now King Henry) participated in the murder of Rizzio, 9 March 1556. On 15 June 1556, Mary Stuart delivered a son: James Charles Stuart (who grew up to become James I of England).

In revenge for voicing his suspicions, Mary Stuart arranged through her boyfriend, the Earl of Bothwell, the assassination of her husband, King Henry (Lord Darnley). Mary coaxed Henry back to Edinburgh, lulled his suspicions and arranged for him to be blown up by explosives. Both Protestants and Catholics in Scotland were outraged. Mary had Bothwell stand a mock trial, at which he was acquitted, then gave him Dunbar Castle and various lands to his associates.

Confronting the Queen

Knox was called before the Queen's Council - where he voiced his suspicions. Then he confronted Bothwell with charges of adultery, complicity in murder, and rape. When Bothwell married Queen Mary, May 1567, the nation became convinced that she had helped murder her husband. There were widespread calls for her to be deposed and the people turned against her. Knox demanded that the Queen stand trial for murder and adultery – both capital crimes. Mary Stuart was forced to abdicate and the

Mary, Queen of Scots declared that she was more afraid of the prayers of John Knox than of an army of 10,000.

The military defeat of Mary Stuart ended the immoral reign of this enemy of the Reformation.

nobles organised a swift coronation of the infant, James VI of Scotland (later he would become James I of England and of the United Kingdom).

The Reformation Triumphs in Scotland

At this coronation, Knox preached from the pulpit about the baby Joash who was anointed and crowned while Queen Athaliah cried treason from her palace. The sermon included details from the Bible as to how the nobles had gone from the coronation of Joash to kill Athaliah, to tear down the temples of Baal and to restore the rule of the prophets in the land. While Knox was calling for the trial of Mary Stuart, she escaped and raised an army of 6,000 Catholics. However, when her army was confronted by the disciplined Protestants, Mary's army melted. She fled to England and sought the protection of her cousin, Elizabeth. Bothwell fled to Denmark.

James Stuart, Mary's half brother, became Regent of Scotland. James Stuart (1531 – 1570) had been an influential figure in Scottish politics. By age 19, he was already a member of the Privy Council. He became Mary Queen of Scots' Chief Advisor when she returned to Scotland. However, as he was won over to the Protestant Faith and became a member of the Lords of the Congregation, he used his power to maintain and extend the influence of Protestantism. When Mary was forced to abdicate in 1567, and her infant son, James VI was crowned, Stuart was appointed Regent. He was described as: *"a Puritan with natural charm and diplomacy."*

Oppression and Insurrection

At the same time, Europe was boiling. The Spanish Duke of Alva had fallen upon the Calvinist rebels of Holland with fire and sword. 8,000 Dutch Protestants were executed. Another 30,000 had their property confiscated. Then in 1568, the Inquisition condemned all 3 million Dutch Protestants to death as *"heretics!"* The Dutch valiantly resisted and declared independence. Philip II was facing a great revolt. Along with the war in the Netherlands, and civil war in France, a papal bull excommunicating Elizabeth inspired a Catholic uprising under the Earls of Northumberland and Westmoreland. The Catholic armies of Northumberland destroyed Bibles and prayer books, re-instituted the mass in Durham Cathedral, and moved to rescue Mary Stuart to make her Queen of England.

Removing the Threat

Elizabeth's army crushed the Catholic rebellion, and after numerous other intrigues and conspiracies to assassinate her and place Mary on the English throne were exposed, Elizabeth reluctantly agreed to Mary's trial and execution.

Assassination

The assassination in February 1570 of the Protestant Regent of Scotland, James Stuart, plunged Scotland into civil war. Later that year, Knox suffered a stroke. But he continued to preach throughout the last months of his life. Even as his health was deteriorating, he insisted on being carried to the pulpit.

John Knox's home in Edinburgh, Scotland. He regularly preached to people in the street from the top of the stairs.

Success

The Reformation Wall in Geneva acknowledges John Knox as one of the four most central Reformers.

Before he died, in 1572, Knox had the joy of seeing the Reforms of 1560 ratified by the Scottish Parliament. Papal authority in Scotland was outlawed. All future rulers of Scotland were to swear to uphold the Reformed doctrine. The day before he died Knox said: *"I have been fighting against satan, who is ever ready for the assault; I have fought against spiritual wickedness and have prevailed."* The dedicated labours of John Knox resulted in Scotland becoming the most Calvinist nation in the world.

The Verdict of History

Otto Scott in *"The Great Christian Revolution"* summarizes his achievements: *"Knox had humbled a reigning monarch, toppled a government, ousted a hierarchy, converted the people and could regard, towards the close of his life, the landscape transformed by his efforts and the teaching of his mentor, Calvin. Knox's triumph in Scotland...severed a tentacle of France and lessened the threat to the Reformation of England."*

At his grave, one man declared: *"Here lies a man who neither flattered, nor feared, any flesh."*

One of Knox's followers had declared that his preaching was *"able in one hour to put more life in us than 500 trumpets continually blustering in our ears."*

The 19th Century historian, Thomas Carlyle, describe Knox as: *"a most surprising individual to have kindled all of Scotland, within a few years, almost within a few months, into perhaps the noblest flame of sacred human zeal and brave determination, to believe only what it found completely believable, and to defy the whole world and the devil at its back, in an unsubduable defense of the same."* To Carlyle, Knox was the very epitome of stalwart leadership, *"the most Scottish of Scots...nothing hypocritical, foolish and untrue can find harbor in this man... fearing God and without any other fear."*

"A man who neither flattered, nor feared, any flesh."

Douglas Wilson in his biography of Knox *"For Kirk and Covenant"* describes Knox as: *"like Daniel in the Old Testament, he was forthright in his condemnation of sin, unguarded in his pronouncement of truth, and single-minded in his adherence to the Word of God. Like King Josiah, in ancient Israel, he did what was right in the sight of the Lord, never turning aside to the right hand or to the left. Like the great general Joshua, he dutifully obeyed the clear commands of Scripture, always steadfast and unwavering. But such character traits and such stands, however compelling, are inevitably costly. It nearly cost Knox everything during his lifetime and it has earned him the odium and ire of virtually every secular historian in the years since...a simple compromise here or there might well have saved him from imprisonment, exile and anathema. But he refused to compromise. He could have tried to work within the system. He could have tried conciliation, accommodation, or negotiation. But he refused to compromise, risking everything for the sake of principle."*

God's Firebrand

John Calvin described Knox as: **"God's firebrand"** and as a *"brother...labouring energetically for the faith."*

Mary Stuart, Queen of Scots, had been heard to declare, trembling and in tears: *"I am more afraid of the prayers of John Knox than of an army of 10,000."*

John Knox's famous prayer: *"Give me Scotland or I die!"* was thoroughly answered in his lifetime.

"I have fought the good fight, I have finished the race, I have kept the faith." 2 Timothy 4:7

"Give me Scotland, or I die!"

Chapter 19
ALBERT DÜRER
Evangelist and Reformer in Art
(1471 - 1528)

Albert Dürer was the oldest son and third of 18 children born to a goldsmith in Nuremberg, Germany. His father, Albert Dürer, the elder, worked hard in his precious metals business, but faced severe trials and suffered the loss of many of his children. Only three of his 18 children survived to adulthood. Yet Mr. Dürer was an honest man who trusted in God and handled his trials with courage and faith.

Brought up to Love and Honour God
His son, Albert wrote: *"My father lived an honourable Christian life. He was a man patient of spirit, mild and peaceable to all, and very thankful toward God... He was a man of few words and a God fearing man... This man, my dear father, was very careful of his children to bring them up to love and honour God."*

Apprenticed in Art
Albert was trained as an apprentice in his father's goldsmith shop, but his longing was to be an artist. So in 1486 his father sent Albert to study for three years at the studio of the famous Michael Wolgemuth. Then Dürer spent the following few years travelling from town to town with other artists

"The Adoration of the Magi."

to develop his craft. In Mainz, where just 35 years earlier, Johannes

Gutenberg had invented the Printing Press, Dürer worked with the famous Erhard Reuwich, whose book *Travels in The Holy Land* was full of sketches depicting the architecture, clothing and landscape of Israel.

Marriage and Masters
In 1494, Albert returned to Nuremberg and married the beautiful Agnes Frey. Together they spent the next 11 years in Nuremberg where Albert developed woodcut illustrations and copper plate engravings. In 1505 he travelled to Venice to study alongside some of the great Renaissance masters.

A Disciple of Martin Luther
As Martin Luther launched his Reform, Dürer paid close attention.

"The Crucifixion."

When Prince Frederick of Saxony sent Dürer one of Luther's books in 1520, Dürer wrote to him and thanked him: *"I pray and humbly beg that you will protect the praiseworthy Dr. Martin Luther for the sake of Christian truth. It matters more than all the riches and power of this world, for with time everything passes away; only the truth is eternal. And if God helps me to come to Dr. Martin Luther, then I will carefully draw his portrait and engrave it in copper for a lasting remembrance of this Christian man who has helped me out of great distress. And I beg your worthiness to send me as my payment anything new that Dr. Martin may write in German."*

"Removing Christ from the Cross."

In his journal, Dürer describes Luther as: *"enlightened by the Holy Ghost to be the continuer of the true Faith... he has suffered... for the Christian truth against the unchristian papacy, which works against the freedom of Christ, exacting from us our blood and sweat, therewith to nourish itself in idleness, while the people famish."*

Christ Centred

Dürer returned to the Netherlands in 1521 and spent the remaining years of his life in pursuit of his ministry in art, engraving, painting, devoting all of his work to various aspects of the life of Christ, the Resurrection and the last Day of Judgment.

Artist of the Reformation

It is in part due to Dürer's influence, and to the spiritual and intellectual character of Nuremberg, that it was the first free city to become officially Protestant. Dürer was also one of the first artists publicly to identify with the Reformation.

Dürer developed a special relationship with Philip Melanchthon. Dürer wrote: *"No man can ever execute a beautiful picture relying on his own imagination, unless he has stirred his mind from a study of Divine work in nature...the mysterious treasure welled up in the heart is made known by the man's work – for the mind and the heart must be in union with the life and power of God, and then the artist's hand will form that thing of beauty which is indeed a joy forever."*

The Gospel in Art

Dürer has provided the church with some of the most striking works representing the life and ministry of Christ in pictures. Clearly, Albert Dürer was a humble and dedicated Christian who loved the Saviour with all his heart. His art proclaims the greatest story ever told.

"Declare His glory among the nations, His wonders among all peoples. The Lord is great and greatly to be praised..."

1 Chronicles 16:24 – 25

"The Horsemen of the Apocolypse."

Chapter 20
ANNE ASKEW
A Daughter of the Reformation
(1520 – 1546)

Anne was born during the reign of King Henry VIII to an honoured knight, Sir William Askew.

Attractive

Anne was described as attractive in form and faith, a beautiful and high-spirited young woman, well educated, with unusual gifts, and *"very pious."* Her father arranged that she should be married to the son of a friend, Thomas Kyme, to whom her deceased sister had originally been promised.

Faithful

Anne endeavoured to be a faithful wife, and bore her husband two children. However, despite an initially happy marriage, her husband, Kyme, threw her out of the home because of her Protestant Faith.

Dedicated

Anne had acquired a copy of the English Bible and had studied it enthusiastically. She abandoned her formal Catholic religion for the life-changing Protestant Faith in a personal Lord and Saviour, Jesus Christ. Her enthusiastic

Anne Askew: *"Attractive in form and faith."*

witness drew the attention of the priests who warned her husband about her *"sedition."* When challenged she confessed that she was no longer a Romanist, but *"a daughter of the Reformation"*. At this, her husband threw her out of the home. However, he acknowledged that he had never known a more devout woman than Anne.

Arrested

In 1545, Anne was examined by church leaders concerning her beliefs. Her answers were full of wisdom and quotes from the Holy Scriptures, and she often out-manoeuvered the inquisitors pointing out the contradictions in their own position. This only served to enrage them more. Lord Bonner was determined to see her burned for heresy.

Blameless

After failing to prove any heresy, he resorted to insinuating that she was immoral. Looking him full in the face, Anne answered calmly: *"I*

Calm and steadfast under interrogation and torture, Anne Askew answered every challenge of her inquisitors with bold and Biblical Faith.

would, my lord, that all men knew my conversation and living in all points; for I am so sure of myself this hour, that there is none able to prove any dishonesty in me. If you know any who can do it, I pray you bring them forth." He could not find anyone who could question her morals, and so he had to have her released.

Newgate prison where Anne Askew was incarcerated.

Interrogated

Thomas Wriothesley, the Lord Chancellor of England, was determined to crush the Reformation. He summoned her before the council and subjected her to an examination that lasted five hours. One of the council, Mr. Paget, challenged Anne: *"How can you avoid the very words of Christ, take, eat, this is My Body which is broken for you?"*

Steadfast

Anne answered: *"Christ's meaning in that passage is similar to the meaning of those other places of Scripture, 'I am the door', 'I am the vine'. 'Behold the Lamb of God.' 'That rock was Christ.' And other such references to Himself. We are not in these texts to take Christ for the material thing which He is signified by, for then we will make Him a door, a vine, a lamb, a stone, quite contrary to the Holy Ghost's meaning. All these indeed signify Christ, even as the bread signifies His body in that place."*

Imprisoned

Anne was charged and imprisoned in Newgate Prison. Her enemies were determined to see her burn. On 28 June, she was taken to Guild Hall to be examined again by the council. She was taunted with being a heretic. She responded that she had done nothing for which the Law of God required her death.

Faithful

When asked directly if she denied the doctrine of Transubstantiation, that the sacrament of the Eucharist was the actual body and blood of Christ, Anne responded: *"God is a Spirit, not a wafer cake. He is to be worshipped in spirit and in truth – John 4:24 – and not by the impious superstitious homage paid to a wafer converted, by popish jugglery, into a god."*

Condemned

That very day, 28 June, the council condemned Anne Askew to be burned to death at the stake.

Tortured

However, before that sentence was to be carried out, Lord Wriothesley ordered her to be stretched on the rack. As the levers were turned and the torture began, Anne remained silent. Wriothesley was so angered by his lack of success that he ordered the torture to be increased. Then the officer of the rack was so moved by the sight of this pious woman enduring such torture in silence, he refused to intensify the torture. Wriothesley himself grabbed the levers and mercilessly stretched her body until her joints were pulled asunder and her bones were broken. Yet, despite the intense sufferings, all the cruelties of her enemies failed to change the patient sweetness of Anne's Christian demeanour.

Martyred

When the day of her execution arrived, Anne was so crippled as a result of her tortures on the rack that she had to be carried in a chair to the stake. One who witnessed her death wrote: *"She had an angel's countenance and a smiling face."* She was offered one last chance at a pardon if she would renounce the doctrines of the Reformation and embrace Catholicism. This she boldly refused. *"I believe all those Scriptures to be true which He hath confirmed with His most precious blood. Yea, and, as St. Paul sayeth, those Scriptures are sufficient for our learning and salvation that Christ hath left here with us; so that I believe we need no unwritten verities with which to rule His Church."*

Anne Askew

The woodcut in Foxe's Book of Martyrs depicting the martyrdom of Anne Askew and others, at Smithfield.

Courageous

All who witnessed her noble martyrdom were impressed and inspired by the courage of this beautiful woman who gladly gave her life for Christ of one as the truest and purest witnesses of the Gospel of the Christian Church.

"Only let your conduct be worthy of the Gospel of Christ…Stand fast in one spirit, with one mind striving together for the Faith of the Gospel, and not in any way terrified by your adversaries, which is to them a proof of their perdition, but to you of salvation and that from God. For to you it has been granted on behalf of Christ not only to believe in Him, but also to suffer for His sake." Philippians 1:27 – 29

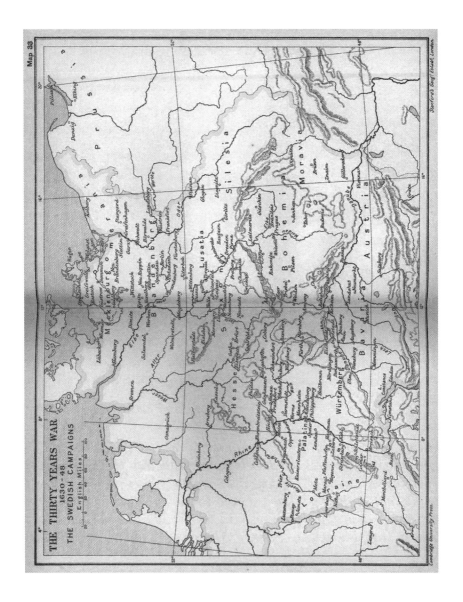

THE THIRTY YEARS WAR
1630-48
THE SWEDISH CAMPAIGNS

Chapter 21
GUSTAVUS ADOLPHUS
The Lion from the North
(1594 - 1632)

Gustavus Adolphus is one of the most inspiring characters of the Reformation. The rapid rise to fame of Gustavus Adolphus, the young King of Sweden, his military innovations and dramatic victories in battle turned the tide in The Thirty Years War and saved Protestant Germany from annihilation.

A Military Strategist

Military strategist Carl von Clausewitz and French emperor Napoleon Bonaparte considered Gustavus Adolphus one of the greatest generals of all time. Gustavus II is famous for employing mobile artillery on the battlefield, and very aggressive tactics where attack was stressed over defence and mobility emphasized over the usual linear tactics. His musketeers were widely known for their shooting accuracy and reload speed, three times faster than any contemporary rivals.

Leading from the Front

Gustavus Adolphus was an active participant in his battles, and chose to lead charges himself at crucial moments. He was repeatedly wounded in battle, including gunshot wounds to the neck, throat and abdomen. Because of an early wound where a musketball was lodged in his neck near the spine,

Gustavus Adolphus, King of Sweden, saved the Protestants in Germany from annihilation in the Thirty Years War.

179

The Swedish infantry were well trained in rapid fire and mobile warfare.

due to the extreme pain, he chose to avoid wearing the customary two part metal armour cuirass, adopting a flexible leather armour instead.

Tactical Innovations

Gustavus II is credited with a number of technical innovations, including the paper bullet cartridges, and light mobile artillery, lightening the muskets and abolishing the musket rest. He also innovated administrative reforms, conscripting large standing armies, developing the infantry brigade, improving military logistics and standardizing artillery calibers. Gustavus' tactical innovations included perfecting dashing cavalry charges, and smaller, more flexible and offensive infantry formations, using concentrated devastating volley fire and close artillery support to clear the way in front of rapid infantry or cavalry advances. Numerous military historians have gone so far as to call him "the Father of Modern Armies." His military innovations proved devastating to his enemies forces in battle.

A Great Christian King

To Protestants, Gustavus Adolphus is one of the greatest examples of a Christian king. He was known in his lifetime as "the Lion from the North", "the Protector of Protestantism" and "the Deliverer of Germany". His timely intervention stopped the onward march and devastation caused by the Catholic League and the Austrian Empire. There is no doubt that Gustavus Adolphus helped change the course of European history. He is comparable to other great Christian military commanders: Oliver Cromwell, Robert E. Lee, and Stonewall Jackson; but as a Reformer-King he can also be compared to King Alfred the Great of England.

An innovative military leader.

Gustavus Adolphus (1594-1632) was born at Stockholm Castle on the 9th of December, 1594, the oldest son of King Charles IX of Sweden and of Queen Christina (daughter of the Duke of Schleswig-Holstein.)

Gustavus Vasa

Gustavus was born during a turbulent time. His grandfather, Gustavus Vasa (1496-1560) had escaped from a Danish prison in Jutland, and succeeded in delivering his country from the yoke of tyranny. He drove the Danes from Sweden, and restored their freedom, and was chosen by the grateful country to be their king. Gustavus Vasa had been discipled by one of Luther's students. He was determined to make Sweden a Protestant nation and he instituted reforms in all his states. He required all his subjects to accept this profession of faith: *"To serve God by being obedient to His Law, and by loving Him above all else; to believe in Jesus Christ as our only Saviour; to study and teach the Word of God with zeal; to love our neighbour as ourself, and to observe the Ten Commandments- such is the true worship that we should render unto God."*

Sweden Adopts the Reformed Faith

However, despite Gustavus Vasa's sincere faith, the Reformation lacked widespread popular support in Sweden until after his death, when under his son, Charles IX, the Swedish Church adopted the Lutheran Augsburg Confession of 1530, as its statement of faith.

Trained to Fight for the Faith

Gustavus Adolphus was schooled in the classics, law, history and Lutheran Theology. By age 16 he was not only fluent in his native Swedish and German, but he'd also mastered Latin, Italian, Dutch, Spanish, Russian and Polish. His austere parents ensured that he was carefully nurtured to champion the cause of the Protestant Faith. He was trained as a prince and as a soldier. From 9 years old he was introduced to public life and accompanied his father on official business of state, receiving petitions, conversing with foreign ministers and even joining his father on military campaigns.

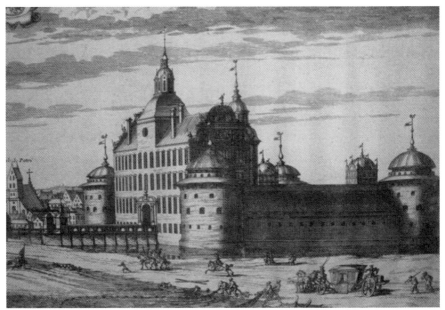

Gustavus was only 16 years old when he was crowned king of Sweden.

A Kingdom in Peril
Gustavus Adolphus was only 16 years old when his father died and he succeeded to the throne. He inherited a country facing critical external threats and internal disintegration. In the West, there was the war with Denmark; in the East, a war with Russia. The country was bankrupt and riots threatened the internal stability of the kingdom.

Godly Counsel
His father's last letter to him is still extant. It counsels Gustavus: *"Fear God. Honour thy father and thy mother. Love deeply and sincerely your brothers and sisters. Esteem the faithful servants of your father, and reward each one according to his merits. Be humane toward your subjects. Punish the wicked, love the good. Trust everyone, but not without caution. Observe the law without respect of person Deprive no one of privileges if they are well founded and not contrary to the general good."*

War Against Russia and Poland
Gustavus terminated the fratricidal struggle against Denmark with the Peace of Knarred, 1613. He then turned his full attention toward the war in Russia against the sworn enemy of Sweden – Sigismund III, the King of Poland, and brother-in-law of Emperor Ferdinand II of Austria. Gustavus insisted on a strict code of conduct and regular worship services in his military camps. Morning and evening his entire army knelt before Almighty God and reverently implored His aid and favour.

Victory in the East
Gustavus was seen digging in the trenches, helping to build the fortifications, and frequently in the front line of battle. He was severely wounded on a number of occasions, but by 27 February 1617, he concluded this war with the Peace of Stolboba - which was very advantageous for Sweden. Finland, Latvia and Estonia were now under Swedish control, and Russia was excluded from the Baltic Sea. King Gustavus' first concern was to ensure that the authorities of all

The road to war – native Swedish troops 1626
1 Corporal of musketeers
2 Pikeman 4 Drummer
3 Captain 5 Musketeer, colonel's squadron

Gustav led the Swedish Army to victories over Denmark, Russia, Poland and Austria.

conquered cities returned to the Protestants their places of worship and freedom of religion.

Defeating the Polish Threat
During a decade of protracted war with Poland, King Gustavus developed into a formidable and brilliant military commander. His infantry, artillery and cavalry won stunning victories against overwhelming odds and earned widespread respect for Sweden's military capabilities.

A Gracious Victor
Both contemporaries and historians have commented on the extraordinary generosity and magnanimity of Gustav. He treated his conquered enemies with a mildness that astonished both friends and foes. However, he would not tolerate any profanity, nor any

disrespectful jesting concerning the Bible or true religion. He often commented that we should work and live as under "the eye of God." *"God has given me the crown, not that I should fear or remain in repose, but that I may consecrate my life to His glory and to the good of my subjects."*

A Man of the Word

Gustavus was often found studying the Word of God and quotations from the Scripture saturated his conversation and instructions. He was described as a huge man, blond and broad-shouldered, with a handsome beard and a piercing eye. Other written descriptions include *"of lofty stature, tidy, well proportioned and noble in all his manners and actions. He loved music, and played some instruments very well."*

Gustavus Adolphus,
"the Protector of Protestants."

Marriage

In 1620, Gustavus visited Germany to marry Maria Eleanora of Brandenburg. His marriage was celebrated on 28 November 1620, at his palace in Stockholm. However, their happy marriage was grief-stricken by the first two children being stillborn. Gustavus wrote: *"Sorrow has come to my house. God has punished me in giving me a dead child."* He accepted this loss as *"a chastisement"* from the Lord and humbled himself under the Almighty. When Maria and Gustavus were blessed with a healthy daughter, Christina, Adolphus rejoiced greatly.

The Thirty Years War

During this time, what would later be known as The Thirty Years War was threatening to engulf the whole continent of Europe. Germany was the battleground between the mainly Protestant North and Catholic South. Spearheaded by the Jesuits, the Catholic Counter Reformation was beginning to mobilise a militant counter-attack against the Protestant princes of Germany. They sought to reverse the Peace of Augsburg (1555), which had been forced on Emperor Charles V when he abdicated. The Counter-Reformation Catholics were led by Archduke Ferdinand - a Hapsburg who became Holy Roman Emperor ín 1619 - and his rival Duke Maximilian of Bavaria. The Lutherans were led by Elector John George of Saxony. The Calvinists were led by Prince Frederick of the Palatinate. The Protestants formed a defensive union in opposition to the Catholic League.

Protestants in Peril in Bohemia

With Spain seeking to reconquer Holland, the Dutch sought to support fellow Protestants in Bohemia who were resisting the imposition of Catholicism by Ferdinand. The Bohemians elected Prince Frederick of the Palatinate as their king. The Catholic Emperor Ferdinand declared, *"It were preferable to rule over a desert than over a country of heretics."* With this he unleashed a wave of religious persecution and political oppression, which raised the indignation and opposition of the Protestant majority of Bohemia. They called to their Protestant brethren in Hungary, Moravia, Silesia and the Evangelical Union in Germany to aid them in their fight against their common enemies, the Emperor and the Pope.

A Reversal of Fortunes

The first two battles of this war were won by the Bohemians. The Evangelical Union sent 4,000 men under Count Mansfeld who seized Polsem, one of the strongest Catholic cities in Bohemia. Count Thurm led the Bohemian armies from victory to victory to the very gates of Vienna. With the Austrian army defeated, Ferdinand was at the mercy of the Protestants when a Flemish army from Belgium appeared in the city and saved the Catholic Emperor from total defeat. At this point the new king of Bohemia, Frederick V, from the Palatine, gave offence to the Hussites and Lutherans and soon found himself abandoned by all the Protestant princes.

Overwhelmed and Oppressed

At their greatest hour of need, Bohemia found itself alone against the united troops of Austria and the Catholic League. Overwhelmed and discouraged, the Bohemians were defeated and Prague was taken on 9 November 1621. Ferdinand had 27 of the most prominent leaders of Bohemia beheaded, much property was confiscated and many were exiled or executed. All Protestant churches were closed and Bohemia groaned under the oppression of Emperor Ferdinand II as he tore up and burned the pieces of their Bill of Rights guaranteeing religious freedom.

Devastating the Land of the Reformation

Count Tilly from Belgium, swept over Germany, pillaging and devastating towns, churches and villages. The Protestants knew that this was only the prelude to their extermination. Spain and Austria's early

The Catholic Emperor Ferdinand declared that *"it were preferable to rule over a desert than over a country of heretics!"*

The Cathlic League devastated Protestant Germany.

military successes, and their plans to occupy naval bases on the North Sea and the Baltic coasts, led the Dutch to encourage King Christian IV of Denmark to open a second front against the Hapsburgs. This ill-fated campaign (1625-1629) ended with imperial generals Tilly and Wallenstein chasing the Danes back to their own land. These staggering imperial successes, and the Edict of Restitution of 1629, handing all Protestant churches and schools over to Catholic control, provoked a violent backlash.

Sweden – The Champion of Protestants

German Protestants appealed to King Gustavus Adolphus for protection. After winning wars against Denmark, Russia and Poland, Sweden, despite having scarcely more than one million inhabitants, had emerged as a great power. King Gustav's military achievements were already legendary and he was perceived as the last hope of the devastated Protestant cause.

Catholic armies devastated the land of the Reformation in the Thirty Years War.

Murder and Mayhem

Wallenstein's imperial army, 50,000 strong, had defeated and dispersed the troops of Mansfeld, and occupied Silesia, lower Saxony and Holstein. Denmark had sued for peace at Lubeck 22 May 1629. Enormous, ruinous taxes had been imposed on the occupied Protestant areas. Soldiers were ordered *"in the name of the Emperor: be active... and if any resist you, kill them and throw them into a fire hot enough to melt the stars..."* Even the Emperor's brother objected in a letter: *"Your Majesty can have no idea of the conduct of the troops... For mere amusement, windows are broken, walls thrown down, noses and ears cut off; when persons are tortured, violated, assassinated, these are certainly irregularities which superiors should and can prevent... who fill their purses with the blood and sweat of the poor people... Discontent is everywhere increasing at an alarming rate, my conscience permits me no longer to conceal from you the true state of affairs."*

The Threat of Spain and Austria

Cardinal Richelieu, the French chancellor, an enemy of the Huguenots, was also concerned at this resurgent power of Spain and Austria. He wrote in his memoirs: *"All the princes of Germany injured and ravaged, looked toward the King of Sweden in their misery, as navigators toward the port of safety."*

A Clear and Urgent Danger

Many persecuted Protestants fled to Sweden for safety. Gustavus called his senate together at Upsala and described the increasing injuries suffered by their brethren in Germany and the imminent danger which threatened Sweden if she awaited Catholic control of the Baltic ports. Gustavus determined to rescue the German Protestants from this war of annihilation being waged by the Austrian Emperor. He was aware that he was about to enter a struggle against a sovereign feared by all of Europe and who was thought to be invincible.

A Just War

He put his affairs in order, streamlined the government and established the council as a permanent cabinet to make decisions in his absence. With his 4-year-old Christiana in his arms, he addressed the leaders in the Hall of Assembly: *"I've not thoughtlessly engaged in this perilous war which calls me far from you. Heaven is my witness that it is neither for my satisfaction, nor personal interests that I go into this conflict... Ready to sink under the weight of oppression which hangs over them, the German Protestants stretch suppliant hands to us. If it please God, we will give them aid and protection. I'm not ignorant of the dangers that await me; I have already been in many others, and by the grace of God I have ever come happily out of them. But I feel that I may lose my life there, and this is why, before leaving you, I recommend you all to the protection of the omnipotent One..."* He exhorted to pastors to ever preach the pure Gospel to their flocks and to be examples of true Christian conduct. He wished his citizens prosperity in business and abundant harvests. *"Finally, I send up to God most ardent prayers for all my subjects... farewell from the depths of my heart, and-- perhaps forever."*

In Defence of the Faith

Gustavus assembled 15,000 soldiers and, with 30 vessels of war and 200 transport ships, set sail for Europe. As they landed he knelt and prayed: *"Oh Thou that rulest over the heavens and the earth, over winds and over the seas, how can I worthily thank Thee for the marvellous protection which Thou hast shown during this perilous voyage? My heart is full of gratitude for Thy favours. Oh, deign to favour my undertaking here, so that it may turn out, not to my, but to Thy glory. Grant, through me, to deliver Thy oppressed Church, and to be to Thy faithful servants a source of great consolation....."* He noted that their disembarking took place on 24 June 1630 - exactly one century after the Protestants had made their celebrated Confession of Faith at Augsburg.

Napoleon considered Gustavus one of the greatest generals of all time.

Courageous Christian Soldiers

He exhorted his soldiers: *"Pray without ceasing. The more prayers, the more victories... Think not that I undertake this war for myself or for my kingdom. We go to succour our oppressed brethren. By brilliant victories you can accomplish this generous project... Fear not the enemy that we are going to meet in battle; they are the same that you have already conquered in Russia. Your bravery has just compelled Poland to conclude a truce of 6 years. If you still show the same courage and perseverance, you will secure, to the Evangelical Church and to our brethren in Germany, the peace and security for which they are now suffering."* The King followed up this speech with a proclamation of the military rules and regulations. The soldiers were warned that any murder or looting or attempt against life or property would be punishable by death. Their conduct was to be blameless as they were Christian soldiers fighting in a sacred cause.

First Gustavus secured his communication lines with Sweden by chasing the imperial troops off the islands in the Baltic Sea and capturing Stettin. His army disembarked at Peenemünde on 6 July 1630.

Fearless

As multiple plots to assassinate Gustavus were uncovered, his officers urged him to take precautions. Gustavus retorted: *"I trust in God, I fear nothing; what shall man do unto me?"* While conquering Pomerania, Gustavus was scouting with 70 of his cavalry when they were suddenly surprised and surrounded by 500 of the enemy. The King's horse was shot out from under him. Many of his men fell all around him during the furious fighting. The Swedes were about to be completely overwhelmed when 200 Finns, alerted to the danger by the firing, arrived, dispersed the enemy and saved the King.

Divine Protection

Several times during his military career Gustavus was saved from what seemed like certain death by some miracle. On one occasion, men all around fell under a shower of cannon balls and musket shots so that his clothes were splattered with their blood. He himself was shot in the neck, in the shoulder and in the stomach. He suffered a sabre wound on the hand and numerous other injuries.

From Victory to Victory

As Gustavus secured northern Germany, the Catholic League mustered two massive armies, under General Pappenheim and Count Tilly, to destroy the Swedes. Gustavus led his men from victory to victory, deeper into central Germany, securing Brandenburg and seizing Frankfurt on the Oder after a short siege.

The Siege of Magdeburg

The destruction of Magdeburg by Count Tilly's Catholic forces.

Meanwhile, Tilly was besieging Magdeburg, one of the most important and richest Protestant centers in Germany. However, while Gustavus sought to hasten to the aid of besieged Magdeburg, the suspicious electors of Brandenburg and Saxony refused him passage through their states. Frustrated by the obstructive timidity of these electors, Gustavus hesitated to employ force against two Protestant princes. Tragically, after a heroic resistance, Magdeburg fell to Tilly's imperial troops. Betrayed by traitors and undermined by the procrastination of its neighbours, the richest city in Germany at that time was overcome by fury and savagery as drunken soldiers of 9 nations purged the Protestants.

The Massacre of Magdeburg

The victims were so numerous - estimated at 25,000 - that they were thrown in wagonloads into the river Elbe. In one church 53 young girls were beheaded. Croatians laughed as they cast little children into the midst of flames. The tortures and horrors perpetrated in Magdeburg were so shocking that several imperial officers besought Tilly to put an end to them. He replied: *"I've promised three days for pillaging and slaying. The soldiers must have some amusement after so many fatigues!"* Within 12 hours Magdeburg was a roaring furnace which reduced that vast and opulent city to smouldering ruins and ashes. The fate of Magdeburg was reported throughout Europe as a great triumph in the Catholic areas, and as a frightful tragedy to all Protestants.

Overcoming Obstructionism

Gustav Adolphus declared his grief and frustration over the obstructionism which had prevented him from rushing to the aid of these beleaguered brethren. At last the Protestant princes entered into an alliance with the King of Sweden. However, when the elector of Brandenburg persisted in a neutrality too favourable to Austria to be tolerated, Adolphus moved against Berlin. At the sight of the Swedish army, George William consented to make a treaty with his brother-in-law. By this stage the imperial armies had devastated Thuringia. Gustav moved to rescue Hesse from the advancing Austrians. Tilly turned on Saxony. On 27 July 1631, the Swedes made a devastating night attack on Catholic cavalry at Burgstall.

Magdeburg, one of the most important and richest Protestant centres in Germany was beseiged and brutally massacred by Catholic forces.

**Gustavus led the charge that routed the enemy's left wing
and seized the heights with the artillery.**

A Fight for the Future of the Faith

The elector of Saxony welcomed Gustav to the fortress of Wittenburg which put him in possession of the Elbe. On 17 September at the Battle of Breitenfeld, near Leipzig, the Saxons and Swedes combined to confront Tilly's Catholic League. This battle was to determine the future of Protestantism and Catholicism in Europe. Gustavus addressed his troops and reminded them that the very existence of the Reformation in Germany depended upon the outcome of this battle. *"We battle not for the honours of this world, but for the Word and the glory of God, for the True Faith which alone can save us, the Faith which the Catholics have cruelly oppressed, and which they would gladly blot out of existence."*

The Battle of Leipzig

An artillery barrage lasting two hours opened the battle. A west wind blew the smoke of the cannons and clouds of dust from the newly worked fields toward the Swedish lines. Gustav made such a rapid movement of his troops covered by this smoke that the enemy had no time to prevent it. As Tilly's forces attacked the Swedes, they were received by the most violent fire. General Pappenheim attacked the

At the decisive Battle of Leipzig, the forces of Gustavus Adolphus destroyed the united armies of the Catholic League and the Holy Roman Empire.

right wing of the Swedes with his cavalry, but without any effect. Seven times the imperial cavalry charged and seven times the Swedes repulsed them. Gustavus himself commanded the right wing in person to respond to this threat. Tilly threw all his forces against the left wing of the Swedes, but Gustavus reinforced with three regiments just in time to block this move.

A Decisive Victory

Then King Gustavus himself decided the victory by putting to flight the enemy's left wing and seizing the heights on which Tilly had placed his artillery. Soon the Catholic forces had to endure the fire of their own cannon. Battered by cannon fire and a general advance of the Swedes, the imperial forces broke and were routed. A general retreat was ordered. The imperial army disbanded and fled in disorder leaving their wounded, their baggage and all their artillery behind.

Humble Gratitude to God

Gustavus' victory at Leipzig was complete. He fell on his knees, in the midst of the dead and the wounded, and surrounded by his men, poured forth aloud his gratitude to God in an ardent prayer for this decisive victory. Then he rose to pass from rank to rank thanking his brave soldiers for their sacrifices. In his dispatch to his chancellor Gustavus wrote: *"Although we have to deplore the loss of so many brave men, we should before all and above all, thank God for His divine protection; for we were never in so great a danger."*

The Empire Defeated

The results of the victory at Leipzig were immense. The united forces of the Catholic League and of the Emperor of the Holy Roman Empire had been annihilated. Barely 2,000 remained of their previously invincible army. Tilly had lost all his artillery and over 18,000 men. He could only retreat towards Bavaria. With no imperial army left to stop him, Gustavus liberated the lower Palatinate, took Marienberg and Frankfurt

(on Main) and Wűrtzburg. On 10 December he entered Mainz. The Saxon army marched into Bohemia and liberated Prague by November 1631. The speed and extent of these Swedish victories greatly alarmed Richelieu, who had supported Sweden as a counter to the rising power of the Hapsburgs, but he was shocked at this dramatic reversal of fortunes.

Triumph

Gustavus' march to the Rhine was triumphal. After decades of suffering under the imperial troops, even Catholics welcomed

"the new Gideon, this second Joshua ...."

Gustavus as a liberator. In Thuringia the Duke of Saxe-Weimar became one of Gustavus' most able generals. Historians have noted that the irreproachable conduct of the Swedish army inspired admiration and confidence. Soldiers who engaged in looting received the death penalty. When Gustavus captured Catholic strongholds such as Würtzburg, he organized a government composed of an equal number of Catholics and Protestants. While he insisted on Protestants being returned their churches which had been confiscated under the so-called "Edict of Restitution", he ensured that Catholics received the same freedom of worship and security in their property. At one Catholic town where the rulers had persecuted the Protestants most cruelly, his officers urged Gustavus to punish them. The King replied: *"I have come to break the chains of bondage and not forge new ones. Let them live as they have lived."*

Frankfurt

Frankfurt on the Main resisted Gustavus and declared their desire to remain a commercial ally of the Empire. Gustavus responded indignantly: *"I am astonished to learn that Frankfurt prizes more highly its wealth than it does the duties which religion and patriotism impose upon it. It is, indeed, little to its honour to talk of its sales shops and its fairs when the liberty of Germany and the future of the Reformation are at stake....It is for the wellbeing of Germany, and for the independence of the Protestant Faith, that I do battle. No obstacle can stop me. For I am conscious of the justice and nobleness of my cause."* Frankfurt soon opened its gates and received Gustavus with great honour.

Courageous

When a Jesuit priest was captured attempting to assassinate the King, Gustavus responded, *"The King cannot live shut up in a box. The wicked have not so much power as ill will, and confidence in God is the best safeguard... God knows perfectly well how long He wishes to employ my frail arm. If I fail He will raise up another instrument more worthy and more powerful than I. His work does not depend on the life of one man."* Alexander Leslie, one of his Scottish volunteers described King Gustavus as: *"The best and most valorous Commander that any soldiers ever had."*

The Death of Tilly
At the beginning of 1632, Gustavus pursued Tilly into Bavaria, where he defeated the imperial forces at the Battle of Lech, in the face of Tilly's strongly entrenched camp at Rain. He pursued the fleeing enemy to their fortress of Ingolstadt where Tilly died of his wounds a fortnight later.

Protestant Cities Liberated
Gustavus then liberated the long-oppressed Protestant cities of Augsburg and Ulm. In May he occupied Münich, the capital of Bavaria. The magistrates and citizens of Nuremberg received Gustavus and his forces with great rejoicing, with the thunder of cannon and the ringing

**Gustavus and his soldiers were welcomed with great rejoicing
and the ringing of church bells.**

of bells mingled with applause and songs from the enthusiastic crowds. He rejoiced to be in the centre of Germany in one of the most powerful cities of the Empire, among his fellow Protestants.

Nuremberg

Printed copies of Gustavus' address to the city of Nuremberg remain: *"I thank you... I can wish nothing better in return than perseverance in the Evangelical Faith. Let nothing turn you from it; neither threats nor promises, nor any of the passions to which the human nature is subject... Let not the riches of earth make you forgetful of the still more precious treasures of heaven... You have wicked and wily enemies, whose aim is the annihilation of Protestantism. Their hope is to found a peace upon the ruin of all Protestants, and they seek their end by the destruction of millions of souls... God has entrusted to you the administration of an opulent and powerful city... So govern it as not to fear to give an account which you one day have to render at the tribunal of God... In these misfortunes...God has aimed to make us feel how much we are sinners. For you, for the defense of the Gospel, I left my peaceful home and came into your agitated country. I've sacrificed the resources of my poor subjects, their blood, my life and love of my family. I will do for you all that the grace of God will give me power to do. On your side, be willing to suffer for a while, if need be, for a sacred cause. Remain faithful to it. Then God will bless you; He will cause your city to flourish. His Name will be everywhere revered, and after the glory and honour of earth, will come that of heaven."*

The Soldier King

Poems and songs composed at that time described *"the good King of Sweden, a glorious protector... this new Gideon...this second Joshua...who directs the battles of the Lord; this other David who has brought Goliath low; this valiant man whose heart is without fraud and who seeks only the glory of God..."*

Augsburg

After seeing Tilly, the butcher of Magdeburg, suitably punished, Gustavus rode into Augsburg as the citizens sang Psalm 103 and rejoiced greatly over their liberation. Gustavus entered this city, where the princes were first called Protestants for resisting the Emperor Charles V, and where Melanchthon had presented the Augsburg Confession just over 100 years before, with great emotion and rejoicing.

In the Face of Death

At the Battle of Ingolstadt, a 24-pounder cannon ball had swept the King's horse from under him. The man next to him, the Duke of Barden, had his head shot off a few moments later. The King was covered with blood and dust and all around feared that Gustavus had been killed. He rose and declared: *"The apple is not yet ripe... Neither my high birth, nor my royal crown, nor my weapons, nor my many victories, can save me from death. I submit to the will of God. If He takes me from the world, He will not abandon the sacred cause which I defend... I know that I can count upon the aid of the All-powerful, and that it is He who has sent me into Germany."*

Merciful

Despite cruel treatment meted out to his soldiers when captured by the Catholics, Gustavus resolved to respond to their most bitter hatred by inexhaustible mercy.

The valiant King Gustavus was frequently in the thick of battle.

Many sought to persuade the king to avenge upon Münich the sacking of Magdeburg. He steadfastly refused this call to revenge and forbade, under pain of death, any crime against life or property. Even the Bavarian priests praised the nobility of so generous an adversary. Gustavus visited the priests and engaged in Evangelical discussions with them in fluent Latin. When some of his generals complained that *"the King would do better to put to flight these Jesuits, than to discuss with them thus."* Gustavus replied: *"Why would you persecute these men? Do you not see how much they injure the cause which they defend, and how much they help the cause which they oppose?"*

A New Threat

At this point the Catholic League was dissolved and Austria lay open on all sides. No army stood between Gustavus and the Emperor Ferdinand in Vienna. However, at this point the old enemy, Albrecht Wallenstein, defeated the Saxons in Bohemia and marched with 60,000 men on Saxony. Gustavus had only 20,000 men, but he could not allow Nuremberg to suffer the same terrible fate as Magdeburg, so he moved with all haste to prevent Wallenstein reaching it. *"Nuremberg is the apple of my eye, and I will defend it with all my power,"* declared Gustavus.

A War of Attrition

But Wallenstein stopped short of Nuremberg and encamped in an impregnable position, threatening the Swedes from the heights occupied by several hundred cannon. There were frequent skirmishes and vicious fighting as the Swedes attempted to take the entrenched positions of the Imperials. Thousands of soldiers were lost on both sides. As famine began to affect their camps, discipline broke down. King Gustavus confronted his men and allies concerning these complaints which afflicted his heart: *"I would rather lose life than sully by crime the sacred work which God has entrusted me. I pray you, in the Name of divine mercy, to look within yourselves, question your own consciences. Remember that you must render an account to God for your conduct, and that you must one day appear before the tribunal of that Judge Who sees all things."*

To the Rescue of Saxony

As Wallenstein began to lay waste Saxony, Gustavus marched 20,000 men to Erfurt. He ensured that all people and their possessions en route were respected. His troops prayed morning and evening and no disorderly conduct was reported thereafter. On the march, the King saw a bird of prey pursuing a lark. Incredibly, the lark flew straight down and rested on his shoulder. The King tenderly took the lark in his hands and declared: *"Poor little bird, may God protect you."* He thanked God for giving him even this opportunity of saving one of His creatures from harm. He saw in this a symbol of the work that he was called to accomplish, protecting Protestant Germany from the Austrian eagle.

Gustavus' soldiers were renowned for their speed of reloading and accuracy.

Erfurt

In Erfurt, Gustavus was welcomed by his Queen, but he could only stay one day as the threat from Wallenstein was so severe. As he took his leave, Gustavus declared to his Queen: *"Be of good courage, we shall see each other again; if it may not be in this life, it will at least be, sooner or later, in the abode of eternal blessedness."* He kissed her one last time and rode fast to rejoin his troops.

The Battle of Lützen

At Lützen, on the 16th of November 1632, Gustavus summoned his chaplain and spent one hour with him in prayer before attending the regular religious services held every morning for his soldiers. He remained upon his knees during the whole service.

The Battle Hymn of Gustavus

Before his men deployed, he had them sing the battle hymn he himself had composed:

"Not withstanding the tumult and the threatening cries which resound around you fear nothing, little flock. Your enemies rejoice in you destruction, but their joy shall be of short duration. Let not your courage fail you.

"Your cause is the cause of God! Accomplish your mission, place yourselves in the hands of God, and you shall fear no danger. He will find another Gideon to defend the people and the Word of God.

"We hope in the Name of Jesus, the violence and snares of the wicked will turn against them. They will thus become an object to be despised. God is with us, we are with Him; victory belongs to us."

"God is with Us"

A thick fog covered the plain on which the battle was to take place. As the Swedes sang Psalms, Wallenstein's cannon announced their impending assault. Gustavus gave the command: *"God is with us."* As

A contemporary sketch of the battle lines.

he mounted his horse without armour, his officers pleaded with him to wear armour. He replied: *"The Eternal One is my armour."* He then rode along the lines to encourage his men.

"Do Your Duty"

He announced: *"The day has arrived on which you are to show what you have already learned in war… hold yourselves ready; conduct yourselves as worthy soldiers; fight valiantly for your God, your country and your King….I beseech you, in the name of a Christian conscience and of your honour, to do your duty today as you have done heretofore… March with courage! …. I myself will show the way. I am ready to risk my life and to shed my blood with you. Follow me, have confidence in God and bear away a victory whose fruits you and your posterity will gather forever."*

The evening after the battle of Leuthen.

"Forward!"

The soldiers responded with shouts of joy and enthusiasm. At 11am the fog had dissipated and the sun brilliantly illuminated the field of Lützen. Gustavus raised his eyes towards heaven, and cried aloud: *"Jesus! Jesus! Be Thou my help this day, while we battle for the glory of Thy sacred Name."* He then brandished his sword high above his head and commanded: *"Forward now, in the Name of the Lord!"*

In the Front Line

The King placed himself on the right wing of his army and led them across the trenches that had been dug by the Austrians. When his infantry did not advance fast enough, he dismounted and charged with them to inspire them with a better example. Continually in the front line, Gustavus sought to strengthen each weak point and inspired his men to throw back the enemy.

King Gustavus was killed in battle leading a charge.

Killed in Action

At a crucial point in battle, he became separated from his troops while leading a cavalry charge into a dense cloud of gunpowder smoke. Hit by gunfire, he fell and was killed while lying severely wounded on the ground.

Like Furious Lions

As word spread throughout the Swedish army that their King was dead, they hurled themselves like furious lions upon the left wing of the enemy and cut the Imperial forces to pieces. Duke Bernard de Weimar took command of the army and charging the right wing, seized the artillery of the Austrians. Wallenstein was preparing to retreat when Pappenheim arrived with 8 regiments of reinforcements. Pappenheim was immediately wounded and forced to withdraw, dying the next day. All hope of bringing the Imperial forces back into line dissipated. The Catholic forces fled the field leaving all their baggage and artillery behind. Wallenstein abandoned Saxony to the Protestants who finally retook all the strong places that had been occupied by the Austrians. Wallenstein was later assassinated on orders of the Emperor in 1634.

Victory

The victory of Lützen was more a cause of grief than joy to the Swedes. Nothing could compensate for the loss of their beloved King. However, true to his vision, he had remained faithful to his mission and successfully fought for religious freedom in Germany. He had championed the cause of Protestantism and secured religious freedom for centuries to come.

Gustav Adolf the Great

Following his death in battle, the Swedish Riksdag of Estates named him Gustaf Adolf den Store (Gustav Adolf the Great). He remains the only Swedish monarch honoured with the title: The Great. Gustav Adolphus is commemorated by city squares named after him in Stockholm, Helsingborg and Gothenburg. In St. Peter, Minnesota, a Lutheran College is named: Gustavus Adolphus College. Gustavus Adolphus day is celebrated in Sweden, Estonia and Finland each year on 6 November.

This plaque in Luther's Stadtkirche in Wittenberg marks where the body of King Gustavus lay in state after being killed in action at the Battle of Lützen.

A Great Christian Soldier King

Gustavus Adolphus was a dedicated Christian, a Reformer-King and a great general. He transformed the art of warfare, changed the course of history and liberated Protestant Germany from the threat of annihilation. The whole course of modern history would have been dramatically different had not the Lord worked in such a tremendous way through the courageous crusade of this Lion from the North

The return in honour of the body of the king of Sweden.

"Blessed be the Lord my Rock, who trains my hands for war, and my fingers for battle, my lovingkindness and my fortress. My high tower and my deliverer, my shield and the one in whom I take refuge. Who subdues my people under me". Psalm 144:1-2

In this famous portrait of key Reformation leaders Gustavus Adolphus stands out as the only military leader and the only person from the 17th Century. From back left: John Hus, Philipp Melanchthon, Gustavus Adolphus, Ulrich Zwingli, John Wycliffe, John Calvin, Martin Luther and William Tyndale.

Chapter 22
OLIVER CROMWELL
The Protector
(1599 - 1658)

Oliver Cromwell (1599-1658) was one of the greatest leaders ever to rule England. He was a dedicated Puritan, deeply and fervently devoted to carrying out the will of God. He was relentless in battle, brilliant in organization and had a genius for cavalry warfare. With a Psalm on his lips and a sword in his hand he led his Ironsides to victory after victory, first against the Royalists in England, then against the Catholics of Ireland, and finally against the rebellious Scots.

Oliver Cromwell pursued religious toleration which helped to stabilize the fragile country after the King was executed. His foreign policy in support of beleagured Protestants in Europe and against Muslim pirates in the Mediteranean was successful and he restored the supremacy of the seas to England.

A Distinguished Family
Oliver Cromwell was one of the few people who could trace his family origins to pre-Norman Conquest times. His family were frequently active in the fight for liberty. Six of his cousins were imprisoned for refusing the Forced Loan of 1627. When he was first elected as Member of Parliament from Huntington in 1628, nine of his cousins were Members of

Oliver Cromwell was the ultimate Puritan statesman who championed Religious Toleration.

The home of Oliver Cromwell near Cambridge.

Parliament. Seventeen of his cousins and nine other relatives served at one time or another as Members of the Long Parliament.

Born towards the end of Queen Elizabeth's reign, Cromwell grieved England's decline from those golden years. His mother, his wife and one of his daughters were all named Elizabeth. He frequently referred to *"Queen Elizabeth of famous memory."*

A Country in Crisis

England in the early 17th century was deeply troubled. King James had left his realm embroiled in the conflict in Europe against Spain that launched The Thirty Years War, the Crown was bankrupt and England was universally disgraced. James' heir, King Charles I, had married a French Catholic princess less than three months after he had inherited the throne. All of England had been against a Catholic marriage but Charles evidenced contempt for the opinions of all. He lied, entered into war without Parliamentary approval, made secret concessions with the Catholics, undermined and interferred in the churches, sent out his agents to collect Forced Loans, bypassing Parliament, and sent rich people to prison until they paid the ransom he demanded.

Under a Tyrannical King

Land confiscations multiplied under Charles, and an increasing number of men were sent to prison for refusing to hand money over to the Crown.   Arbitrary imprisonments and depriving men of property without any semblance of the Law jeopardized the rights of everyone in the realm.   Charles summarily dissolved Parliament whenever it interfered with his will. He scorned a Petition of Rights and said that Parliament had no rights, merely privileges granted by the Crown! The King did not seem to consider himself to be bound by any promise or subject to any law.

Challenging Charles

In March 1629 Parliament passed a Bill that declared: *"Whoever brought in innovations in religion, or introduced opinions disagreeing from those of the true and orthodox Church; whoever voluntarily paid those duties; was to be counted an enemy to the kingdom and a betrayer of it's liberties."*

The Cruelty of Charles

Immediately the motion was passed, the King dissolved Parliament and extracted a furious vengeance on Sir John Eliot who had proposed the motion, and others who had supported it. Eliot and other MP's were thrown into prison. Eliot remained in prison for the rest of his life, dying in the Tower of London in December 1632. Charles' pettiness was seen in how he even refused the widow the right to take her husband's body to be buried at their Cornish home. Charles appointed and dismissed judges at will. His appointed Archbishop Laud banned the publication of Calvinist sermons that had been collected since the time of Elizabeth and Edward VI.

The Star Chamber

The cruelty of Archbishop Laud's Star Chamber can be seen in the treatment of Calvinist minister Alexander Leighton for writing a Puritan book. Leighton was chained in solitary confinement until his hair fell out and his skin fell off. He was tied to a stake and flogged until his back was raw. He was branded in the face, had his nose slit and his ears cut off and was condemned to life imprisonment.

War Against Calvinism

From the moment that Laud was consecrated Archbishop of Canterbury in 1633, the Arminians assumed full control over the Church of England and declared war on Calvinism. Calvinist pastors were dismissed from their parishes. Calvinist writers and speakers were excommunicated, placed in the stocks and had their ears cut off.

The treatment that Calvinists received at the hands of the Arminian Star Chamber was remarkable as Arminians accused Calvinists of being *"cruel"* in believing that God's Salvation could be selective. The Arminians had also accused the Calvinists of being in favour of a Theocracy, in which the church ruled the state. They claimed to be less ambitious, but in practice these Arminians ruled the people through the state. For example Archbishop Laud had author John Prynne hauled before the Star Chamber for *"seditious libel."* Prynne was barred from further practice of law, had his university degrees rescinded, was fined an impossible £5,000, was pilloried, had his ears cut off and was then sent to prison for life. All this because of one book he had written.

Ruling Without Parliament

All of these abuses took place during the eleven years that Charles ruled England without Parliament. These eleven years were the longest years without Parliament in English history.

The Scots Rebel

However, when the Scottish rebelled against the imposition of what they saw as Roman Catholic superstition and ritual on their churches in

Parliament at Westminster was the focal point of a contest of wills between the tyrannical king Charles and the elected representatives of England.

Scotland, Charles was forced to recall Parliament to raise new taxes and an army.

The Short Parliament
The Short Parliament was summoned 13 April, 1640. Instead of providing Charles with the money and men to fight the Scots, they immediately started talking about the crimes of Charles' government, the atrocities of Archbishop Laud, the illegal taxation of the people, the excesses of the High Commission, and the terrors of the Star Chamber. This Parliament lasted only 23 days before the King dissolved it on 5 May.

A Kingdom in Crisis
A whole series of crisis situations compelled Charles to call a new parliament. Turkish pirates were raiding the Irish and Cornish coasts and carrying Christians off into Islamic slavery. English settlers were being slaughtered by the Catholics in Ireland. A Scottish army had seized Northern England. There was a general belief that a Catholic

King Charles showed contempt for the privileges and powers of Parliament, once suspending Parliament for eleven years.

conspiracy was at work to destroy English liberties and to install an absolutist Catholic monarchy.

The Long Parliament Seizes the Initiative

For eleven years newspapers had been banned. The secret circulation of pamphlets helped keep people informed. King Charles was being out-manoeuvered and cornered. The Long Parliament moved swiftly and impeached the Earl of Strafford, the King's dictator of Ireland, as a secret Papist plotting to bring his Catholic army from Ireland to alter the laws and religion of England. The House of Commons also charged that the Arminian changes in the Canons of the Church of England were illegal and impeached Laud, the Archbishop of Canterbury, of popery and treason. He ended up in the same tower to which he had consigned so many others. Censorship was abolished and pamphlets on religion and government couldn't be produced fast enough, the demand was so great. London became a fountain of Puritan publications dealing with God and government, faith and morals.

The King's government collapsed and his ministers fled the country. Systematically Parliament dismantled the instruments by which the King had oppressed the nation. No taxes could be levied without Parliamentary consent. The Star Chamber, and its torture, was abolished. The Privy Council was deprived of its power. The Court of High Commission was abolished and the king left financially dependent on Parliament. Parliament also took control of the militia.

Oliver Cromwell played an increasingly pivotal role in Parliament. The Long Parliament, which began its sitting on 3 November 1640, was the fifth Parliament of Charles's reign. Cromwell had been in two previous Parliaments which had been summarily dissolved by King Charles.

The Puritan Politician
Oliver Cromwell was described as having penetrating eyes of steely blue, being profoundly religious, well-read, eloquent, full of fervour, and with an iron conviction - which his character turned to steel. He

The home church of Oliver Cromwell.

was a graduate of Cambridge University, a descendant of Henry VIII's Chancellor Thomas Cromwell and a dedicated Puritan. In 1620 Oliver married Elizabeth Bourchier. Cromwell proved himself an affectionate husband with a deep love for his children. When he was 28, Cromwell was elected to Parliament as a Member for Huntingdon. This Parliament lasted less than five months before the King dissolved it.

It was eleven years before the Short Parliament was summoned. By the time the Long Parliament was summoned on 3 November, 1640, Oliver Cromwell was nearly 42 years old. Up to this point he had no military experience, but that was about to change.

War
As war became inevitable it seemed that the King's forces had the great advantage of trained and experienced cavalry. The Royalist officers were experienced at fencing and riding. Leading the King's cavalry was his cousin Prince Rupert of the Rhine. Prince Rupert had brought over 100 professional officers experienced in the Dutch and German wars.

Edgehill
In the first serious battle at Edgehill on 23 October, 1642, the King's forces, led by Prince Rupert descended upon the Parliamentary infantry so effectively that it was almost a massacre. But, after thundering through Essex's men, the cavalry stopped to plunder baggage. This gave Captain Cromwell the opportunity to counter-attack with his cavalry and halt the Royalist effort to march on London. Cromwell observed to his cousin John Hampden that they never would be able to beat these gentlemen's sons schooled in sword fighting and horse riding with old, decaying serving men. Oliver Cromwell declared that he was going to set out to find honest men who feared God and were full of the Holy Spirit.

The disastrous battle of Edgehill provoked Cromwell to select and train a special force.

Selecting and Training a Special Force

Cromwell's initiative earned him a promotion to Colonel. Richard Baxter noted that Oliver Cromwell *"had a special care to get religious men into his troops because these were the sorts of men he esteemed and loved; and...from this happy choice flowed the avoidings of those disorders, mutinies, plunderings and grievances of the country which debased men and armies are commonly guilty of."* By May 1643 Cromwell had selected and trained 2,000 brave, disciplined and dedicated men .

Battles

In May 1643 Cromwell, heavily outnumbered, attacked a Royalist force at Belton and killed over a hundred at a cost of only two men. Cromwell's men quickly earned a reputation for being religious, obedient, fearless and disciplined. In October 1643 Cromwell won a victory at Winceby.

Prince Rupert led the King's forces to massacre the Calvinists of Bolton, at Clothington.

Cromwell's Ironsides were victorious at the Battle of Gainsborough on 28 July 1643.

Religious Freedom

Cromwell rose in Parliament in December 1644 to propose a self-denying ordinance in which all members should resign their military commands. He argued for religious freedom: *"Presbyterians, Independents, all here had the same spirit of Faith and prayer...they agree here, know no names of difference; pity it should be otherwise anywhere. All that believe have the real unity, which is most glorious because inward and Spiritual...As for being united in forms, commonly called uniformity, every Christian will, for peace sake, study and do as far as conscience will permit; and from brethren, and things of the mind, we look for no compulsion but that of light and reason."*

A New Threat

Cromwell was horrified to see that Parliament was seeking to impose Presbyterianism on the nation. Baptists, Congregationalists, Anglicans and other Believers had fought on the field of battle for religious freedom, against Catholicism and Episcopal tyranny. Were they now going to replace that with Presbyterian tyranny?

Cromwell demanded the restructuring of the Army. He castigated those sections of the Army where: *"profaneness and impiety and the absence of all religion, drinking and gambling, and all manner of license and laziness"* had led to poor performance and defeat. He argued for a New Model Army. Cromwell was appointed second-in-command of the Parliamentary Forces, under Lord Fairfax. Out of the total Parliament Forces of over 88,000, Cromwell selected and trained a quarter (22,000) as a New Model Army.

Time and again Oliver Cromwell led his disciplined Ironsides to victory over the Royalist Cavaliers.

Victory

At Marsdon Moor, on 2 July 1644, Oliver Cromwell led his cavalry to victory over the Royalists in a most decisive battle. By now Cromwell was a Lieutenant-General and his disciplined Bible-reading, Psalm-singing troops won the day. His new Model Army again won a most decisive Battle at Naseby on 14 June 1645. This ended the first civil war.

Presbyterian Tyrany

Meanwhile Parliament established the Church of England as Presbyterian, with orders to persecute Baptists, Congregationalists and other non-conformists who were to be imprisoned for life, and on some occasions, even to be put to death! No laymen were to be allowed to preach or expound on the Scriptures.

Liberty of Conscience

Oliver Cromwell was horrified. This was not what his army had been fighting for! He argued most passionately for religious freedom and liberty of conscience. The Army did not want to see Arminian absolutism replaced with a Presbyterian version. The Independents no longer wanted a national church but all varieties of the Protestant Faith to be free of state interference and limitations. When the Parliament sought to disband the New Model Army which was overwhelmingly composed of Congregationalists, Baptists and other Independents, the Army Council sent a message to Parliament demanding liberty of conscience for its members.

Cromwell wrote: *"He that ventures his life for the liberty of his country, I wish he trust God for the liberty of his conscience, and you for the liberty he fights for."*

Checks and Balances

The Army Council proposed a Council of State, free elections and an enlarged franchise, the right to disagree with both King and Lords, no bishops, no compulsory orders of service, and no compulsory obedience to Presbyterianism. Although one of the king's advisors observed *"never was a Crown so nearly lost, so cheaply recovered"* the king contemptuously dismissed these, and all other, proposals for settlement.

Cromwell then became the power-broker between the army, Parliament and the captive Charles in an attempt to restore a constitutional basis for government. However, dealing with the slippery and inflexible Stuart monarch exhausted Cromwell's patience.

A Second Civil War

In 1647 Charles escaped and sought to restart the war with the Scottish Presbyterians in support. Defeating the Royalist Welsh and Scottish rebels in 1648, Cromwell supported a trial for treason of the King which ended in the execution of Charles on 30 January 1649.

In 17 August 1648, Cromwell achieved a tremendous victory at Preston. He quickly broke up the Royalist Army and seized 10,000 prisoners. As on any other occasion Cromwell was always very careful to give all the glory to God. He wrote: *"It pleased God to enable us to give them a defeat..."*

On 6 August, 1647, the Army 18,000 strong, with the King in their midst, entered London. Despite the illusions of the Presbyterians in Parliament, the Army knew that it alone had defeated the King. The Army included officers and men who had previously been excluded from the religious and political consensus. They were determined not to have Parliament send them back to the pattern of the past that they had so successfully fought against.

Independent Congregations and a Qualified Franchise
Cromwell emerged as the Leader of the Independents, favouring freedom of religion for all Protestants. John Milton, Henry Ireton, and Oliver Cromwell argued for *"rule by the virtuous, selected by men of standing."* They rejected the universal franchise proposed by the Levellers observing that a man with no more fixed property than what *"he may carry about with him"*, one who is *"here today and gone tomorrow"* would be enabled by numbers to enact confiscatory laws. Therefore they advocated a qualified franchise based upon the ownership of property.

Treachery and Duplicity
While Parliament was arguing over the form of their future Faith and freedoms, King Charles was negotiating with the Scots, promising to accept and impose Presbyterianism over England, suppressing all non-conformists. The Scots who had launched the war against Charles in the first place, now decided that it was God's will that Presbyterianism should be enforced over England - through restoring Charles to the throne.

On 3 May, 1648, the Scots issued a Manifesto calling on all England to accept their Covenant and suppress all religious dissent from Presbyterianism. They also demanded that the New Model Army be disbanded. The Royalist Cavaliers, both from within and outside of England hurried to join the Scots in this new conflict against the Parliamentary Forces. This Second Civil War saw the Presbyterians allied with the Arminians against the Independents and the new Model Army. How these two theological opposites expected to settle their differences with one another if they ever defeated the New Model Army was a question no one dared even ask, let alone attempt to answer at that time.

Cromwell led part of the army to Wales where he lay siege to Pembroke Castle. This nearly impregnable stronghold took an agonizing six weeks to subdue. Cromwell then had to force march his army across the country to intercept the invading Scottish army. In a ferocious three-day battle Cromwell's forces defeated the Scots.

Now the Army was outraged that the duplicity and treachery of the King had led to a new war, even against their previous allies, the Scots. The Army demanded a trial of *"this man of blood."*

True Unity of Believers
Cromwell wrote to his cousin Robin Hammond, who was guarding the King on the Isle of Wight: *"I profess to thee a desire from my heart, I've prayed for it, I have waited for the day to see the union and right understanding between the Godly people (Scots, English, Jews, Gentiles, Presbyterians, Independents, Baptists and all)."*

Placing the King On Trial
135 Men were nominated to the High Court of Justice, and the trial of the King began on 8 January, 1648. The trial was held in the ancient Westminster Palace which had originally been built in the time of the Norman William Rufus. In it Sir Thomas More, Guy Fawkes and the Earl of Strafford had been tried.

Oliver Cromwell

The Westminster Confession was produced by some of the most learned minds under the protection of Parliament.

Convicting Charles of Treason

The indictment against the King read that he had by *"wicked design"* erected and upheld in himself *"an unlimited and tyrannical power...to overthrow the rights and liberties of the people."* That he had *"traitorously and maliciously levied war against the present Parliament and the people..."* and that he was *"a tyrant, traitor and murderer, and a public and implacable enemy to the Commonwealth of England."*

Evidence was brought forward of the illegal taxes, arbitrary imprisonments, mutilations, tortures and executions of people whose only crime had been to disagree with the King on matters of Faith and ethics, and that he had trampled upon the Common Law of England and the Chartered Rights guaranteed by the Magna Carta.

The prosecutor argued that *"there is a contract and a bargain made between the King and his people...a bond of protection...is due from the*

Sovereign; the other is the bond of subjection that is due from the subject....if this bond is ever broken, farewell sovereignty!...The authority of a ruler is valid only so long as he can provide protection in return. " But the King had made war against his own subjects.

Despite Charles' attempt to disrupt and derail the proceedings, the death warrant was signed by 59 of the Commissioners. Cromwell described the execution of Charles on 30 January 1649 as *"a cruel necessity."*

New Threats

When Charles II promised that he would impose Presbyterianism upon the Realm, the Scottish Presbyterians mobilized to fight their Protestant Brethren in England. A Catholic uprising in Ireland also threatened the new Republic. The Council of State appointed Oliver Cromwell as Lord General of a new army to deal with the Catholic threat in Ireland.

Knowing that he still had to deal with the Scottish threat, Cromwell determined to subdue the Irish as quickly, and as finally, as possible. His first action on reaching Ireland was to forbid any plunder or pillage. Two men were hanged for disobeying that order. At Drogheda, Cromwell's forces crushed the Catholic stronghold in a ferocious battle. He then moved to Wexford, long a thorn in the side of English traders as a centre of Piracy. As the town refused to surrender, after an intense 8-day siege it was put to the sword. Cromwell prayed that *"this bitterness will save much blood through the goodness of God."*

After subduing the major strongholds of resistance in Ireland, Cromwell learned that Charles II had landed in Scotland. He left Ireton to complete the mopping operations in Ireland and returned to England.

The Scottish Campaign

Young Charles II had signed the Scots National Covenant and Solemn League and Covenant, swearing to maintain Presbyterianism in his household and in all his dominions. Charles II was crowned King at

Scone, in Scotland. Lord Fairfax, the Supreme Commander of the Parliamentary Forces refused to lead an English army into Scotland – because he was a Presbyterian. Fairfax was relieved of command and Oliver Cromwell was appointed Supreme Commander of the Parliamentary Forces.

Cromwell Conquers Scotland

With his usual fearful efficiency, Oliver Cromwell led 16,000 well-equipped and well experienced, determined troops into Scotland. Despite being heavily outnumbered, and trapped by superior forces, Cromwell decisively defeated

At the Catholic stronghold of Drogheda, Cromwell led his men to victory in a ferocious battle.

the Scottish Army at Dunbar on 3 September, 1650. He seized 10,000 prisoners and soon occupied Edinburgh and Leith.

Reasoning with the Scottish Presbyterians

Cromwell attempted to reason with his Scottish neighbours: *"Our brethren of Scotland, are we to be dealt with as enemies because"* we do not agree with you on all points? *"Are you sure that your league with wicked and carnal men is a Covenant of God? I pray you read Isaiah 28."*

"I beseech you in the mercies of Christ, think it possible that you may be mistaken...are you troubled that Christ is preached? Is preaching so inclusive in your function?" He argued and reasoned for liberty of

conscience and religious toleration. Cromwell's persuasions were somewhat successful as numerous Covenanters chose neutrality thereafter.

The Victory of the Independents
On 3 November, 1651, a year after the battle at Dunbar, Cromwell's forces defeated another Scottish army at Worcester. Charles II's massive army of 30,000 was put to flight and scattered. It was remarkable that the Presbyterians, the Arminian Episcopals and the Catholics had co-operated to fight the Protestant Parliament of England. Each of these three groups believed in the tradition of a single faith in a single land. They were willing to co-operate with their most determined enemies in order to crush the Independent Calvinists, Baptists and Congregationalists of Parliament.

Cromwell's Triumph
The victory at Worcester was to be Oliver Cromwell's last battle. He was now 52 years old. In campaign after campaign Oliver Cromwell had triumphed, often over vastly superior forces numerically. Cromwell's tactics had proven themselves time and again. He was welcomed back to London in triumph in September 1651. He was now at the height of his power and prestige. As Captain General of the Army and as a member of the Council of State, Oliver Cromwell's position in England was unassailable.

The English Royalists had been bled white, decisively defeated time and again. Charles I had been executed, Charles II had fled to France. The Second Civil War had ended. England was firmly under the control of the Parliamentary Forces. Ireland was subdued. Scotland had been conquered. The three kingdoms of England, Ireland and Scotland were united under the Parliamentary government in London.

Parliamentary Dilemmas
However, the situation that confronted Oliver Cromwell upon his return to London was most disturbing. In his absence England had declared war on Protestant Holland. This was the first war in English history that

was fought primarily for economic reasons. Cromwell was horrified that the English Republic should have waged war against the Protestant Dutch. He deprecated the Licensing Acts and Treason Acts, which overrode customary liberties. The war with Holland was resented by the New Model Army. The soldiers wanted to know when they would see the Reforms for which they had fought.

When Parliament refused to renew the Commission for the Propagation of the Gospel in Wales – the army's favourite instrument for evangelising that politically unstable country - it created a storm. Oliver Cromwell was outraged: *"This we apprehended would have been throwing away the liberties of the nation into the hands of those who never fought for it."*

Parliamentary Intolerance

As parliamentary intolerance and interference in the religious liberty of the Independents increased, Oliver Cromwell gathered some soldiers and, accompanied by Major-General Thomas Harrison, he entered Parliament, sat down and listened to the discussions. At length he rose and calmly began to speak of his concern that Parliament had become *"a self-perpetuating Oligarchy"* unfit to govern England. He condemned the members of Parliament as drunkards and whoremasters.

CROMWELL DISSOLVES PARLIAMENT.

Ending the Long Parliament

"You are no Parliament. I say, you are no Parliament! I will put an end to your sittings." He turned to Harrison and ordered *"call them in; call them in."* Soldiers appeared and Cromwell told them to clear the room. The members left, some under protest. This ended the Long Parliament that had dethroned the King, abolished the House of Lords, created a new government and won a revolution – only to be itself abolished.

A New Parliament

Cromwell called for a new Parliament of 140 members. Some of these were chosen by churches, others by various generals, 5 were from Scotland, 6 were from Ireland; London Puritans predominated. In short order this Parliament reviewed the judicial system and voted to abolish the Court of Chancery. Tenants were provided protection against arbitrary expulsions. For the first time in English history, marriages were made possible by civil ceremony. Their proposals not to execute pick-pockets and horse thieves for first offences shocked the lawyers. Many of these reforms were constructive, but they alienated the population by seeking to abolish tithes. Concerned that Parliament was seeking to undermine the Church and secure ownership of property, the Army grew impatient and persuaded the members to dissolve voluntarily.

A New Constitution

A committee produced a constitution, titled The Instrument of Government. On 16 December, 1653, Oliver Cromwell was proclaimed Lord Protector of the Commonwealth of England, Scotland and Ireland. This was an elective position and not for life, nor hereditary. The Lord Protector was to be the Chief Executive, assisted by a Council of 15 members (8 civilians and 7 army officers). Parliament alone was to retain the power to levy taxes and grant supply to the government. The Protector could not dissolve Parliament while it was in session.

Religious Freedom

Oliver Cromwell believed in an established, non-Episcopal, Evangelical church with full toleration of dissent and separate congregations. His position was fully supported by the Baptists, Congregationalists and other Independents. The new government was silent on rites, ceremonies and sacraments. How to administer the Lord's Supper or Baptism was left to each congregation. Church government was to be congregational, allowing for Presbyterian, Independent, Baptist and Episcopal congregations. Any form of Protestant worship was permitted.

The Arts Flourished

Writers found the Protectorate under Oliver Cromwell far more lenient than his bureaucratic predecessors. Literature flourished and the Calvinist love of poetry appeared everywhere. Christmas once again became festive. Musical entertainments and theatre, which had been prohibited under the Presbyterian Parliament, were now encouraged under the Puritan Protectorate. The first full-length, five-act English opera (*The Siege of Rhodes*) in 1656 premiered under the Protector. Women were again allowed to wear make-up. Even play readings which satirized the government were allowed. It was during the Commonwealth that the violin became popular and solo singing began to be enjoyed.

Foreign Policy

In terms of foreign policy, Oliver Cromwell promptly made peace with Holland. The British Navy crossed the ocean and restored Virginia and the Barbados Islands to England. In the summer of 1654, the Lord Protector summoned the Spanish Ambassador and told him that Englishmen in Spanish territories should have the liberty to worship as they pleased, free of the Inquisition, and that English traders should no longer be molested. The negative response of the Ambassador prompted Cromwell to send an English fleet to San Domingo, and to Jamaica. The expedition to Jamaica succeeded in conquering this previously Spanish territory. Cromwell dreamed that Calvinists from

New England would settle there. Unfortunately, it became another Barbados, a place for the English to ship their criminals and rebels.

Defeating the Barbary Pirates

In April 1655, Admiral Blake led the English Navy into the pirate stronghold of Tunis, in North Africa, destroying the Bey's ships and forcing the sultan to release all English prisoners and slaves. Oliver Cromwell sent his warm congratulations on this decisive act against the Barbary pirates, and ordered Blake to proceed to Cadiz to intercept Spanish ships carrying treasure from the New World.

Defending the Waldensians

In May 1655 the Catholic Duke of Savoy unleashed a vicious persecution against the Protestant Huguenots in the Vadois (or Waldensians') Valley. Newspapers in England reported *"a devilish crew of priests and Jesuits leading unspeakable atrocities"* against their Protestant brethren. Oliver Cromwell immediately sent an agent to the scene whose report verified the persecution. The Lord Protector headed a subscription list that raised several hundred thousand pounds for the relief of the Waldensian victims. He then brought pressure to bear upon the Duke to stop the campaign. The threat of mobilizing English Navy and the New Model Army quickly sobered the Duke of Savoy and the Waldensians survive to this day.

Social Justice

Oliver Cromwell turned his attention to cruelty to animals and banned cock fights and bear baits. Vagrants who often were involved in drunkenness and theft were swept up by the military, evaluated by officers and either imprisoned or sent to forced labour outside the country.

Freedom for the Jews

Cromwell then invited Jews to return to England. Jews had been officially expelled from England in 1290. The Puritan Protector now

Oliver Cromwell intervened at a critical stage to save the Waldensians from annihilation at the hands of Catholic Savoy and France.

launched a campaign for their return. Cromwell did not theologically approve of Jews, Unitarians, or any group that denied the Divinity of Christ, but he favoured freedom of religion and longed to see the fulfillment of prophesy by Jews being brought to Salvation in Christ.

Cromwell hosted Menasseh Ben Israel at White Hall. This earned Cromwell much opposition, especially from London merchants who foresaw fearsome competition from this close-knit network. On 4 December, 1655, Oliver Cromwell made a speech, sometimes described as one of his best, which smothered the objections of the Council to the re-admittance of Jews to England.

Surviving Conspiracies and Threats
Cromwell was frequently burdened by the costs of war against Spain. His Head of Security, Thurloe, uncovered numerous plots to murder the Protector. Those Jews who returned to England flourished, and many

proved most useful to England's survival by providing vital intelligence, through their international commercial network, of the conspiracies against the Commonwealth from Spain.

A Refuge for the Persecuted
The Protector not only welcomed Jews to England, but Protestants of all nations. The University of Oxford received an influx of distinguished foreign Protestant professors. Education profited immensely from the Commonwealth and the Calvinists.

Refusing the Crown
Cromwell refused offers of the Crown declaring that he *"cannot undertake this government with the title of King."* The whole of Europe was astonished, but Calvinists hailed the decision as proof that Cromwell did not bow down before the honours of this world.

Victory against Spain
In June 1658, 6,000 English soldiers defeated the Spanish in Mardyk, Gravelines and Dunkirk. This finally secured the freedom of Protestant Holland from what had previously been the Spanish Netherlands.

The House of Lords Restored
Oliver Cromwell restored the House of Lords, declaring: *"Unless you have such a thing as balance, we cannot be safe..."*

The Limits of Tolerance
Cromwell's religious toleration even led to him having talks with George Fox of the Quakers. When a well-known Quaker preacher, James Naylor, rode in triumph into Bristol on a donkey to the cries of *"Hosanna!"* from his hysterical supporters who changed Naylor's name to *Jesus*, the parliamentary authorities arrested Naylor for blasphemy and sentenced him to whipping, branding, and life imprisonment. Cromwell was appalled and sought to alleviate the sentence, but was informed that he could not.

Cromwell refusing the crown of England.

Oliver Cromwell has frequently been blamed for many of the excesses of the Commonwealth Parliament. However, many of these extreme measures, such as the banning of Christmas and closing down of theatres were put in place by the Presbyterian Parliament, and rescinded by the Puritan Protector.

The Protestant Alliance

Oliver Cromwell sought to build up a Protestant League throughout Northern Europe. He settled disputes between Denmark and Sweden, concluded an alliance with Sweden, restored the supremacy of the seas to England, and even challenged the Catholic powers and Muslim pirates in the Mediterranean.

During the times of Oliver Cromwell, England was feared and respected throughout Europe. Cromwell formed a strong alliance between Holland and England, negotiated peace between the Protestant nations,

The Navy under Cromwell's Protectorate cleared the English Channel and the Mediterranean Sea of pirates.

cleared the English Channel and the Mediterranean Sea of pirates, expanded foreign trade and worked enthusiastically for the evangelism of Indians in North America. During the time of Oliver Cromwell's Protectorate, the whole world learned to respect British sea power. Cromwell became known as the Champion of Protestantism, an arbiter of Europe, a patron of learning and of the Arts and a tireless worker to lay legal foundations and checks and balances for the Parliamentary rule of England.

The Protector

While some have sought to describe Oliver Cromwell as dictator, there was no attempt to make any kind of party around the personality of Protector. Respect was always shown for private property and an effective and vocal opposition was always tolerated. Very few people were put to death under the Protectorate, and none for purely political crimes. No one was cast into prison without trial.

A Heritage of Freedom

Liberty of conscience and freedom of the press flourished under Oliver Cromwell. Religious toleration reached new heights - unprecedented up until that time. It is remarkable that in that bitter time of conflict, Oliver Cromwell could write: *"We look for no compulsion but that of light and reason."*

Parliament, through the English Civil War, had swept away the remains of Feudalism. Oliver Cromwell pioneered the New Model Army, created the world's first global sea power, laying the basis for both the Industrial Revolution and the British Empire, and preserved the Common Law.

Otto Scott in *"The Great Christian Revolution"* concludes that: *"Luther and Knox and Cromwell and Calvin lifted millions from the swamps in which they were placed by elegant men in power."* He noted that the foundational work of Oliver Cromwell in establishing checks and balances for the Rule of Law triumphed in the United States of America as people, inspired by his example, instituted many of the same principles of government and restrictions on power in their nation as Cromwell had worked so hard to achieve in England.

Otto Scott writes: *"Our War of Independence...raised men like Cromwell's, who fought like Cromwell's, for the same reason that Cromwell fought. The men at Philadelphia echoed the history of the 1640's and 1650's when they wrote the constitution with its limitations on the powers of congress, the presidency and the court.... when they said in the constitution that this nation would not have an established church, they reflected the experience of their forebears with Laud and his successors. When they spoke about open doors to all, open careers to all, they spoke in accents of Cromwell and the Calvinists, the Independents and the Congregationalists and the Puritans and the Presbyterians and the Levellers and those who fought under these banners. All this and more came from the great Christian Revolution; all the liberties that men know have come from Christianity, from its lessons about the individual and the state; God and His Covenant...to fulfill God's Word by bringing justice, truth, faith and joy to the world."*

A Vision for World Missions
Under Oliver Cromwell *The Society for the Propagation of the Gospel in New England* was established. An enormous sum of money was

donated towards this first Evangelical missionary society. Cromwell was keenly interested in evangelisation of the Red Indians and he proposed a comprehensive plan for world evangelism – dividing up the world into four great mission fields. Unfortunately, the death of Oliver Cromwell and the restoration of the Monarch in England under Charles II set back the cause of missionaries.

Chief of Men
John Milton wrote:
"Cromwell, our chief of men, who through a cloud
Not of war only, but detractions rude,
guided by Faith, and matchless fortitude,
to peace and truth, the glorious way hast plowed,
And on the neck of crowned fortune proud,
Hast reared God's trophies, and His work pursued,
while Darwen stream, with blood of Scots imbued,
And Dunbar field, resounds thy praise loud,
And vistas Laureate Wreath.
Yet much remains to conquer still; peace hath her victories
No less renowned than war; new foes arise,
Threatening to bind our souls with Secular chains.
Help us to save the conscience from the poor
Of hireling wolves, whose gospel is their naw."

One of the Greatest English Leaders of All Time
President Theodore Roosevelt in his book on Oliver Cromwell described him as: *"The greatest Englishman of the 17th century...the greatest soldier statesman of the 17th century..."* whose sacrifices and achievements *"have produced the English speaking world as we at present know it."*

Theodore Roosevelt makes comparisons with the Confederate General Stonewall Jackson and Oliver Cromwell, and the American War of Independence with the English Civil War.

Oliver Cromwell

Theodore Roosevelt concluded that, in his opinion, Oliver Cromwell was: *"one of the greatest of all Englishmen, and by far the greatest ruler of England itself, ...a man who, in times that tried men's souls, dealt with vast questions and solved tremendous problems; a man who erred...but who strove mightily towards the Light as it was given him to see the Light; a man who had the welfare of his countrymen and the greatness of his country very close to his heart, and who sought to make the great laws of righteousness living forces in the government of the world."*

The statue of Oliver Cromwell is one of only two within the grounds of the Palace of Westminster, which includes the House of Commons and the House of Lords.

"I will love you, O Lord, my strength, the Lord is my rock and my fortress and my deliverer; my God, my strength, in whom I will trust; my shield and the horn of my salvation, my stronghold. I will call upon the Lord, who is worthy to be praised; so shall I be saved from my enemies." Psalm 18:1-3

Oliver Cromwell, *"the chief of men"*, was a dedicated Puritan, relentless in battle, the Protector of Protestants, sponsor of foreign missions and champion of Religious Toleration.

Chapter 23
GEORGE FREDERIC HANDEL
The Musician who produced *"Messiah"*
(1685 - 1759)

Lutheran Musicians
Incredibly, two of the greatest musicians in all of history were born in the same year, in the same country – Germany, and both were Lutherans. George Frederic Handel and Johann Sebastian Bach were both born in 1685. However, they never met. And while Bach came from a musical family, Handel was the first musician in his family.

From Law to Music
George Frederic Handel's father was a surgeon-barber, who discouraged his son's musical career at every turn. He intended his son to become a lawyer. George studied law until 1703. However, he was permitted to take music lessons from age 9. By age 12, Handel was substituting for his organ teacher and had written his first composition.

Against the Fashions of the Time
After studying music in Germany and Italy, Handel moved to England, where he stayed for the rest of his life, becoming a composer for the Royal Chapel. However, his great interest in the opera was apparently ill-timed, as the form was falling out of fashion in England at that time. Into the 1740's Handel continued to compose operas, losing more and more money. When his friends expressed concern that the concert halls

George Frederic Handel was convinced that he had been called to set Scripture to music.

241

were nearly empty, Handel responded that an empty venue meant great acoustics!

From Bankruptcy and Boycotts to Success
In 1737 Handel's opera company went bankrupt and he suffered a stroke. His first oratorio, *Esther*, was condemned by church leaders for allowing the Word of God to be spoken in a theatre! The Bishop of London prohibited the oratorio from being performed. However, when Handel proceed with *Esther* anyway, the Royal Family attended and it met with success. In 1739 advertisements for Handel's *Israel in Egypt* were torn down by church leaders, who also disrupted his performance.

Setting Scripture to Music
George Handel was convinced that his call was to set the Scriptures to music. *"I have read my Bible very well and will choose for myself."* Handel declared that he knew his Bible as well as any bishop.

Despite great opposition and serious debt, Handel produced one of the greatest musical masterpieces of all time.

Facing Failure
However, their attacks had the effect that he was threatened with the debtor's prison. By 1741 George Frederic Handel was a failure. He was financially bankrupt, in great physical pain and the victim of several plots to sabotage his career. Deeply depressed, Handel began to plan his farewell appearance in London for April 1742.

The Messiah
That summer, however, he composed *Messiah,* which was at once hailed to be *"The epitomy of Christian Faith."* Handel began

George Frederic Handel

composing *Messiah* on 22 August 1741. Within six days, part 1 was finished, in nine more days, Part 2. Six more days and part 3 was completed. Handel composed like a man obsessed. He rarely left his room and seldom touched his meals. In 24 days he had composed 260 pages of what has been recognised as one of the greatest compositions ever. When he had finished writing what would become known as the *Hallelujah Chorus*, he exclaimed: *"I did think I did see all Heaven before me, and the great God Himself."*

Messiah is *"the epitomy of Christian Faith."*

Standing for the Anthem of the King of Kings
The premiere of *Messiah* on 13 April 1742, to an over-capacity crowd of 700, was a sensation. The demand for tickets were so great that men were asked not to wear their swords, and women not to wear hoops in their skirts, to allow 100 extra people into the audience. When *Messiah* was performed in London, the King attended, and when he stood at the opening notes of the *Hallelujah Chorus,* he began a tradition that has been carried on in the English-speaking world ever since.

More Powerful than many Sermons
Evangelist John Wesley attended a performance of *Messiah* at Bristol Cathedral, commenting afterwards: *"I doubt if that congregation was ever so serious at a sermon as they were during this performance."*

Seeing Heaven Before Him
By the time of his death Handel had conducted 30 performances of *Messiah*. He died on the day before Easter Sunday 1759, hoping to *"meet his good God, his sweet Lord and Saviour, on the day of His Resurrection."*

A friend remarked that George had *"died as he lived – a good Christian, with his true sense of his duty to God and to man, and in perfect charity with all the world."*

"Let everything that has breath praise the Lord. Praise the Lord!"
Psalm 150:6

"A good Christian, with his true sense of his duty to God and to man …"

Chapter 24

JOHANN SEBASTIAN BACH
The Greatest Musician
(1685 - 1750)

One of the Greatest Musicians of All Times
Johann Sebastian Bach was without question the greatest organist and composer of the Baroque Era. He was also widely recognised as one of the most productive geniuses in the history of music.

From a Family of Musicians
Johann was born and schooled in Eisenach, Thuringia, at the same Latin school that Luther had attended two centuries before. Johann Sebastian Bach was born on 21 March 1685 and died in 1750. Johann was part of a family that, in seven generations, produced 53 prominent musicians. He received his first musical instruction from his father Johann Ambrosius Bach. Orphaned at age 10, Johann went to live and study with his uncle Johann Christoph Bach, an organist in Ohrdruf. Johann was the eighth and youngest child of his parents.

Talented and Innovative
By age 15, Bach was displaying tremendous talent and became a soprano in the choir of Lüneburg's Church of St. Michael. Three years later he became a violinist in the chamber orchestra of Prince Johann Ernst of Weimar. A few months later he was invited to become a church organist at Arnstadt. In October 1705, Bach was invited to study under the renowned German organist and composer, Dietrich Buxtehude. Upon his return he was severely criticized for his new organ flourishes and harmonies

Johann Sebastian Bach was one of the most productive and innovative musical geniuses of all time.

that accompanied the congregational singing.

Marriage
In 1707 he married Maria Barbara and went to Mülhausen to become organist in the church of St. Blasius. After 13 years of happy marriage, Maria died in 1720 and the next year he married Anna Magdalena Wilcken, an accomplished singer.

Leipzig
He finally settled down in Leipzig in 1723 where he remained for the rest of his life. Anna Magdalena bore him 13 children, in addition to the 7 he had had by Maria. In addition to running a busy household, Anna also helped copy music for Johann's performances. Four of Bach's surviving ten children became well-known composers.

Johann Sebastian Bach's desk and chair where he composed many of his compositions.
"Soli Deo Gloria" **(for the Glory of God alone).**

Johann Sebastian Bach

Johann Bach was a family man who delighted to sing with his children.

"A Second Rate Musician"

In Leipzig Johann Bach was music director and choir master of St. Thomas's church and a teacher at their school. This was not an easy time, and he was involved in constant conflict with the town council and the populace, who did not seem to appreciate his musical genius. The council paid him a very inadequate salary and, even when he died, they contrived to defraud his widow of her meagre inheritance. (At his appointment one of the town councillors famously said: *"As the best musicians are not available, I suppose we must take one of the second rate."*)

"Continual Vexation"

Bach wrote to a friend: *"The authorities are odd and little interested in music, so that I must live amid almost continual vexation, envy and persecution."*

Soli Deo Gloria

Yet, in this unpromising setting, Johann Sebastian Bach wrote some of his most enduring music. For a time he averaged a cantata a week.

Bach was renowned for "opening the stops" of an organ and playing wholeheartedly.

Today a composer who writes a cantata a year is highly regarded. Nearly three-fourths of Bach's 1,000 compositions were written for use in worship. All of his music was closely bound to Biblical text. At the end of most of his music Bach wrote: *Soli Deo Gloria* (To God alone be the glory), or the initials SDG.

The Passion of St. Matthew

It was in Leipzig that Bach composed *The Passion of St. John* and *The Passion of St. Matthew* for use in worship services. *The Passion of St. Matthew* has frequently been called *"The supreme cultural achievement of all western civilisation."* Even the skeptic Frederic Nietzsche admitted upon hearing it: *"one who has completely forgotten Christianity truly hears it here as Gospel."*

God-Pleasing Music

When he was 48, Bach acquired a copy of Cavlov's 3-volume Luther translation of the German Bible, with parallel Luther commentary. This he studied most carefully. Next to 1 Chronicles 25 Bach wrote in his Bible, *"This chapter is the true foundation of all God-pleasing music."* At 2 Chronicles 5:13 Bach wrote: *"At a reverent performance of music, God is always at hand with His gracious presence."*

A Resurgence of Appreciation

After his death, his music was generally neglected, although a few musicians, such as Mozart and Beethoven, admired it. However, it was in 1829, when German composer Felix Mendelssohn arranged a performance of *The Passion of St. Matthew*, that there was a massive resurgence of appreciation for Bach's compositions. Bach was not only one of the most creative and prolific musicians in all of history, but he was also acknowledged as an expert in organ design.

The Fifth Evangelist
Today Johann Sebastian Bach is recognised as one of the greatest musical geniuses in all of history, a devout Christian theologian whose music has had such a deep impact that he has been described in many circles as *"The Fifth Evangelist."*

The Father of Modern Music
Many music critics declare that Bach was the greatest musician that ever lived. J.S. Bach was an unsurpassed

genius and is acknowledged as the Father of Modern Music. *"He left no musical form as he found it"*, says one critic. On the other hand, with every form he touched, he seemed to have said the last word. Bach's teaching notebooks and violin books have been the basis for music theory and practice ever since.

A Modest Musician
Bach was modest about his achievements, offering this classic understatement: *"I was obliged to be industrious. Whoever is equally industrious will succeed equally well."*

The Lutheran Church in Leipzig where Bach composed *"The Passion of St. Matthew."*

For the Glory of God and the Refreshment of the Soul

Johann Sebastian Bach was a dedicated Protestant Christian, a Lutheran. Most of his library consisted of Protestant writings, including all of Luther's books. Bach taught his pupils that music is an act of worship and that all musicians need to commit their talents to the Lord Jesus

Christ. *"The aim and final end of all music should be none other than the glory of God and the refreshment of the soul."*

The Greatest Musician

As one critic said: *"Bach is to music what Shakespeare is to literature. They are both the greatest."* And they were both Protestant Christians.

"Speaking to one another in psalms and hymns and spiritual songs, singing and making melody in your heart to the Lord, giving thanks always for all things to God the Father in the Name of our Lord Jesus Christ,"
Ephesians 5:19-20

Johann Sebastian Bach, *"The Fifth Evangelist"* who *"left no musical form as he found it"*, yet with every form he touched seemed to have said the last word.

Chapter 25

JONATHAN EDWARDS
A Mind on Fire for Christ
(1703 - 1758)

America's Greatest Theologian

Jonathan Edwards (1703-1758) played a leading role in The Great Evangelical Awakening (1735-1744) and in defending the Reformed Faith against the attacks of Deists and Arminians. Jonathan Edwards has been recognised, even by secular historians, as one of the most original thinkers and influential intellectuals in the history of New England and of American theology. He has also been described as: *"America's greatest theologian."*

Certainly the writings of Jonathan Edwards have attracted more attention and study in England, Europe, and further afield, than any other American theologian over the last two and a half centuries.

The Making of a Genius

Jonathan was born on 5 October, 1703, the fifth child of Timothy and Esther Edwards. Jonathan was their only son out of eleven children. He had ten sisters!

Jonathan's father, Timothy Edwards, was a third generation New Englander, a pastor, who served his East Windsor parish faithfully. Jonathan's father, Timothy Edwards, also served as a chaplain during an Indian war.

Jonathan preached one of the most famous sermons in history, which sparked a remarkable Revival.

Jonathan's grandfather, on his mother's side, was Solomon Stoddard, a famous Puritan minister who served as a pastor for over 55 years.

Jonathan's mother, Esther Stoddard grew up in a home filled with books and frequented by New England's elite. She was described as *"highly educated"* and she instilled in her young son Jonathan her own great love for books.

Even before he was a teenager, Jonathan was fluent in Latin, Greek and Hebrew. From a very early age he was very methodical and showed astonishingly early maturity in making both scientific observations and philosophical speculations.

As a young boy, Jonathan built little forts in the woods to hold prayer meetings with his friends. He entered the Collegiate School of Connecticut (which later became Yale University) at age 13 and graduated at 17 years old at the head of his class.

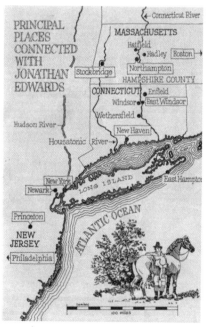

Converted to Christ

Shortly before his graduation, at age 17, he was soundly converted. As he was reading: ***"Now unto the King, eternal, immortal, invisible, the only wise God, be honour and glory, forever and ever. Amen."*** 1 Timothy 1:17, *"There came into my soul...a sense of the glory of the Divine Being, a new sense, quite different from anything I'd experienced before...from about that time I began to have a new kind of apprehension and ideas of Christ, and the work of Redemption and the glorious way of Salvation by Him."*

The doctrines of God's sovereignty,

which had previously appeared *"repugnant"* to him suddenly became *"exceeding pleasant, bright and sweet"* to his soul. He rejoiced in God's sovereignty, glory and majesty. From this point on Edwards noted that he continually saw in nature: *"God's excellency, His wisdom, His purity and love...in everything; in the sun, moon and stars; in the clouds and blue skies; in the grass, flowers, trees; in the water and all nature"* and this greatly fixed his mind. The next time he experienced a thunderstorm he was captivated to see the spectacular lightning and *"hear the majestic and awesome voice of God's thunder...my great and glorious God...it always seemed natural for me to sing..."*

A Puritan Faith

From the beginning Jonathan Edwards bucked the trend among the students away from the Puritan faith of the college's founders. Jonathan went against the spirit of his time and began to devour the writings of the Reformers and the Puritans. The glory and majesty of God became Edwards' compelling passion in life.

Jonathan Edwards entered Yale University at age 13 and graduated at 17 years old at the head of his class.

Called to the Ministry

After studying Divinity for two years, Edwards was called to be an assistant pastor to his grandfather, Solomon Stoddard, in Northampton, Massachusetts. He was mentored by his grandfather in the pastorate for two years. Upon the death of Solomon Stoddard at 85 years (after being a powerful preaching influence in Massachusetts for over 55 years), the church in Northampton called Jonathan Edwards to become its pastor.

By all accounts, Jonathan Edwards was a dedicated and dutiful pastor. He spent an average of 13 hours a day in study and sermon preparation. Edwards described the minister's calling: *"To rescue lost souls and bring them to eternal happiness."*

He was distressed by the wickedness and worldliness of the society he was called to reach. This spiritually-minded pastor preached harsh and scathing sermons which cut to the heart of many. He saw the people of his congregation as immersed in immorality.

"The Gospel seemed to me the richest treasure; the treasure that I have most desired...the way of Salvation by Christ...glorious and excellent, most pleasant and beautiful." Holiness was described by Jonathan as *"a sweet, pleasant, charming, serene, calm...inexpressible purity, brightness, peacefulness and ravishment to the soul."*

The preaching of Jonathan Edwards was described as *"arresting"*, *"awakening"*, *"remarkable"* and *"instructive"*. He employed no *"theatrics"* in his preaching, but convinced *"with overwhelming weight of argument and with much intenseness of feeling."* He preached against sin as an affront to the sovereign majesty of God. He proclaimed the need for divine grace through Christ Jesus. At an ordination sermon Jonathan Edwards proclaimed: *"Ministers are only sent on His errand. They are to preach the preaching that He bids them. He has put into their hands a Book containing a summary of doctrine and bids them go and preach that Word."*

An Uncommon Marriage

When Jonathan Edwards was 20 he met Sarah Pierrepont. After four years of often agonizing courtship he married Sarah and thus began what was described as an *"uncommon union."* Jonathan and Sarah were blessed with eleven children. (In 1900, a study tracked down the 1,400 descendants of Jonathan and Sarah Edwards and revealed that this one marriage has produced: 66 physicians, 30 judges, 65 professors, 13 college presidents, 100 lawyers, 1 Dean of the top law school, 1 Dean of a Medical School, 3 US senators, 3 mayors of large cities, 3 state governors, 1 controller of the US Treasury, and 1 Vice-President of the USA - who the very next year became President of the USA – Theodore Roosevelt. In addition, members of the family had written 135 books and edited 18 journals. They had entered the ministry *"in platoons"* and sent out over 100 missionaries overseas).

George Whitefield wrote of his time in the Edwards' home as having been a tremendous blessing and inspiration. Of Jonathan and Sarah Edwards he wrote: *"a sweeter couple I have not yet seen."* He described their children as *"examples of Christian simplicity."* He described Sarah Edwards as: *"Adorned with a meek and quiet spirit. She talked solidly of the things of God, and seemed to be such a helpmeet of her husband, that she caused me to renew those prayers...that He would be pleased to send me a daughter of Abraham to be my wife."*

Jonathan and Sarah Edwards enjoyed an "Uncommon" marriage which produced an incredible list of illustrious descendants.

Sarah saw it as her spiritual duty to keep her home peaceful and pleasant so Jonathan could devote the maximum amount of time to his studies and ministry. How she was able to do this with eleven children whom she home schooled is a wonder. At the end of each day, Jonathan and Sarah would ride on their horses through the nearby woods and they would encourage one another with the spiritual riches they had discovered that day.

Revival

In 1734 Jonathan Edwards' preaching on Justification by Faith sparked a Spiritual Revival in his parish. In December there were six sudden conversions. By Spring there were about thirty per week. *"The town seemed to be full of the presence of God; it never was so full of love, nor so full of joy...there were remarkable tokens of God's presence in almost every house...God's Day was a delight...everyone earnestly intent on public worship, every hearer eager to drink in the words of the minister."*

This work of the Holy Spirit spread throughout the Connecticut River Valley, across the whole of North America, and then across the Atlantic to the British Isles.

Edwards' careful account of this Revival: *"A Faithful Narrative of the Surprising Work of God"* was published in 1737. Soon it was republished in England (edited by the famous hymn writer Isaac Watts). English Evangelist George Whitefield read Edwards' book and made it a point to visit him when he came on his preaching tour to America.

When Whitefield preached at Edwards' church it was reported: *"The congregation was extraordinarily melted...almost the whole assembly being in tears a great part of the time."* Through the itinerant preaching of George Whitefield, the Great Awakening spread throughout the English colonies in North America and further abroad.

The Most Famous Sermon

It was shortly after Whitefield's visit that Jonathan Edwards preached his most famous sermon, possibly one of the most famous sermons in history, *"Sinners in the Hands of an Angry God."* It was 1741. The style was similar to the sermons preached to a condemned criminal just before execution. The minister would be expected to stress their imminent encounter with the Judgement Seat of God and he would exhort them to repent. As these sermons were often publicised, most would have recognised the style.

Jonathan Edwards preached *"Sinners in the hands of an angry God"* – which sparked the Great Evangelical Awakening.

In a most shocking move, Edwards applied this form of sermon to the *"respectable"* church going people and relentlessly hammered home the instability of their position before a Holy God. The total depravity of man, the holiness and wrath of God and the only way of Salvation through Christ was most powerfully presented in this devastatingly effective sermon. Lives were transformed, previously lukewarm and worldly church members abandoned questionable practices and communities were dramatically transformed.

Many of Edwards' Bible studies and sermons were later published. This included *Justification By Faith* (1737), *The Distinguishing Marks of a Work of the Spirit of God* (1741), *Thoughts on the Revival* (1742), and *Religious Affections* (1746).

David Brainerd

In 1749 Jonathan Edwards published the diaries of missionary David Brainerd (1718-1747). In Brainerd, the young dedicated missionary who brought the Gospel with great impact to the Indians, Jonathan Edwards found a living example of all that he had preached and written about concerning a Christian's transformed life of holiness. Brainerd was engaged to be married to Jonathan Edwards' daughter, Jerusha, but contracted tuberculosis and died in the Edwards' home at age 29. Shortly afterwards Jerusha died from the same tuberculosis that she had contracted while caring for her fiancé.

Edwards' book: *The Life and Diary of Rev. David Brainerd"* was mightily used to inspire the 19th century missionary movement. It galvanised countless missionaries, including the Father of the Modern Missionary Movement, William Carey, into foreign fields.

A Dedicated Pastor

Jonathan Edwards was convinced that he could accomplish the greatest good by studying, preaching, writing, counselling and through prayer. Much of this was accomplished in his study where he poured out his soul in fervent prayer and counselled many members of his congregation.

His sermons were carefully written out, reasoned, doctrinal statements, based on solid Biblical exegesis and with the characteristic Puritan application to head and heart, to faith and practice. He divided his sermons into three sections: Text, Doctrine and Application – each saturated with Scripture. His style was described as: restrained and powerful. Edwards encouraged the intellectual development of his members by lending out his books.

A Strict Disciplinarian

When it became apparent that some of the conversions in his midst were not sincere, Edwards forbade their participation in the Lord's Supper. This caused much dissension amongst his congregation. He insisted that only persons that had made a public profession of faith, which included a description of their personal conversion experience, could receive Communion. This reversed the Open Communion position of his grandfather and led to him being voted out of the church by an overwhelming 230 to 23.

Rejected

Some complained about Edwards' practice of not visiting the homes of congregants, but rather receiving those seeking counsel in his study. In order to make more time for

Missionary David Brainerd preaching to the Indians

his writing ministry, Edwards preferred those needing counsel to come to his study, rather than travelling to visit every member in the congregation as a matter of routine. Others were offended by Edwards' *"harsh"* dealing with several young men, who had transgressed accepted ethical standards, by reading their names from the pulpit. As several of these were from well-placed Northampton families, it earned him the enmity of many status-conscious, established families did not like being reminded that their personal achievements amounted to *"filthy rags"* in God's sight. Edwards' conscientious insistence on congregational purity had embarrassed many of the Northamptonites who were more concerned with their social standing.

Exiled

On 1 July, 1750, with no post to move to, Edwards preached his farewell sermon to the church at Northampton. He then became a missionary to Housatomic Indians in the frontier town of Stockbridge. This began seven years of hardship and practical exile. He was regarded as a worldly failure, having been dismissed from the pastorate, and forced to live in abject poverty. And yet, in many ways, this missionary posting on the frontier led to the most productive time of his writing ministry.

True and False Conversions

In his *"Distinguishing Marks of a Work of the Spirit of God"* (1741), Jonathan Edwards distinguished between true and false conversions. *"In the main, there has been a great and marvellous work of conversion and Sanctification among the people here."* However, he reported irregularities and excesses requiring one to ***"Try the spirits whether they be of God."*** 1 John 4:1

Edwards wrote the biography of missionary David Brainerd which inspired many into pioneer missions.

Outwardly, the saved abandon old vices and contentious ways. Inwardly they testify to a new and lively sense of God's presence and a new attitude and disposition towards spiritual matters. However, the Revival was marred by emotionalism and disorderly behaviour by some. Edwards pointed out that God created the soul with two faculties: intellect and will. One could possess speculative knowledge without a transformed heart.

For example, we may memorise a mathematical formula or the Ten Commandments, but the mere knowledge may not necessarily influence our motives and actions.

Edwards discussed non-signs that neither confirm, nor deny, the presence of the Holy Spirit. Amongst these Edwards included intense religious experience, *"bodily manifestations"*, extensive and fervent religious conversation, devotion to religious practices, knowledge of Scripture and even direct communication by God. As he pointed out, in the Scriptures, God even spoke to reprobates.

It was Edwards' practice to not visit the homes of his congregation but to counsel them in his study.

The Marks of a True Christian

The signs of a true Christian Edwards identified as wholehearted love for God and our Lord Jesus Christ, not for the benefits of peace, comfort or eternal life – though these do come as by-products of salvation. Rather, however, the true believer loves God for who God is. Not only for what God does.

Spiritual affections incline one's sinful self away from self-interest towards God's glory. The real distinguishing marks of a true believer can be seen in the Fruit of the Spirit: love, joy, peace, patience, kindness, goodness, faithfulness, gentleness and self-control (Galatians 5:22-23).

Holiness comes from the heart, or the will, rather than from our understanding. Holy affections (emotions and the will) are the substance of genuine faith.

The work of the Spirit of God is seen in those who are: humble, loving in spirit, spiritually hungry, self-reflective and steady, and abiding in holy affections. The chief sign of all the signs of grace, the true mark of a Christian, is found in Christian love in action. *"Godliness in the heart has direct a relationship to practice as a fountain has to a stream or as the luminous nature of the Sun has to beams sent forth, or as life has to breathing."*

True Love is Seen in Sacrifice

Christian faith in action, lived out consistently, amidst the trials of life, is the most convincing evidence of true Christianity. A person may feel intensely, talk, listen, sing and pray, but unless they are accompanied by integrity and works of love and mercy, these are not convincing proof of the work of regeneration. Edwards encouraged his readers to distinguish genuine Christian experience from the counterfeit, not so much by what people said, but by what they did.

A Joyful Faith

Jonathan Edwards insisted that believers should expect joy from their faith. True Christianity *"begets love and peace, goodwill one towards another, brotherly kindness, mutual benevolence, generosity and a concern for one another's welfare."*

A Matter of the Heart

Edwards taught that *"true religion"* is first and foremost a matter of the heart. One can see one in whom the Spirit of God is working because the Holy Spirit re-orientates our soul. The most important evidence of regeneration is the turning of the heart, transforming our affections, causing us to love God's will and take delight in pursuing His ways.

God Himself

God Himself is the source of all that is good, true and beautiful. A loving union with God brings unprecedented joy and personal fulfillment and a Biblical love of God and our neighbour. He quoted Augustine's *Confessions*: *"You have made us for yourself, and our heart is restless until it rests in you."*

Edwards taught that God has created us to have a longing that only He can satisfy. However, we sinners try to fill this God-shaped vacuum with idols of pride, greed and lust. He taught that goodness can never be separated from godliness. That which is not done to serve Christ can in no way be called good.

Creation Testifies to the Creator

Edwards taught that everything in nature and history speaks of Christ and His Gospel, if only it is rightly understood. He showed images, types and shadows of Divine things in nature and history.

For example, he taught that springtime's gradual progress is ordained by God to illustrate the gradual increase in the Kingdom of God on earth. The *"filth"* in which newly born babies are covered is God's way of stressing to us the sinfulness of all men.

Calvinism vs Arminianism

He taught that the Calvinist doctrine of predestination provides the greatest support for true morality. Better than any other alternate view, he showed that Calvinism holds human beings responsible for their own actions. Freedom and predestination are essentially compatible. His book, *Original Sin*, is a solid defence of the controversial doctrine of predestination. He showed the logical incoherence of Arminianism.

The preaching and teaching of Jonathan Edwards had a dramatic impact throughout New England.

Edwards was not a fatalist. People are accountable to God and we are fully responsible for our own actions. Yet it is God's grace alone which saves sinners.

Emotion vs Emotionalism

Many of Edwards' works defended the Revivals against those who would have no emotion in their religion, and those who would have nothing but emotion in theirs.

Jonathan Edwards was a very disciplined person who maintained a life-long habit of rising at 4am. Most of his days were devoted to intensive studying, sermon preparation and writing. He insisted that true Christianity is rooted in a changed heart. His *Treatise on Religious Affections* (1746) is a masterpiece of spiritual discernment. Jonathan Edwards combined intellect and piety, head and heart, doctrine and devotion in an extraordinary balance. He encouraged the singing of new Christian hymns, notably those of Isaac Watts.

During his seven years missionary work in Stockbridge, Edwards ministered to the last of the Mohican tribe.

With the Last of the Mohicans

During his seven years of missionary work in Stockbridge, Jonathan Edwards was associated with the last of the Mohicans. Mohican children boarded at the mission school, and his son, Jonathan, spent a year in Mohican villages learning their language. When the French and Indian War broke out, the Mohicans abandoned Stockbridge, some to fight alongside the English.

The writings of Jonathan Edwards are some of the clearest on Revival and true and false conversions ever written.

Called to Princeton

Finally, after seven years of exile at Stockbridge, Jonathan Edwards' intellectual stature was finally recognised when he was invited to become President of the new college at Princeton. He arrived in January 1758, but due to an experimental inoculation against smallpox, which he received on 13 February, he died of the disease 22 March. He was just 55 years old.

Called to Glory

His last words spoke of his love for his wife Sarah (who was still packing up their belongings in Stockbridge in preparation for their move to New Jersey) and urged his children to find faith in God. He asked her not to give him an elaborate funeral, but that what money was available rather be given to charity. His last words to his daughter, who was caring for him, were: *"Trust in God, and you need not fear."*

He Still Speaks to Us Today

Tragically, the major work which Jonathan Edwards was beginning, that of arranging a synthesis of Christian doctrine and ethics arranged historically, was barely begun. However, numerous of his other works which were almost complete at his death were later finalised and printed including: *The End for Which God Created the World* (1765); *Nature of True Virtue* (1765) and *History of Redemption* (1774). Because of his writings, his personal example of holiness, and his influence as a dedicated church leader, Jonathan Edwards has continued to exert a tremendous influence on Reformed churches in America and Great Britain. His defence of historic Calvinism held back the oncoming tidal wave of rationalism and romanticism. In many ways Edwards' long years of isolation on the mission field helped produce some of his greatest writings, which continue to bless the church today.

Edwards' call for prayer for Revival: *A Humble Attempt to Promote Explicit Agreement and Visible Unity of God's People in Extraordinary*

Prayer for the Revival of Religion (1749) was widely circulated throughout the British Isles and had a tremendous influence on William Carey who carried this book to India. Jonathan Edwards' insistence on a vibrant faith of head and heart, holiness and service, continues to challenge and rebuke Christians to this day.

"Now to the King eternal, immortal, invisible, to God who alone is wise, be honour and glory, for ever and ever. Amen." 1 Timothy 1:17

America's greatest Theologian and one of the most influencial original thinkers in North American history.

Chapter 26
GEORGE WHITEFIELD
Calvinist, Evangelist and Revivalist
(1714 – 1770)

Dynamic Preacher

George Whitefield was described by his contemporaries as: *"the marvel of the age."* Whitefield was an eloquent preacher who electrified his audiences. He drew some of the greatest crowds ever assembled up to that time, across two continents, without any institutional support, through prayer and the sheer power of his personality. The Great Evangelical Awakening that swept across the British Isles and North America in the 18th Century has been attributed primarily to the dynamic ministry of George Whitefield.

"Probably not since Luther and Calvin has there been such a vessel chosen for bearing the errands of mercy to the multitude. By the power of the Holy Spirit, he changed sterile religious wastes into verdant, heavenly pastures, and sowed on good ground those seeds of practical piety, whose fruit bless and encourage us in the institutions and habits that have been handed down to us from the Christianity of past generations." Gene Fedele

Raised in an Inn

George Whitefield was born the youngest of seven children, at Gloucester, the son of an innkeeper. His father died when he was just two years old. His mother remarried, but that resulted in a disastrous divorce. His

Despite being raised by a single parent in an inn, George Whitefield grew up to be one of the most influential evangelists in all of history.

mother, Elizabeth Whitefield, struggled to maintain the Bell Inn, with George mopping floors, cleaning rooms and serving customers food and drink. Whitefield later recalled how his mother endured 14 weeks sickness after giving birth to him, and that she would often say to him that she expected more out of him than any of her other children. George expressed his desire to *"follow the example of my dear Saviour, Who was born in a manger belonging to an inn."*

Oxford
Through the efforts of his mother, young Whitefield entered Pembroke College, Oxford, as a servitor. He would be put through college by serving the wealthier Oxford students.

The Holy Club
Even before he arrived at Oxford, he had heard of *"the Holy Club"* (the Methodists) of John and Charles Wesley, who were generally despised and ridiculed. George felt strongly drawn to defend them in argument. In time Whitefield was welcomed to their *"Holy Club"* and sought to live by their strenuous rules.

Studying at Oxford University, George Whitefield joined *"the Holy Club"* of John and Charles Wesley.

Born Again

At this time, while reading *"The Life of God in the Soul of Man"* by Henry Scougal, Whitefield declared: *"God showed me that I must be born again."* George later commented that at Oxford it became clear that he was no scholar, but that he was called to be a communicator of the Gospel. He determined to be a missionary to America. However, his great devotional excesses and lengthy fastings broke down his health and he was laid aside by a long and wearisome sickness.

The Boy Preacher

When Whitefield recovered, Dr. Benson, Bishop of Gloucester, offered him ordination as a deacon.

Whitefield's open air preaching began when over a thousand people could not fit into the church at Bermondsey.

After a short time as a temporary pastor to a congregation in Hampshire, Whitefield sailed for America. He had already risen to great prominence as a popular preacher. Huge crowds had gathered in and around London wherever he spoke. Newspaper articles had been written concerning the sensation of the *"boy preacher"* and his intense and emotional presentations of Biblical characters and stories were attended by huge crowds and unprecedented emotional responses. Before departing for America, Whitefield published his first message: *"The Nature and Necessity of Our Regeneration or New Birth in Christ Jesus."*

Georgia

In Georgia, Whitefield preached five times a week to crowded congregations. Multitudes followed him.

Open Air Preaching

When he returned to London, churches were opened on week days and constables were placed at the doors to prevent too many people from forcing their way into the buildings. At Bermondsey church, nearly 1,000 people stood outside the church, unable to hear his message. Whitefield felt a strong compulsion to go out and preach to this crowd from the tombstones. This was the beginning of his open-air preaching.

Field Preaching

Soon, at Kingswood, near Bristol, Whitefield began his field preaching to about 200 coal miners. The second time he preached 2,000 people assembled to hear him. The third time, the audience numbered up to 5,000. The numbers gathering increased until more than 20,000 people were assembled on the fields to hear this powerful preacher.

Excluded from Pulpits

Although the common people thronged to hear him, the church authorities took great offence to George Whitefield's innovations of preaching the Gospel outside of the sanctuary of a church building and determined to prevent him preaching from any of their pulpits in future. What Whitefield had adopted by choice, now became a necessity. At the time, the idea of outdoor, extemporaneous preaching, with no wooden pulpit or even sermon notes, between him and his congregation, seemed revolutionary and undignified to the established church.

Itinerant Preaching in America

It was at this point early in 1738 that George Whitefield concluded that his calling was to be an itinerant preacher to urban areas throughout the Anglo-American world. It was during his preaching tour of the American colonies in 1739 – 1740 that the Great Evangelical Awakening erupted. Whitefield's first stop was Philadelphia – a major port city, the most cosmopolitan city in the New World, with a thriving market economy. At every stop along Whitefield's ministry tour from Philadelphia to New York, and back again, record audiences, often exceeding the population of the towns in which he preached, assembled.

George Whitefield

With pulpits closed to him, Whitefield preached in the open air at sporting events and in market places.

The Evangelical Awakening

Observers reported on the remarkable phenomenon of spellbound audiences listening in profound silence in greater numbers that had ever been seen up until that point in North America. Some of the most dramatic spiritual responses occurred during Whitefield's 39-day whirlwind tour of New England. On 17 October 1740, Whitefield preached in Northhampton, Massachusetts, and stayed with the famed theologian Jonathan Edwards. Edwards reported: *"The congregation was extraordinarily melted… almost the whole assembly being in tears for a great part of the time."*

Aiming at the Heart

It was after that visit that Edwards preached his famous sermon *"Sinners in the Hands of an Angry God."* Sarah Edwards observed that Whitefield aimed more at affecting the heart by proclaiming the simple truths of the Bible than any other preacher she had ever heard.

Whitefield's Bethesda Orphanage in Savannah, Georgia, placed such financial burdens and legal complications on him that it almost ended his ministry.

The House of Mercy

It was on this second ministry tour of America that Whitefield acquired a 500-acre plot for his Bethesda (House of Mercy) orphanage 10 miles north of Savannah, Georgia. By 1740 he had nearly 40 children under his care, but it was at this point, while Revival was breaking out in New England, that a disagreement arose between Whitefield and his trustees, who withdrew their support. Supplies bound for the orphanage were stolen.

The Burden of Debt

Soon Whitefield owed about 500 pounds – 20 years wages at that time. Then his primary sponsor for the endeavour, William Seward, died without a will. Whitefield reported: *"I was embarrassed with Mr. Seward's death. He died without making any provision for me, and I was at the same time much indebted for the Orphan House... I am almost tempted to wish I had never undertaken the Orphan House."* The debt against Bethesda placed Whitefield in jeopardy of being jailed for unpaid debt. The financial burdens associated with this orphanage Whitefield described as: *"lying like a dead weight upon me."* It was only by 1768 that Whitefield finally managed to settle the debt.

Revival in Scotland

With Revival sweeping England and North America, Whitefield sailed for Scotland. In 1742 Whitefield's preaching was received with great enthusiasm in Glasgow and Edinburgh. Whitefield's evening services attracted thousands and continued until 2 am. *"There were scenes of uncontrollable distress, like a field of battle... all night in the fields, might be heard the voices of prayer and praise."* Whitefield commented that the responses in Scotland *"far outdid all that I ever saw in America."* At one service 20,000 people attended a meeting that stretched late into the night. On Sunday Whitefield served communion in the fields. It was reported that wherever you walked *"you might have heard persons praying to, and praising, God."* Whitefield made 14 ministry tours to Scotland and 7 to America.

Conflict with Wesley

Early in his ministry a sharp conflict developed between John Wesley and George Whitefield. When Whitefield left England in 1739, he was the recognised leader of the Evangelical Awakening, and he entrusted his thousands of converts to John Wesley's care. When he returned to England in early 1741, he found that *"many of my spiritual children... will neither hear, see, nor give me the least assistance. Yes, some of them sent threatening letters..."* John Wesley had preached and published against the teachings of George Whitefield on predestination and total depravity. Wesley rejected Whitefield's Calvinist convictions and held that sinless perfection may be obtainable in this life.

Gracious Disagreement

Whitefield had always respected John Wesley as his *"spiritual father in Christ"* and addressed Wesley in his letters as *"Honoured Sir."*

Although Whitefield's evangelistic successes far outstripped that of his former instructor, he continued to show John Wesley great respect to the very end of his life, when he requested that John Wesley preach the sermon at his funeral.

Opposition
However, the Arminianism of John Wesley was hostile to Whitefield's Calvinist convictions. In March 1739, while Whitefield was in America, Wesley preached and published a passionately Arminian sermon *"Free Grace."* He testified that this step was only taken with great unease, and after seeking a sign from heaven and drawing lots twice. Wesley feared that Calvinism would discourage growth in holiness. Wesley ensured that *"Free Grace"* was widely published in America, forcing Whitefield to write a response.

Reconciliation
Despite some hot tempers and hard words in the exchanges, George Whitefield and John Wesley were ultimately reconciled. Not that there was any agreement on the two issues of predestination or perfection, but they agreed to disagree. Whitefield refused to build Calvinist Methodist chapels in places that already had a Methodist society. Wesley agreed to do the same. Whitefield was welcomed to preach at many of Wesley's societies. More than once Whitefield acted as a mediator when the Wesley brothers fell out, notably when Charles sabotaged John's marriage prospects to Grace Murray.

A Forgotten Founder of the Methodists
In 1749, Whitefield resigned formal leadership of the Calvinist Methodist Societies and posed no further *"threat"* to Wesley as the chief organiser of the Revival in England. Wesley lent Whitefield one of his best preachers, Joseph Cownley, to minister at the Tabernacle in London. Whitefield laid the foundations for the Kingswood College, Bristol, which became so important to Methodism.

George Whitefield

Whitefield electrified audiences throughout North America and the British Isles.

Benjamin Franklin and George Whitefield
Another interesting friendship of George Whitefield was with Benjamin Franklin. Franklin and Whitefield were clearly on opposite ends of the theological spectrum. Benjamin Franklin proclaimed a religious creed which consisted primarily of good works. Whitefield's last public words, preached within hours of his death, declared: *"Works! Works! A man gets to heaven by works? I would as soon think of climbing to the moon on a rope of sand!"*

Yet Benjamin Franklin and George Whitefield went beyond a partnership in publishing, to a genuine friendship of mutual trust and respect.

Siding with the Americans
As colonial tensions with the Mother Country arose, Whitefield clearly sided with the Americans. When Benjamin Franklin appeared before

Parliament, Whitefield attended every session and gave his old friend public support.

The Christian Work Ethic
Benjamin Franklin commended Whitefield's evangelistic zeal and charitable ministries. He wrote to Whitefield encouraging him to organise *"a strong body of religious and industrious people"* to settle Ohio. *"Might it not greatly facilitate the introduction of pure religion among the heathen, if we could, by such a colony, show them a better example of Christians than they commonly see in our Indian traders?"*

Black Christianity in America
Some historians attribute *"the advent of black Christianity"* in America to George Whitefield's first preaching tour in Philadelphia when he sought out audiences of slaves, preached the Gospel to them and wrote on their behalf.

The Battle of Moorfields
One of Whitefield's classic open-air preaching battles occurred in 1746 in the Moorfields of London. He began preaching at 6 in the morning when some 10,000 people had assembled, waiting for the sports events to begin. Whitefield preached three times for many hours during the day, in spite of drummers, trumpeters, players, hecklers and vulgar attacks with stones, dirt, rotten eggs, pieces of dead animals, and all manner of filth was thrown at him. When a recruiting sergeant marched his men through the midst of the audience in the hope of making a disturbance, Whitefield requested his people to fall back and make way for *"the king's officers"* and then close up again. This manoeuvre trapped the men within a mass of worshippers.

Holding the Field
When the uproar of the heathen became so great that Whitefield could not be heard, he stopped preaching and called the Christians to sing with loud voices, and so, with singing, praying and preaching he held the field throughout the day. More than a thousand letters were handed

George Whitefield

to him by persons who were *"brought under conviction."* 350 people came to Christ and joined his congregation as a result of that day's preaching.

Despite hecklers and attacks, George Whitefield preached to thousands of people throughout the day at Moorfields.

A Tireless Preacher
In his lifetime, Whitefield preached at least 18,000 times. He would preach an average of 12 times a week and spent 20 to 50 hours in the pulpit each week. Whitefield was America's first celebrity.

About 80% of all American colonists heard him preach at least once.

Under Attack
Brutal mobs of non-Christians sometimes attacked Whitefield and his followers. Whitefield received death threats by letters, and once he was stoned until nearly dead. In his lifetime, he was declared: *"the greatest preacher that England has ever produced."* It was calculated that he preached to over 10 million people in his lifetime. Whitefield usually awoke at 4 AM and began preaching at 5 or 6 am.

A Pioneer and Innovator
While John Wesley is known as the founder of the Methodist movement, few remember that it was actually George Whitefield who formed the first Methodist societies and pioneered most of the methods used in the 1700's Evangelical Awakenings. It was Whitefield that pioneered preaching in fields rather than churches, publishing

magazines and holding conferences. Whitefield published the first magazine in North America: *"Christian History"* – containing *"authentic accounts of the most remarkable passages, historical and doctrinal"* from famous Christians of the past.

A Productive Ministry

Whitefield pushed himself so hard and preached with such intensity that he was frequently ill afterwards. Aside from preaching an average of 12 times a week, Whitefield sometimes conducted funerals and performed weddings, often counselled enquirers, oversaw numerous congregations, and maintained a large correspondence, as well as organising his charitable endeavours, and preaching at conferences which Lady Huntington described as times *"of refreshing from the presence of our God... Mr. Whitefield's sermons and exhortations were close, searching, experimental, awful and awakening."*

Yet, despite all that he achieved amidst physical trials and spiritual labours, Whitefield wrote on the occasion of his 37th birthday: *"I am ashamed to think I have lived so long and done so little."*

Burning Out for God

Many times Whitefield travelled through torrential rain and blizzards of snow in order to make his appointments. Much of his correspondence, reading and study was accomplished while travelling, and amidst a *"throng of business."* Frequently, Whitefield ignored the advice of doctors and he continued his 1770 preaching tour in America, declaring: *"I would rather wear out than rust out."* Struggling with breathing, nearly collapsing, needing to be helped onto his horse, Whitefield was heard to pray: *"Lord, if I have not yet finished my course, let me go and speak for Thee once more in the fields, seal Thy truth and then let me come home and die!"*

Finishing the Race

This prayer was answered as he managed to complete one final powerful sermon. The following morning he died at Newburyport. All of the bells in the town tolled, the ships in the harbour fired their cannon in mourning, and flags were hung at half-mast. In Georgia all the black cloth in the stores were bought up and the churches were hung in black. The governor and council met at the State House in deep mourning and marched in procession to hear the funeral sermon. Poet John Green Whittier described Whitefield as: *"That life of pure intent. That voice of warning yet eloquent."*

A Bold Pathfinder

Whitefield has been attributed with pioneering non-denominational, international, para-church ministry. He preached to the heart, and demanded a response. He utilized the media and blazed the trail

"That life of pure intent. That voice of warning yet eloquent."

which future generations of Evangelical Revivalists, chaplains, youth and student para-church leaders and Christian charities have followed. By all accounts, those who were awakened by his burning words to a sense of their spiritual needs and who came to Christ as a result of his Biblical preaching number in, at least, the hundreds of thousands. The lives changed by the Great Evangelical Awakening launched through his itinerant preaching ministry are incalculable.

Words of Whitefield

Some quotable sayings of George Whitefield: *"There is not a thing on the face of the earth that I abhor so much as idleness or idle people."*

"God forbid that I should travel with anybody a quarter of an hour without speaking of Christ to them."

"I hope to grow rich in heaven by taking care of orphans on earth."

"Young Christians are like little rivulets that make a large noise and have shallow water; old Christians are like deep water that makes little noise, carries a good load and gives not way."

"Suffering times are a Christian's best improving times."

In His lifetime, George Whitefield preached at least 18 000 times. He preached an average of 12 times a week and spent from 20 to 50 hours in the pulpit each week.

"So shall My Word be that goes forth from My mouth; It shall not return to Me void, but it shall accomplish what I please, and it shall prosper in the thing for which I sent it."
Isaiah 55:11

Chapter 27
JOHN AND CHARLES WESLEY
Evangelists Extraordinary
(1703 – 1791) (1707 – 1788)

The Wesley brothers were central figures in the 18th century Evangelical Revival in Great Britain. Theirs was one of the most effective partnerships between brothers in ministry.

The Industrial Revolution
The Wesleys grew up during the Industrial Revolution. Their lifetimes and ministries spanned a time of rapid change. Revolutions in smelting, spinning and distilling created whole industries. The 18th century saw some of the first experiments in electricity, photography and the steam engine.

A Desperate Situation
When the Wesleys began their itinerant preaching, there were no railroads and no restaurants. Only five or six members of parliament even went to church. Infant mortality was extremely high. Life expectancy was in the early 40s.

The newly urbanised lived in overcrowded slums.

Unhygienic Conditions
Most dwellings had no running water and few homes used any

The Industrial Revolution transformed the traditionally agricultural society.

soap. The plague, smallpox, cholera and a host of other parasitic and water-borne diseases were common. Rodent and insect control was minimal. It was a world without street lights, and no numbers on the doors of homes. Most bedding was full of lice.

A Harsh Justice System
Corporal punishment was public with the stocks, the whip and the cutting of ears and noses as part of the criminal justice system. No man was safe in the cities, on the highways or even on the high seas. Forcible recruitment into the army and navy was common and those who fell foul of the law could either be hanged, even for very petty offences, or be transported across the seas to convict colonies. Execution of criminals was public.

Immoral Slums

Promiscuity and public drunkenness were common, as was cruelty to animals in bear baitings. Most of the newly urbanized poor, who had crammed into unsanitary slums in the cities, lived in warehouse-like buildings with no plumbing and no privacy.

Immorality and public drunkenness characterised the urban slums.

Reaching the Poor

For the average working man, there was no variety, no vacations, no advancement, and very little wages. It was on this world of little hope and few options that the Wesley brothers' evangelistic ministry had the greatest impact, literally transforming society.

Early Childhood

John Wesley was born on the 17 June 1703, the 15th of 19 children (8 of whom died in infancy). His father, Samuel Wesley, was a stern Anglican minister. His mother, Susanna, was a pious and dedicated disciplinarian. Both of his grandparents were non-conformist Puritan clergy who had been expelled from the Church of England in 1662. Although his parents worked and worshipped within the established church, their Puritan and non-conformist heritage did affect the upbringing of their children.

Home Schooled

From the age of 5, the Wesley children were home schooled and were expected to become proficient in Latin and Greek and to have memorise major portions of the Scriptures. Susanna Wesley interviewed each one of her children on their own once a week in order to evaluate their spiritual progress.

A Brand Plucked From the Flames

At age 5, John Wesley was rescued from the Rectory fire.

A disastrous fire which destroyed their Rectory on 9 February 1709 made an indelible impression upon young John Wesley. At about 11 pm the Rectory roof caught fire and the Wesleys managed to shepherd all of their children out of the house, except for 5-year-old John who was left stranded on the second floor. With the stairs aflame and the roof about to collapse, a parishioner stood on another man's shoulders to lift young John Wesley out of the second floor window. Throughout his life, John thought of himself as *"a brand plucked from the fire"* Zechariah 3:2 and Amos 4:11.

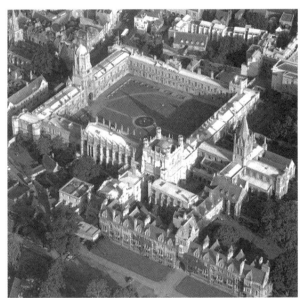

Christ Church, Oxford, where John and Charles Wesley studied for the ministry.

Saved For a Purpose

Charles Wesley, as the youngest child, was the first to be rescued from the Epworth Rectory fire. But his life had almost been snuffed out when he had been born prematurely: After being left for dead, he revived. Both brothers were made aware by their mother that they had been spared for a purpose.

Oxford
John Wesley's formal education began in 1714, when at age 10 he was sent to Charterhouse school in London. By 1720, at the age of 16, he had matriculated at Christ Church, Oxford, where, except for a two year curateship, when he served in the pastorate under the direction of his father, John remained for the next 16 years. He achieved his Bachelor of Arts and Master of Arts, was ordained in 1727, and became a Fellow of Lincoln College, Oxford, where he taught Greek and lectured on the New Testament.

The Holy Club
At Christ Church, Oxford University, Charles Wesley founded the Holy Club, which met for Bible study, prayer and self-examination. When his elder brother John returned from serving as a parish curate, he took over the leadership of the Holy Club. The group met daily from 6 pm until 9 pm for prayer, Psalms and reading of the Greek New Testament. They fasted on Wednesdays and Fridays until 3 pm. In 1730 the group began the practice of visiting prisoners in jail where they preached, educated and cared for the sick.

Charles Wesley started the Holy Club in Oxford.

John Wesley took over the leadership of the Holy Club in Oxford.

Opposition

As spiritual life was at a very low ebb in Oxford at that time, the Holy Club was derided as *"enthusiasts"* – religious fanatics. This opposition exploded into scandal when one of the group, William Morgan, suffered a mental breakdown and died. It was at this time that the critics began to term the Wesleys and the members of their Holy Club as *"Methodists."*

Georgia Colony

In 1733, James Oglethorpe, a renowned soldier and Member of Parliament, led a commission which exposed the horrors of debtors' prisons. He motivated the founding of the colony of Georgia in North America as a haven for imprisoned debtors, needy families and persecuted Protestants from the continent. Oglethorpe proposed settling them in Georgia as a bulwark against Spanish expansion and to help reach Indians for Christ.

Governor James Oglethorpe, Founder of Georgia.

Missionaries to America

The Wesley brothers were recruited to be chaplains for the colony. John wrote that his chief motive for becoming a missionary was: *"the hope of saving my own soul."* He also hoped to *"learn the true sense of the Gospel of Christ, by preaching it to the heathen."* On board ship en-route to America, John and Charles and two other members of the Holy Club continued their Methodist practices, beginning private prayers at 4 am. Their frequent services, readings and exhortations were resented by the other passengers.

Moravian Faith

The Wesleys were impressed with the 26 Moravians, by their *"great seriousness"* and by their exemplary behaviour and *"fearlessness."* During a ferocious storm which disrupted a service, Wesley reported that *"a terrible screaming began among the English, while the Germans calmly sung on."* Wesley could not help but notice the difference between *"those that feared God and those that did not."*

Challenged

Later, John was challenged by the Moravian pastor, Augustus Spangenberg, who questioned his salvation: *"Do you know Jesus Christ?"*
John replied: *"I know He is the Saviour of the world."*
Spangenberg responded: *"True... but do you know He has saved you?"*
Wesley answered: *"I hope He has died to save me."*

Governor Oglethorpe intended to establish Georgia as a bulwark against Catholic Spanish expansion and to reach Indians for Christ.

John Wesley was a missionary to the
Indians before he was converted.

Spangenberg continued to question John closely and Wesley confessed in his diary that he offered *"only vain words"* in reply.

Alienating Americans

In Georgia, John laboured strenuously, but unsuccessfully. His lack of tact alienated the colonists. He insisted upon the total immersion of infants at Baptism and had the only doctor in the colony locked up for violating the Sabbath. When one of the doctor's patients suffered a miscarriage while the physician was detained, John came under even further criticism. At Frederica, a hundred miles inland, conflict arose between Charles and the governor. Charles fell into a nervous breakdown, fever and dysentery. He was shipped back to England in 1736.

Failed Romance

John developed a romantic relationship with Sophy Hopekey, who although she was 15 years younger, returned his affections. There was much affection and discussion of marriage, but then John prepared 3 lots: *"Marry", "Think not of it this year"* and *"think of it no more."* When he drew the third, he abruptly dropped the relationship with Sophy. When Sophy married another suitor, John had her barred from communion, asserting that she had failed to attend some of the 5 am prayers!

Legal Problems

As a result, the Chief Magistrate had Wesley arrested for defamation of character. A Grand Jury returned ten indictments against John Wesley and as the case dragged on, John fled the colony and set sail for England, never to return.

A Crisis of Faith

While sailing for England, Wesley wrote in his Journal: *"I went to America to convert the Indians! But Oh! Who shall convert me?"* In England a young Moravian pastor, Peter Boehler, challenged John as to whether he possessed saving faith. John responded that he only had a *"fair, summer religion"*, not true faith. Wesley asked whether he should not abandon preaching altogether.

"Preach Faith!"

Boehler responded: *"By no means. Preach faith until you have it; and then, because you have it, you will preach faith."* John took Peter Boehler's advice to heart and began energetically to preach the Doctrine of Justification by Faith Alone. However, by May 1738, his enthusiastic preaching had alienated the establishment and he was banned from 9 churches.

Listening to Luther

On 24 May 1738, Wesley went *"very unwillingly"* to a Moravian meeting in Aldersgate. There, as he heard Luther's preface to the Epistle to the Romans read, *"I felt my heart strangely warmed. I felt I did trust in Christ, Christ alone for Salvation, and assurance was given me that He had taken away my sin, even mine, and saved me from the law of sin and death."*

Peace with God

Three days earlier, on Pentecost Sunday, 21 May 1738, Charles Wesley had been reading Luther's Commentary on Galatians. *"I now found myself at peace with God, and rejoiced in hope of loving Christ... I saw that by Faith I stood; by the continual support of Faith."* John Wesley wrote that he now had the faith of a son, rather

The plaque commemorating the conversion of the Wesley brothers.

than that of only a servant. He jubilantly announced to his brother Charles: *"I believe!"* John later wrote that before his conversion experience he was *"not a Christian"*. He had been a minister and a missionary before he had even been saved.

Whitefield Shows the Way

Even before the Wesleys found peace with God, the young George Whitefield, the last person to become a member of the Holy Club, had been flooded with the joy of Salvation. In March 1735, after months of desperately striving, he cast himself on the mercy of God, trusted Christ and received the forgiveness he had so earnestly sought. In 1736, as he was ordained to the ministry of the Church of England, he preached his first sermon and soon crowds overflowed the buildings where he proclaimed Salvation through Christ alone. Then Whitefield sailed to America to continue the work which had been begun by the Wesleys in Georgia. Even on board ship, he brought many to saving faith. Whitefield's preaching in Georgia was crowned with many turning to Christ. His ministry is counted as the beginning of the Great

George Whitefield pioneered open air preaching.

Awakening in America and the Evangelical Revival in England.

The Bristol Revival

As Whitefield returned to England, he found himself barred from London pulpits and began preaching in the open to coal miners near Bristol. George Whitefield begged the Wesleys to come to Bristol and continue and organise the campaign that he had begun. After casting lots, John decided it was God's will to accept this invitation. After arriving in Bristol, 31 March 1739, Wesley witnessed Whitefield's preaching. He wrote in his Journal: *"I could scarce reconcile myself to this strange way of preaching in the fields, of which he set me an example on Sunday; having been all my life, until very lately, so tenacious of every point relating to decency and order, that I should have thought the saving of souls almost a sin if it had not been done in a church."*

John Wesley preached over 40,000 sermons in the last 50 years of his life.

When the pulpit was closed to him, John Wesley preached on his father's gravestone.

Open Air Preaching

The next day Wesley found himself preaching to 3,000 people in the open air. This experience at Bristol transformed John Wesley into an Evangelist who would now focus on proclaiming Salvation and Holiness to the lower classes and to the unchurched. Now 36 years old, John Wesley had found his life's calling. For the next 50 years he energetically preached throughout the length and breadth of the British Isles. Travelling on horseback, Wesley covered over 250,000 miles (400,000km), preaching an average of three times a day, beginning at 5 am each morning. It is calculated that he preached over 40,000 sermons in his life. With pulpits increasingly closed to the unfashionable message of the Wesleys, they turned to the open air, preaching in fields, market places, in parks and at mines. Not since Professor John Wycliffe had mobilised the Lollards, the field workers of the Reformation, had England seen such extensive and effective open air evangelism.

"The World is my Parish!"

From the beginning, John Wesley was seen as a controversial figure and widespread opposition was mobilized against him, frequently with mob violence. When Bishop Joseph Butler of Bristol confronted John and told him that he had *"no business here"* and that he was *"not commissioned to preach in this Diocese"*, John famously replied: *"The world is my parish!"* John Wesley maintained that he had been ordained as a priest of the Church of England, and as a Fellow of Lincoln College he was *"not limited to any particular"* diocese, but had a *"commission to preach the Word of God to any part of the Church of England."*

Organising the Methodist Societies

From the time of the Bristol Revival, the two great gifts of John Wesley became evident: Preaching and Organising. John founded religious societies, similar to the Holy Club, to disciple the converts who responded to his public preaching.

As early as 1739, Wesley required subscriptions for membership in the newly created societies. This simultaneously provided funding for the ministry, particularly for publications, and provided a mechanism for discipline of unworthy members who could have their subscriptions suspended or denied. Membership in the societies was open to all who were *"sincere seekers after Salvation."*

Evangelising England

From 1740 Wesley commissioned lay preachers, and by 1744 there were 77 laypreachers in the field.

John Wesley rode over 400,000km on horseback.

"The world is my parish!"

Also in 1744, Wesley convened the first conference, which consisted of six Anglican ministers and four lay preachers. This conference would become the movement's ruling body. By 1746, Wesley had organised geographic circuits for itinerant preachers, organising Societies in Circuits which in turn were organised in Districts with quarterly meetings, annual conferences, classes, bands and select societies. In addition to classes of a dozen or so society members meeting weekly for spiritual fellowship and guidance, there was also a category of penitents for backsliders.

Women in Ministry
From the beginning the Methodist movement offered opportunities for women to minister. Wesley appointed women as lay preachers.

A New Denomination
John Wesley insisted that the societies remain within the Church of England and he attempted to maintain an inter-denominational identity. Although it had never been his intention to develop a separate denomination, when he began to ordain ministers and missionaries, this inevitably led to separation from the Church of England.

Violent Opposition
The establishment regarded the Wesleys as traitors to their class. Yet Methodist meetings were frequently disrupted by mobs of the poorer classes, the very ones whom the Wesleys were trying their best to help. Methodist buildings were ransacked and their lay preachers harassed, beaten and frequently dragged before the local Magistrate. Methodist-

baiters frequently drove oxen into the congregations assembled for field preaching. In Epworth, as John was barred from speaking in the church, he addressed the large crowd standing on his father's tombstone.

John encouraged Circuit riders to adhere to their schedule regardless of weather conditions.

Fearless

John Wesley proved fearless in confronting hostile mobs. He even converted some of the most vocal ringleaders. Hecklers were shocked when they found Wesley to be educated, articulate and a gentleman.

Relentless

Sometimes John covered 60 miles a day on horseback. He would adhere to his schedule regardless of weather conditions. In rain, sleet, or snow John relentlessly travelled and preached across the country, from coast to coast. He first ministered in Wales, 1741, then Ireland in 1747 and Scotland in 1751. In all, he conducted 42 separate ministry tours of Ireland and 22 to Scotland.

The Wesleyan Quadrilateral

John Wesley preached the Law of God, cleanliness, honesty, thrift, good family relations and above all saving faith in Christ. Although he was well-read, John Wesley saw himself as preeminently a man of one book – The Bible. John Wesley was far too energetic an evangelist to become anything like a Systematic Theologian, however he developed his theology by using the Wesleyan quadrilateral: Scripture, Tradition, Reason and Experience. Scripture was foundational. The Doctrine had to be in keeping with *"orthodox Christian tradition"*, that had to be logical and the truth had to be applied in the personal experience of the Christian.

Sin and Salvation

Wesley affirmed God's Sovereignty and human free agency. He taught that God's loving and merciful interaction with free and responsible human beings does not detract from His glory. He believed that all human nature had been corrupted by original sin, and all human beings are personally guilty because of our violation of God's Law.

Prevenient Grace

Wesley also taught prevenient grace that was free and not meritorious at all, which provided human beings with the power to respond to, or resist, the work of God. Wesley's description of justifying faith as preconditioned by Repentance and the fruits, or works of Repentance, differed from what the Protestant Reformers taught. Whereas Reformers Martin Luther and John Calvin taught that justifying faith includes both Repentance from sin and trust in Christ, Wesley had a narrower view of justifying faith separating Repentance from it.

Christian Perfection

Wesley also argued for the possibility of *"entire Sanctification"*, that is *"Christian perfection"*, where we can be *"perfect as our Father in Heaven is perfect."* He taught that this Christian perfection frees people from *"voluntary transgressions"*, but not necessarily from *"sinful inclinations."* He also maintained that individuals could have a *"second blessing"*, akin to a second conversion, experiencing *"instantaneous sanctification."*

Free Grace

In 1740, John Wesley preached a sermon on *"Free Grace"* in which he condemned the doctrine of predestination. John claimed that the doctrine of predestination undermines morality and dishonours God by presenting *"God as worse than the devil, as both, more false, more cruel and more unjust."*

The Arminian Controversy

George Whitefield urged John never to repeat or publish this sermon. When Wesley published it, it led to the controversy between Whitefield and Wesley. Wesley inclined strongly towards Arminianism and in 1778 began the publication of the *"The Arminian Magazine."* He taught that God wills all people to be saved and that he believed in *"conditional predestination"*, which depended upon human response. He believed that God's grace could be resisted and that a true Believer could fall from grace, even finally *"so as to perish forever."*

Holiness and Revivalism

John Wesley was a pioneer of modern Revivalism and a spiritual father of the Holiness movement, Charismatic renewal and Pentecostalism. His emphasis on Free Grace, Entire Sanctification and Perfection led to the development of denominations such as the Church of the Nazarene.

Social Justice

Methodists became leaders in many social justice issues of the day, particularly Prison Reform, Abolition and Temperance. Wesley had a profound concern for people's physical, as well as spiritual welfare. Holiness had to be lived out and seen in works of mercy. He taught that charities imitate Christ's earthly ministry of healing and helping the needy. Almost all that he received from his publications, at least 20,000 Pounds, were invested in charities. He made provision for the care of the sick and pioneered the use of electric shock for the treatment for illness. He superintended schools and orphanages. He ensured that collections for the poor were regularly taken up in Methodist services. The 'Stranger's Friend' societies provided relief for the poor.

Pews designed by John Wesley.

Charles Wesley was the Hymn Writer of the Evangelical Revival.

Transformation

The effects of Wesley's preaching were dramatic. Swearing stopped in factories. Drunkards became sober. Thieves performed restitution. Neighbours gave one another mutual help through the societies. Wesley's preaching had the greatest impact amongst the poorest classes.

Charles Wesley

Charles Wesley, (1707-1788), John's younger brother, gave music, heart and soul to the Methodist movement. Although overshadowed by his elder brother, Charles directly influenced John throughout his ministry. It was Charles who began what became the Holy Club at Oxford. Charles went with John to Georgia in the Americas and was with him from the beginning of the work of open air preaching in Bristol.

The Hymn Writer

As energetic as John was in keeping his Journals, Charles composed over 6,500 Hymns, many of which are still sung today, such as *Jesu, Lover of My Soul, Love Divine, All Loves Excelling, Hark the Herald Angels Sing* and *Christ the Lord Has Risen Today*. There was scarcely a day in the 50 years following his conversion in which he did not set down some lines in verse. Along with Isaac Watts, he was a major pioneer in Hymn writing.

John and Charles Wesley

Methodism was the antidote to Jacobinism.

Dedicated Service

Charles exercised a distinctive ministry as an Evangelist, a counsellor and a shepherd of souls. For almost 20 years Charles covered the country in his travels and then settled in Bristol, later in London, to support and supplement the dynamic ministry that John so relentlessly advanced.

Defeating the Revolution

The French historian, Elie Halevy (1870-1937), in his *A History of the English People in the 19th Century* (published in 1912), maintained that the Evangelical Revival in 18th century England enabled the British Isles to avoid the political Revolutions that tore France and much of the European continent apart between 1789 and 1848. *"Methodism was the antidote to Jacobinism."* Wesley and his fellow labourers provided hope and encouraged discipline amongst Britain's newly urbanised and industrialised working class. Holiness defeated Humanism.

Church Buildings
John Wesley instructed that churches should be built in the octagonal form (with eight sides), and that the interior should have a rail in the middle *"to divide the men from the women"*. There were also to be no backs for the seats.

The American Question
John Wesley so disapproved of the American colonists' rebellion against the Crown that he wrote a stinging rebuke urging them to submit, and when the Americans broke from Great Britain he ordered superintendent Francis Asbury (1745-1816) to return to England.

Francis Asbury
This Asbury refused to do. Asbury seized the reins of Methodism in the United States and shaped what would become the Methodist Episcopal Church. Although he clashed with Wesley, Asbury was so like him in energy and organisational ability that he has been called the Wesley of America. Francis Asbury rode over 5,000 miles each year on horse

Francis Asbury was known as the *"Wesley of America"* as he averaged 8000km a year on horseback.

back, often in bad health, linking up the congregations from Georgia to Maine.

George Bell

George Bell was a convert to Methodism who turned into an opponent. Bell made extravagant claims for himself and his followers that they had attained *"absolute perfection"*.

The Apostles Creed, The Ten Commandments and Greatest Commandment at Wesley's Chapel.

Wesley had to exclude Bell and his extreme followers. George Bell went on to predict the end of the world on 28 February 1763. Bell did severe damage to the Methodist cause in London.

Social Reformer

John Wesley has been recognised as one of the foremost Social Reformers of the 18th century. On his death the Gentleman's Magazine commended the *"infinite good to the lower classes of the people... By the humane endeavours of him and his brother Charles, a sense of decency and morals and religion was introduced to the lowest classes of mankind; the ignorant were instructed, the wretched relieved and the abandoned reclaimed."*

"I offered them Christ."

Rule for Christian Living

John Wesley's rule for Christian living was summarised as: *"Do all the good you can, by all the means you can, in all the ways you can, in all the places you can, at all the times you can, to all the people you can, as long as ever you can!"*

Legacy
Through faith, endurance and perseverance, John Wesley transformed 18th century British society and left a legacy far greater than the Methodist church. By 1790, a year before his death, the number of members stood at almost 60,000. Today, Methodists number in the tens of millions.

God With Us
In Westminster Abbey, close to the memorial to Bible translator William Tyndale, is a sculptured medallion showing the profiles of the two Wesley brothers. Below it are inscribed John's last words: *"The best of all is God with us"* and another of his well known sayings: *"I look upon all the world as my parish."* A quote from Charles Wesley is also on the memorial: *"God buries His workmen, but carries on His work."*

John Wesley's summary of his life's work was: *"I offered them Christ!"*

"The best of all is God with us."

Chapter 28
WILLIAM CAREY
The Father of Modern Missions
(1761 - 1834)

"It's impossible! It can't be done! Don't be ridiculous – what difference can one person make?"

Have you ever encountered these reactions? Anyone who embarks on a challenging enterprise – especially those determined to end legal abortions, eradicate pornography, establish a Christian school or Christian Teacher Training College, stop the ongoing slave trade in Sudan, work for national Reformation and Revival or evangelise a Muslim nation – will encounter those people who seem to believe that they have *"the gift of criticism"* and *"a ministry of discouragement!"*

Should Christians be Involved in Politics?

Then there are those who maintain that Christians shouldn't even be involved in social issues at all! When you tell them of the abortion holocaust or the pornography plague they mutter that *"all we can do is pray", "just preach the Gospel"* and *"it's a sign of the last days!"*

We suspect that such attitudes are often motivated more by laziness and cowardice or a selfish desire to shirk responsibility and hard work than anything else. Certainly those people who resort to such superficial excuses are being disobedient to the clear commands of Scripture: *"Love your neighbour as yourself"* (Luke 10:27); *"Go and do likewise"* (Luke 10:37); *"Speak*

The man who launched the modern missionary movement and his first convert from Hinduism, Krishna Pal.

up for those who cannot speak for themselves" (Proverbs 31:8); *"Rescue those being led away to death"* (Proverbs 24:11); *"Make disciples of all nations"* (Matt 28:19); *"Anyone, then, who knows the good he ought to do and doesn't do it, sins"* (James 4:17).

Those who maintain that Christians shouldn't be involved in social or political issues display their ignorance of both the Bible and Church history. Over 70% of the Bible deals with social, political and national issues. Abraham used military force to rescue Lot and his family from the four kings (Gen. 14). God raised up Joseph to be Prime Minister of Egypt (Gen. 41). Samuel, Nathan, Elisha, Isaiah, Ezra – in fact almost all of the prophets – were heavily involved in politics as advisors to kings and exerted a godly influence on national affairs. Moses, Elijah, Jeremiah and John the Baptist publicly confronted and rebuked wicked rulers. King David was described as *"a man after God's heart"* (Acts 13:22). Daniel and Mordecai became prime ministers in pagan Babylonian and Persian governments – yet without compromise. God raised up Deborah and Queen Esther to national leadership positions. Joshua, Gideon and Nehemiah also held senior political positions.

"I looked for a man among them who would build up the wall and stand before Me in the gap on behalf of the land so that I would not have to destroy it . . ."   *Ezekiel 22:30*

Those who maintain that Christians shouldn't be involved in political and social issues are not only ignoring the Word of God but also showing their ignorance of Church history.

Slavery and Human Sacrifice

Before the advent of Christianity every culture practised slavery and human sacrifice. In the Roman Empire abortion, infanticide and the abandonment of unwanted babies was legal and commonplace. The Aztec Empire in Mexico, the Inca Empire in Peru and the Mayan Empire in Central America engaged in slavery, ritual rapes and mass human sacrifices. Slaves were marched up the stairs of the pyramid type temples. At the top a priest would rip out their beating hearts – one by one. There were over 80 000 human skulls on the skull racks of just one of King Montezuma's many temples. Only the advent of Christianity introduced a respect for the sanctity of life and ended the rampant infanticide and human sacrifice.

Similarly, slavery was eradicated as a result of the tireless efforts of Christians such as William Wilberforce and David Livingstone. The whole concept of charity was a Christian innovation, as were hospitals (hence the universal healing symbol of a cross to represent hospitals.) But of course these monumental achievements were not easily achieved. Every victory for life and liberty was only accomplished by much sacrifice and ingenuity over many, many years of hard work.

If you sometimes feel overwhelmed by the immensity of the task before you, or discouraged by a seemingly never-ending series of obstacles and opposition, frustrations and failures – take heart! The man whom God used to launch the modern missionary movement faced all this and much, much more.

Launching a Reformation

Undereducated, underfunded and underestimated, William Carey seemed to have everything against him. He was brought up in abject poverty and never had the benefit of high school. He had a thirst for knowledge, read widely and had

As a young cobbler, William Carey prayed for all the nations.

a keen interest in nature. Carey's formal education ended in junior school. Yet, at age 12 Carey taught himself Latin. Then he went on to master – on his own – Greek, Hebrew, French and Dutch! He eventually became professor of Bengali, Sanskrit and Marathi at the prestigious Fort William College in Calcutta (where the civil servants were trained). Carey and his co-workers, William Ward and Joshua and Hanna Marshman, started over 100 Christian schools for over 8 000 Indian children of all castes and launched the first Christian College in Asia – at Serampore. This college continues to this day! Carey finally succeeded in translating the Bible into 6 languages, and New Testaments and Gospels into 29 other languages!

Mission Impossible

Carey's achievements are all the more astounding when you consider that his bold project to plant the Gospel among the Hindus in India was completely illegal! By an act of the British Parliament it was illegal for any missionary to work in India. For the first 20 years, Carey's mission to India had to be carried out with ingenuity and circumspection, based under Danish protection in the small Danish colony of Serampore. At last the British Parliament – under pressure from evangelical Members of Parliament such as William Wilberforce – reversed its policy and compelled the British East India Company to allow missionaries in India.

Passion and Principle

Sometimes his students in England saw him in tears while teaching geography. Carey would point to various places on the map and cry *"And these are pagans! Pagans!"* Carey was considered a radical in his day. He boycotted sugar because he was intensely opposed to slavery and sugar from the West Indies was produced with slave labour. Carey also took the extremely unpopular stand of supporting the American War of Independence against Britain.

Insanity and Disease

He was also subjected to vicious criticism and gossip. Under the extreme heat and in abject poverty, initially with daily dangers from snakes, crocodiles and tigers in a remote and mosquito-ridden jungle house, Carey's wife, Dorothy, went insane. She would rant and rave about the imaginary unfaithfulness of her husband and on several occasions attacked him with a knife. She was diagnosed insane and had to be physically restrained with chains for the last 12 years of her life. The

As a young teacher, William Carey taught his students of the pagan nations that needed missionaries to take them the Gospel.

Careys' also lost their 5-year-old son, Peter, who died of dysentery in 1794. Every family member suffered from malaria, dysentery and other tropical diseases – frequently.

Debt and Discouragement

Carey's first co-worker, John Thomas, squandered all their money and bankrupted the mission, forcing William to work on a plantation to provide for his malnourished family. In their first seven months in India the Careys had to move home five times! And although Carey frequently wrote home, to family and mission society – it was 17 months before they received their first letters! One of these first letters from the Society criticised Carey for being *"swallowed up in the pursuits of a merchant!"*

Toil Amidst Turmoil

Somehow, while often sick, holding down a full time secular job, surrounded by domestic turmoil, with an insane wife screaming from the next room, Carey mastered Bengali and Sanskrit and by 1797 the New Testament was translated into Bengali and ready for printing! Carey had also established several schools and was preaching regularly in Bengali. However, after seven years of tireless toil in India, Carey still did not have a single convert!

Persistence and Productivity

How did William Carey manage to maintain such a productive schedule while having to endure all these crushing disappointments, the endless distractions, the undeserved criticisms, the physical ailments and the heart-breaking tragedies? How did he manage to persevere and to keep on keeping on without even the encouragement of a single convert to justify all his effort and sacrifice? To understand what motivated this most remarkable man we need to look back at what inspired him in the first place.

A Vision of Victory

One of the most influential sermons in world history was preached on 31 May 1792 by William Carey in Northhampton, England. Carey's sermon literally sparked the greatest century of Christian advance. It marked the entry of the English-speaking world into missions. Since that time English speakers have made up 80% of the Protestant missionary work force.

The Sermon that Launched the Greatest Century of Missions

The text of this historic sermon was Isaiah 54:2-3:

"Enlarge the place of your tent and let them stretch out the curtains of your dwellings. Do not spare, lengthen your cords and strengthen

your stakes! For you shall expand to the right and to the left and your descendants will inherit the nations, and make desolate cities inhabited."

The theme of his sermon was summarised as:

"Expect great things from God!
Attempt great things for God!"

William Carey (seated at left) with the eleven other Baptist pastors that launched the first mission society.

Rebuked for Missionary Zeal

Yet, riveting as the sermon was, the result was initially indecision. Carey was considered *"an enthusiast"* (a fanatic) and an embarrassment – because *"he had a bee in his bonnet about missions."* One story recounts how an older pastor rebuked Carey for his missionary zeal: *"Young man, sit down! Sit down. You are an enthusiast! When God pleases to convert the heathen He will do it without your help or mine!"*

The First Mission Society

But Carey persisted until, five months later, 12 Reformed Baptist ministers formed the *"Particular (Calvinist) Baptist Society for Propagating the Gospel among the Heathen."* Their first collection from these pastors amounted to thirteen pounds, two shillings and sixpence.

Inspiration

What inspired Carey's landmark book *"An Enquiry into the Obligation of Christians to use Means for the Conversion of the Heathens"* and this prototype pioneer missionary society was his eschatology of victory. William Carey was a Post-millennialist who believed that God who commanded His Church to *"make disciples of all nations"* would ensure that the Great Commission would ultimately be fulfilled.

The house in which 12 Reformed Baptist pastors formed the *"Particular (Calvinist) Baptist Society for Propogating the Gospel among the Heathen."*

Unwavering Conviction

"The work, to which God has set His hands, will infallibly prosper . . . We only want men and money to fill this country with the knowledge of

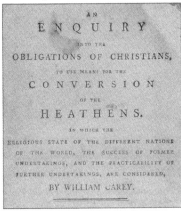

AN
E N Q U I R Y
INTO THE
OBLIGATIONS OF CHRISTIANS,
TO USE MEANS FOR THE
C O N V E R S I O N
OF THE
H E A T H E N S.
IN WHICH THE
RELIGIOUS STATE OF THE DIFFERENT NATIONS
OF THE WORLD, THE SUCCESS OF FORMER
UNDERTAKINGS, AND THE PRACTICABILITY OF
FURTHER UNDERTAKINGS, ARE CONSIDERED,
BY WILLIAM CAREY.

The title page of the book which launched the 19th Century Missionary movement.

Christ. We are neither working at uncertainty nor afraid for the result . . . He must reign until Satan has not an inch of territory!"

Time and again, in the face of crushing defeats, disappointments, diseases and disasters, Carey reiterated his unwavering optimistic eschatology:

"There are great difficulties on every hand, and more are looming ahead. Therefore we must go forward."

"God's cause will triumph!"

Carey's faith was most certainly vindicated. The years of hard work and wholehearted sacrifice were graciously rewarded by God. Carey's ministry literally transformed India.

The Horrors of Hinduism

When Carey stepped ashore at Calcutta on 11 November, 1793, India was in a terribly degraded state. If an infant was sick, it was assumed that he was under the influence of an evil spirit. The custom was to expose sick infants to the elements – perhaps hanging them up in a basket. Near Malda, Carey found the remains of a baby that had been offered as a sacrifice to be eaten alive by white ants. At the *Sagar Mela* where the Ganges river flows into the sea, Carey witnessed how mothers threw their babies into the sea to drown, or to be devoured by crocodiles. This the Hindus regarded as *"a holy sacrifice"* to the *"Mother Ganges"!*

Carey undertook thorough research into the numbers, nature and reasons for the infanticide and published his reports. He presented several petitions to the government until, in 1802, infanticide was outlawed. This marked the first time that the British government interfered directly with religious practice in India. It set a precedent for the abolition of other practices.

Hinduism had an extremely low view of women. It was often stated *"In Hinduism there is no salvation for*

INFANTICIDE IN THE GANGES.

Hindu mothers were taught to sacrifice their children to *"the Holy Ganges River."*

women until she be reborn a man." Her only hope lay in serving men in complete subjection. Many female babies were smothered, strangled or drowned at birth. Girls were married as young as 4 years old! Widows were perceived as bad omens who had brought about the deaths of their husbands. Widows were also seen as an economic liability. Bereaved widows had to shave off all their hair, remove all jewellery and were forbidden to remarry – but a widow was required to cohabit *(niyogo)* with her deceased husband's nearest male relative. Tremendous pressure was exerted on the widow to submit to *Sati* or immolation – to be burned alive on the funeral pyre of her husband. Amongst the Weaver *(Kories)* caste, widows were buried alive.

Because of the Hindu practice of *Sati,* children who had lost their father would also lose their mother and be orphaned at the same time. The Hindu practice of polygamy compounded the problem. On one occasion Carey documented 33 wives of one man burned alive at his funeral. On another occasion an 11-year-old widow was burned on the funeral pyre of her husband!

Lepers were rejected by their families and society and burned alive. Hinduism taught that only a violent and fiery end could purify the body and ensure transmitigation into a healthy new existence. Euthanasia was also widely practised on those afflicted by other sicknesses. The infirm were regularly carried out to the riverside and left exposed to cold and heat, crocodiles or insects.

Believing that a widow should be burned to death on the funeral pyre of her deceased husband, Hindus practised *Sati* for centuries.

Confronting Cruelty

Carey fought against these and many other evils – including child prostitution, slavery and the caste system. He publicly criticised the government for inaction and passivity in the face of murder. He organised public debates and spoke out and wrote often on these atrocities. At first he met with official indifference. The Indian Supreme Court in 1805 ruled that *Sati* had religious sanction and could not be questioned.

A Pioneer for Freedom

Carey established the first newspaper ever printed in an oriental language, the *Samachar Darpan* and the English language newspaper *Friends of India.* Carey pioneered mass communications in India, launching the social reform movement, because he believed that: *"Above all forms of truth and faith, Christianity seeks free discussion."*

Carey was the first man to stand up against the brutal murders and widespread oppression of women through female infanticide, child

William Carey proclaimed the Gospel in India in the native tongue.

marriage, polygamy, enforced female illiteracy, widow burning and forced euthanasia. He conducted systematic research and published his writings to raise public protest in both Bengal and England.

Transforming a Nation

Carey educated and influenced a whole generation of civil servants through his lectures at Fort William College. He fought against the idea that a woman's life ceases to be valuable after her husband's death.

He undermined the oppression and exploitation of women by providing women with education. He opened the first schools for girls.

Education was a major emphasis of his mission. Carey wrote in 1805 that his chief objective was *"the forming of our Indian brethren to usefulness, fostering every kind of genius, and cherishing every gift and*

Serampore College, the first Christian College in Asia.

grace in them; in this respect we can scarcely be too lavish in our attention to their improvement. It is only by means of native preachers that we can hope for the universal spread of the Gospel through this immense continent."

In 1800 Carey was invited to lecture on Bengali, Sanskrit and Marathi at Fort William College. In 1806 he was made a Professor. In 1818 he and his colleagues launched Serampore College which taught Theology, Botany, Zoology, Sanskrit, Arabic and English literature. Carey produced a 1000 page Sanskrit Grammar. William Ward produced a book on *Manners and Customs of the Hindus.*

Working for Reformation
It was Carey's relentless battle against *Sati* – for 25 years – which finally led to the famous Edict in 1829 banning widow burning.

Carey was also the first man who led the campaign for a humane treatment for leprosy and ended the practice of burning lepers alive.

Carey certainly had a comprehensive view of the Great Commission. He ministered to body, mind and spirit. Carey introduced the idea of Savings Banks to India and made investment, industry, commerce and economic development possible. He founded the Agric–Horticultural Society in the 1820's (30 years **before** the Royal Agricultural Society was established in England)! He introduced the steam engine to India. He pioneered the idea of lending libraries in India. He persuaded his friends in England to ship out tons of books to regenerate and reform India.

A Pioneer for Scientific Advance and Conservation
Carey also introduced the study of Astronomy into India. He saw that the prevalent astrology with its fatalism, superstitious fears and inability to manage time had terribly destructive consequences. Hinduism's astrology makes us subjects – with our lives determined by the stars. However, the Christian science of astronomy sets us free to be rulers – to devise calendars, identify directions, study geography and better plan our lives and work.

Carey was the first man in India to write essays on forestry. Fifty years **before** the government made its first attempts at forest conservation, Carey was already practising conservation, planting and cultivating timber. He understood that God had made man responsible for the earth. Carey was also a botanist who cultivated beautiful gardens such as the Serampore Gardens and the Calcutta Botanical Gardens.

He frequently lectured on science, botany and zoology because he believed that *"all Thy works praise Thee, O Lord."* He knew that nature is worthy of study. Carey pointed out that even the insects are worthy of attention – they are not souls in bondage but creatures with a God given purpose.

Carey Baptist Church in India continues to this day.

Innovation

William Carey was also the father of print technology in India. He introduced the modern science of printing, built what was then the largest printing press in India and devised the fonts.

Destruction

In 1812 a devastating fire destroyed Carey's warehouse with his printing presses, 55 000 printed sheets, 1200 reams of paper, whole sets of type for 14 languages and manuscripts for a Bengali dictionary, 2 grammar books and several Bible translations representing many years of work.

Determination

Even in the face of this catastrophe, Carey praised God that no lives had been lost and quoted Psalm 46: *"Be still and know that the Lord is*

After seven years of faithful service Carey's labours were rewarded with the first baptisms.

God." He resolved to do better translations than the ones that were now ashes and consoled himself: *"Every branch that beareth fruit, He purgeth it, that it may bring forth more fruit"*; *"The Lord has laid me low, that I might look more simply to Him"*; *"However vexing it may be, a road the second time travelled is usually taken with more confidence and ease than at the first,"* declared Carey, He quoted Isaiah 61:1-4 and trusted God for better printing presses and more accurate translations – a *"phoenix rising out of the ashes."*

Calamities and Conflicts

Not only was Carey hit by the fire, but there were deaths in each of the seven missionary families at Serampore. Carey himself had just buried a grandson. Carey also had to endure unjust and unbalanced criticisms from new young missionaries who actually split from the Serampore Mission, and slanderous accusations from the Mission Society in England, as well as an earthquake and a flood. One of his sons, Felix, caused much embarrassment when he backslid, adopted a lavish lifestyle and began drinking heavily. Ultimately, however, Felix came back to the Lord and became fully committed to the mission.

Monumental Achievements

Yet despite the controversies, calamities and conflicts, William Carey's monumental achievements outshine all his critics. He was a dedicated

Christian whom God used in extraordinary ways to launch the greatest century of missionary advance, to translate the Scriptures into more languages than any other translator in history and to save literally millions of lives by his compassionate social action and tireless labours. He excelled as a missionary strategist. He was humble, hard-working, industrious and persistent, persevering for over 41 years in the field, without any furlough. Carey succeeded in producing and distributing over 200 000 Bibles, New Testaments or Gospels in 36 languages, in addition to many books and tracts.

We need to follow his example by ministering to body, mind and spirit and persevering through all disappointments and opposition with an unshakeable faith in God's sovereign power.

In 1993, the government of India commemorated the 200th anniversary of William Carey's arrival in India by issuing this postage stamp which honours Carey's translation work and educational ministry.

"Those who sow in tears shall reap in joy. He who continually goes forth weeping, bearing seed for sowing, shall doubtless come again with rejoicing, bringing his sheaves with him." Psalms 126:5-6

Chapter 29
DAVID LIVINGSTONE
Pioneer Missionary and Explorer
(1813 - 1873)

David Livingstone was a great missionary pioneer pathfinder whose greatest desire was granted only after his death: the cessation of the slave trade and the opening up of Africa to Christianity and lawful commerce.

Livingstone the Liberator
He had the grace to see that his mission was part of a divine plan to set many souls free from slavery, both physical and spiritual. Livingstone's great goal of bringing to the world's attention the scourge of the Islamic slave trade in Africa was achieved largely through the work of his convert, American journalist Henry Morton Stanley.

Upbringing in Scotland
David was brought up in a pious but poverty-stricken home in Scotland. He was an avid reader and borrowed extensively from the local library. By age 9 he had already committed to memory Psalm 119 and won a copy of the New Testament as a reward. By age 10 David was employed 14 hours a day, 6 days a week, at the local cotton spinning factory. David managed to read in the factory by placing his book on a portion of the

"A man of resolute courage."

spinning jenny so that he could catch sentence after sentence as he passed at his work. He maintained fairly constant study, undisturbed by the roar of the machinery. His conversion at age 12 inspired him to resolve to devote his life to the alleviation of human misery.

Dedication

Three themes dominated his life: **evangelisation, exploration** and **emancipation.** He wrote at the time: *"The salvation of men ought to be the chief desire and aim of every Christian."* He therefore made a resolution: that he would give to the cause of missions all that he might earn beyond what was required for his subsistence.

"Fire, water, stonewall would not stop Livingstone in the fulfillment of any recognised duty."

Theology and Medicine

After 10 years of daily drudgery at the cotton mill, David set out to study theology and medicine. Medical science in the 1830's was, by today's standards, primitive. Surgical operations were performed at hazardous speeds because of the lack of anaesthetics. Chloroform and ether were not introduced until several years later and the discovery of antiseptics lay 25 years ahead. The study of chemistry was growing, but biochemistry and bacteriology were unknown. Nothing at all was known about the tropical diseases he was to encounter, such as malaria and blackwater fever.

Diligent

It was not in Livingstone's character to relax. He took his task and calling most seriously and whatever he did he performed thoroughly. He was uncompromising, diligent and inflexible in his adherence to his word.

Resolute

Friends described him as: *"a man of resolute courage"; "fire, water, stonewall would not stop Livingstone in the fulfillment of any recognised duty."*

To Africa

It took him 3 months by sailing ship to reach Cape Town and another 4 months by ox cart before he even reached Robert Moffat's mission station at Kuruman where he would begin his work for the Lord in Africa. When he landed in South Africa, on 17 March 1841, David Livingstone was coming to a continent that was plagued with problems. Africa was still a place of mystery to the Europeans. The Arabs south of the Sahara never ventured far from the coast inland. The rivers were riddled with rapids and sand bars. The deadly malaria disease was widespread and inhibited travel. Entire expeditions of 300 to 400 men had been wiped out by malaria. The African terrain was difficult to negotiate. Floods, tropical forests and swamps thwarted wheeled transport.

Dr. David Livingstone was dedicated to opening up Africa for the Gospel of Christ.

Fearless Faith

Livingstone soon acquired a reputation for fearless faith – particularly when he walked to the Barka tribe (infamous for the murder of 4 White traders whom they had mercilessly poisoned and strangled). As the first messenger of mercy in many regions, Livingstone soon received further challenge. Chief Sechele pointed to the great Kalahari desert: *"you never can cross that country to the tribes beyond; it is utterly impossible even for us Black men."* The challenge of crossing this obstacle began to fascinate Livingstone.

Livingstone wrote: *"I shall try to hold myself in readiness to go anywhere, provided it be forward."*

Frustration

Livingstone is reported to have had a steadfast manner and folk knew where they stood with him. His plans to establish a Bible college for Africans were frustrated. However, the Sovereignty of God was seen in this. Had Livingstone's wishes been carried out, he might have spent his

David Livingstone was the first missionary to proclaim the Gospel in many remote regions of Africa.

David Livingstone

Medical Missionary David Livingstone committed his life to Evangelism, Exploration and the Emancipation of slaves.

life's work teaching in a Bible college rather than traversing Africa and dealing a death blow to the slave trade.

Daily Challenges
His three great daily challenges he described as: **heat, harsh conditions** and **hardness of hearts.**

Determination
"I hope to be permitted to work as long as I live beyond other men's line of things and plant the seed of the Gospel where others have not planted. But every excursion for that purpose will involve separation from my family for periods of 4 or 5 months."

"I am a missionary, heart and soul. God had an only Son, and He was a missionary and a physician. A poor, poor imitation of Him I am, or wish to be. In His service I hope to live; in it I wish to die."

Family Matters

During his first missionary journey with his wife and children, their 4th child, Elizabeth, was born. Within a few weeks she had died and the rest of the family were sick. He received much criticism for the *"irresponsibility"* of taking a wife and 4 children on a missionary journey in the wilderness. Later he was criticised for sending his family back to Britain while he pioneered the hinterland of Africa. When his wife rejoined him for his second great missionary expedition in the Zambezi Valley she died of malaria.

Conviction

"I shall open up a path into the interior or perish," he declared. *"May He bless us and make us blessings even unto death." "Shame upon us missionaries if we are to be outdone by slave traders!" "If Christian missionaries and Christian merchants could remain throughout the year in the interior of the continent, in 10 years, slave dealers will be driven out of the market."*

Overcoming All Obstacles

Battling rains, chronic discomfort, rust, mildew and rot, totally drenched and fatigued, and laid low by fever, Livingstone continued to persevere across the continent. Hostile tribes demanded exorbitant payment for crossing their territory. Some tense moments were stared down by Livingstone, gun in hand. Trials tested the tenacity of the travel wearied team. *"Can the love of Christ not carry the missionary where the slave trade carries the trader?"*

Occupational hazards of pioneer missionary work in Africa during the 19th Century included attacks by hippopotamuses.

A Man of Principle

After 2 years of pioneering across the hinterland of Africa, Livingstone reached Luanda. The *"Forerunner"* ship was ready to take him to England. However, Livingstone chose to return overland to bring his guides and porters back to their village. Rather than risk their being sold into slavery in Portuguese West Africa, he preferred to take another 2 years crossing the continent that had almost killed him on his first journey!

However, had Livingstone chosen to return he might well have ended his ministry. The ship sank with all hands lost (and with his journals)! By God's grace, Livingstone still had a copy of his journals that he had laboriously written out – just in case!

"These privations, I beg you to observe, are not sacrifices. I think that word ought never to be mentioned in reference to anything we can do for Him, who though He was rich, yet for our sakes became poor."

Deprivation

Often Livingstone endured excessive and unnecessary suffering and deprivation, hacking through dense jungle on foot because lack of funds prevented him from affording the "luxury" of a canoe!

Confronting Slave Traders

Livingstone often saw the sickening results of the Islamic slave trade: burned out villages, corpses floating down rivers and long lines of shackled slaves being

Islamic slave raiders axe a straggler near the Ruvuma River, 1866.

Livingstone escaped countless attempts on his life.

herded through the bush. Livingstone's mere presence often sent the Yao slave raiders scurrying into the bushes. Many hundreds of slaves were set free by Livingstone and his co-workers. On one occasion a war party of Yao warriors attacked the missionary party. While attempting to avoid confrontation, the team found themselves cut off and surrounded by the aggressive and bloodthirsty mob. Finally, Livingstone was forced to give the command to return fire. The slave traders fled.

"More Light Might Enter Your Mind"
This incident led to much criticism in England. Charles Livingstone, his brother, on hearing one outburst from Britain replied: *"If you were in Africa and saw a host of murderous savages aiming their heavily laden*

Arab slave raiders in East Africa.

muskets and poisoned arrows at you, more light might enter your mind . . . and if it didn't, great daylight would enter your body through arrow and bullet holes!"

Three Slave Trades in Africa
It was Livingstone's great desire to see the slave trade cease. Firstly, there was the internal slave trade between hostile tribes. Secondly, there were slave traders from the coast, Arabs or Portuguese, for whom local tribes were encouraged to collect slaves by marauding raids. Thirdly, there were the parties sent out from Portuguese and Arab coastal towns with cloths, beads, muskets and ammunition to exchange for slaves.

The Shortest War
Incidentally, Livingstone inspired the shortest war in history – in 1872 – when the British Navy presented an ultimatum to the Sultan of Zanzibar to close the flourishing slave market. When the Sultan refused, his palace was shelled – resulting in a record breaking surrender within the hour!

Twin Concerns
In his writings and public speaking engagements, Livingstone regularly spoke on his twin concerns – to enlighten people on the evils of the slave trade, and to spread the Christian Gospel amongst the heathen. Although he was renowned for his **exploration,** in his mind it was only a means to **evangelism** and to *"disciple the nations."*

Livingstone the Liberator set many captives free from Arab slave traders. This incident was in the Shire valley.

Body, Mind and Spirit

Dr. Livingstone believed in comprehensively fulfilling the Great Commission – ministering to body, mind and spirit. Along with his Bible, surgical kit and medicine chest, Livingstone always carried a microscope and sextant – with which he observed God's spectacularly diverse creation with awe and wonder. His books are filled with fascinating scientific, medical, botanical, anthropological and geographic observations and details. Livingstone was the first to map the great Zambezi river and many other parts of the vast hinterland of Africa. He was one of the first scientists to make the connection between mosquitos and malaria, and he pioneered the use of quinine as a treatment – often experimenting on himself!

Not a Sacrifice!

The challenge of Livingstone rings out to us today: *"Can that be called a sacrifice which is simply paid back as a small part of a great debt owing to our God, which we can never repay . . . it is emphatically no sacrifice. Say rather, **it is a privilege!**"*

Henry Morton Stanley enthusiastically continued Livingstone's crusade to expose and eradicate the slave trade in Africa.

A Vision of Victory

The optimistic eschatology of Livingstone the Liberator, comes as a stern rebuke to the prevailing escapist eschatology of defeat and retreat.

An Inspiring Example

Livingstone's steadfast example has been used by the Lord to inspire hundreds of men and women to devote their lives to African missions. Mary Slessor, for

Dr. Livingstone's medical case which he carried with him on all his missionary journeys.

example, went to Calabar (present day Nigeria) and ended the practice of murdering twins (believed by animists to be bewitched.)

Galvanised Back to the Field

Peter Cameron was inspired to return to Africa after his first mission failed, when he read the inscription on the tomb of Livingstone in Westminster Abbey: ***"Other sheep I have which are not of this fold; them also I must bring and they shall hear My voice."***

The Challenge of Africa

"I beg to direct your attention to Africa: I know that in a few years I shall be cut off from that country, which is now open; do not let it be shut again! I go back to Africa to try to make an open path for commerce and Christianity: ***will you carry out the work which I have begun? I leave it with you!"***

"Also I heard the voice of the Lord saying: 'Whom shall I send, and who will go for Us?' Then said I 'Here am I! Send me.'"   **Isaiah 6:8**

Chapter 30

FLORENCE NIGHTINGALE
The Lady with the Lamp
(1820 – 1910)

Few people realise the enormous debt which the whole world owes to Florence Nightingale. This courageous Reformer transformed hospitals and pioneered the modern nursing profession. No other person in history has done more to alleviate suffering and establish so high a standing of health care for the sick.

The Degraded State

Before Florence Nightingale the condition of hospitals and the nursing profession was in a degraded state. Hospitals were dirty and over-crowded. Antiseptics were unknown. Scarcely any facilities for the training of nurses existed, and their pay was less than that for a common labourer in the field. Nurses were drawn from the *"undesirable sections"* of society and were commonly regarded as *"vulgar"*, *"uneducated"*, *"unclean"* and were notorious for their drunkenness and immorality.

Florence

Florence Nightingale was named after the town in Italy where she was born on 12 May 1820. Until that time, Florence was always understood to be a man's name, but through her parent's tendency

Florence Nightingale pioneered the modern Nursing profession.

333

to name their children after their town of birth, Florence has become an honoured woman's name.

Home Education

Florence's parents were wealthy and well-connected. Florence was highly educated. A governess taught her music and art, and her father, William, taught her Greek, Latin, German, French, Italian, grammar, history, mathematics and philosophy. Florence loved books and immersed herself in her studies. She felt alienated from those around her and was profoundly dissatisfied with *"the emptiness"* of her existence. She was distressed at the pettiness of social life. She developed a passion for neatness and accuracy. Visitors described her as: *"Stubborn"*, *"Strong willed"*, *"very intelligent,"* and *"Extraordinary!"*

"God spoke to me and called me to His service."

Called

On 7 February 1837, just before she turned 17 years old, Florence wrote: *"God spoke to me and called me to His service."* Florence travelled widely throughout Europe and even to Egypt. She was well aware of the misery of the poor. She became convinced that God had called her to reform the nursing profession and devote her life to the alleviation of suffering for the sick. Her parents were horrified and expressly forbade her to pursue such a degrading occupation. So Florence carried on her investigations, studies and correspondence concerning Hygiene, Sanitation and Nursing in secret.

Intelligence and Intergrity
In her 20's, Florence was described as: *"Tall, slender, elegant and very straight, her hair of a rich brown, her complexion delicate, her grey eyes pensive, yet ready to light into mirth with a smile the sweetest and most winning."* Her personal charm, intelligence, wide reading and sincerity attracted many friendships and marriage prospects – which she spurned.

Seeking First God's Kingdom
At the age of 30, Florence wrote: *"I am 30, the age at which Christ began His mission. Now, no more childish things, no more vain things, no more love, no more marriage. Now Lord, let me think only of Thy Will."*

Training in Germany
Florence travelled to Germany to enrol at a college for Deaconesses. She was a star student at the Lutheran Deaconess Training Institute at Kaiserswerth on the Rhine in Germany. She lived a spartan life in this college, rising at dawn, doing all the menial services, sharing the frugal meals of the sisterhood and attending lectures on nursing. On her return to England she set up a Sanatorium for Sick Governesses run by a Committee of Fine Ladies. This establishment for gentlewomen in Harley Street, London was used to test her innovative ideas on health care. At first there was conflict with the Committee, but in time all the members came to respect her innovations and skill in management.

Hygiene and Fresh Air
In the treatment of the sick, her first principles were cleanliness and fresh air. Contrary to all the tenets that then held sway, Florence began by insisting upon large and open windows for all hospital wards. *"Thoroughness, initiative and hygiene"* characterised the routines established by her. She produced the most detailed study into the state of health care in Europe

The Crimean War

Florence was just about to assume the superintendence of Kings' College Hospital when the Crimean War broke out. After the Battle of Alma, in September 1854, *The Times* correspondent wrote on the shameful lack of proper provision for the care of the wounded after their heroic victory.

Disaster and Disgrace

"There were not sufficient surgeons; no dressings and no nurses; no linen for bandages – and yet, no one was to blame!" This was the first war in which the telegraph was used to wire dispatches back home, so for the first time up-to-date reports kept the people in England informed on the course of the war and the horrors of having no proper medical care for the wounded.

To Care for the War Wounded

As an outcry of indignation arose throughout the country, the Secretary for War, Sir Sydney Herbert, wrote to Florence asking if she would go to organise the care of the wounded in the Crimea. Within two days of receiving the letter of appointment from the War Office, Florence

During the Crimean War, Florence Nightingale was commissioned by the British government to travel to Turkey and organise the care of British war wounded.

Nightingale set out (21 October 1854) for Turkey. She was accompanied by 38 hand-picked volunteers, whose abilities she had proved. Her sister wrote that Florence *"was as calm and composed in this furious haste...as if she were going out for a walk."*

Controversy

With the announcement of her government appointment, Florence Nightingale came under national attention and became the target of much controversy. It was only after

The Crimean War exposed the colossal calamity of the medical services.

Queen Victoria gave Florence her personal support that most of the accusations against her subsided. Many high officials objected to a woman taking charge of what was essentially *"a man's job."* Others were astounded that a rich, popular, young and attractive gentlewoman

Florence Nightingale took decisive action to ensure efficient medical care was given to sick and wounded soldiers.

was prepared to abandon her life of ease and luxury in England to face dangers, horror and fearsome toil on the battlefield.

Scutari

Apparently Florence took no notice of her critics. She reached Scutari on 4 November, just in time to receive a flood of wounded from the Battle of Balaclava. While struggling to cope with the Herculean task of tending these casualties, a further 600 wounded arrived from the Battle of Inkerman. She endured the prejudice and opposition of military surgeons, endured unimaginable squalor, a devastating cholera epidemic and battled against bureaucratic bungling from the start.

Colossal Calamities

She reported that: *"Far more soldiers had died of disease than on the battlefield."* She described the hospitals as *"colossal calamities."* There was no furniture, and no cooking utensils. Toilets were blocked and overflowing. Rats were everywhere. The filth and stench of rotting

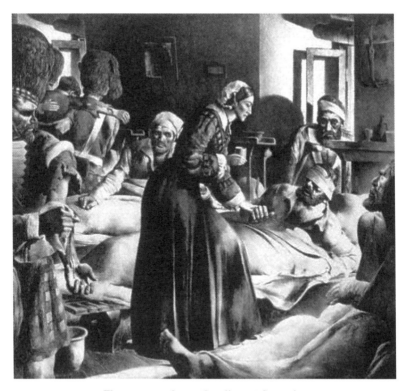

Florence saved countless lives at Scutari.

wounds were overwhelming in the overcrowded, rat, cockroach and lice invested corridors and wards.

Decisive Action

When informed that essential items that she needed would take weeks of delay, authorisation from England, and that she needed to await official reaction to the Commission of Enquiry, Florence Nightingale used her own funds to set up a house in Scutari as a laundry, and requisitioned a consignment of 27,000 shirts, which had not yet been released by the Board of Survey. Florence ordered that the bales be opened at once, and the materials delivered to the hospital: *"Red tape or no red tape."* Many officials were incensed: *"Is this the way to manage the finances of a great nation! Miss Nightingale coolly draws a cheque!"* In fact, Florence paid for many of the supplies out of her own funds.

Overcoming Obstructionism

Apparently unconcerned by the controversies and furore surrounding her, Florence continued her work of cleaning up the shambles she had found. Those of her helpers who would not submit to the strict discipline, or endure the necessary privations, were promptly sent home. Official obstructionism impeded her efforts at every step, but she overcame all opposition with her persistence and determination. As Florence wrote: *"I have no compassion for men who would rather see hundreds of lives lost than waive one scruple of the official rules."*

Organisation

She organised staff, oversaw purchases, set up housekeeping, ordered furniture, supplied clothing, supervised daily routines, working an average of 20 hours every day, performing the duties of cook, housekeeper, washerwoman, general dealer and storekeeper along with scavenger and nurse. Florence began and ended each hospital day routine with prayers. She also provided reading rooms and library books for the patients.

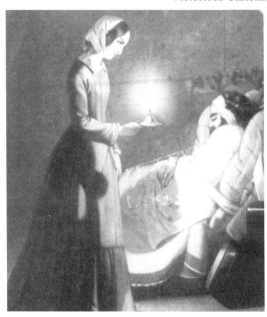

The Lady with the Lamp personally checked patients each night.

Personal Care

It was her custom before retiring to make a last tour of the wards. Her tall slender figure in nurse's uniform, rich brown hair covered by a white cap, passing, lamp in hand, down the long isles between the rows of beds, bestowing comfort on the wounded seemed like an angel to the hundreds of wounded and sick soldiers.

Battlefront Reforms

Florence visited the battlefront to set in place further reforms. Hospital mortality (the death rate of patients) before she took over the care of war-wounded in the Crimea was as high as 42%. Soon Florence brought hospital mortality down to only 2%,

Saving Lives

As Dr. Benjamin Jarved of Oxford declared: *"Nobody knows how many lives are saved by your nurses in hospitals, how many thousands of soldiers who would have fallen victim to bad air, bad drainage, and ventilation are alive owing to your forethought and diligence."*

Fever

Towards the end of the war, Florence succumbed to a severe fever, which could have easily taken her life. She recovered, but her health was so damaged that she would never be the same again.

Steadfast

In spite of her sickness and weakened condition, Florence refused to leave her post of duty until the British army evacuated Turkey at the end of the war in July 1856.

Avoiding Publicity

Travelling under a false name, as *"Miss Smith"*, she avoided the enthusiastic receptions that had been arranged for her, but was received by Queen Victoria, whom she persuaded to support hospital reform. Prince Albert described Florence as *"extremely modest."*

St. Thomas's Hospital in London was the site where many of Florence Nightingale's innovations and reforms were first tested.

Nurses Training

Florence's work in the Crimea was, to her, only a beginning. She founded the Nightingale Home for Training Nurses at St. Thomas's Hospital and published an 800 page report entitled: *"Notes on Matters Affecting the Health, Efficiency and Hospital Administration of the British Army."* This formed the basis of a Royal Commission to reform medical care in the military. The Army Medical Corp was transformed as a result of her efforts.

India

Florence took a deep interest in the sanitary and health measures adopted in India and was in constant communication with the Secretary of State for India to reform sanitation and health in that vast country.

Health Care Reform

Florence launched the most significant campaigns to improve health care and prevent patients dying from causes which could have been prevented. She strove to learn from the past in order to save lives in the future. It was her goal to ensure that those who had suffered in Crimea had not suffered in vain. She changed forever the status of the nurse and the fate of the soldier.

Transforming Hospitals

Her *"Notes on Hospitals"* revealed that civilian hospitals were as bad, if not worse, than military hospitals. She worked late into the night establishing effective training for nurses, setting new standards for sanitation and drainage. Her research reports dramatically improved working conditions for the poor and health care for the sick. Her requirements for nursing included that they must be: *"Sober, honest, truthful, trustworthy, punctual, quiet and orderly, clean and neat."*

In Spite of Ill Health

Struggling against ill health herself, and surrounded by a colony of cats, Florence Nightingale continued her crusade to save lives and provide efficient, effective health care for the infirm.

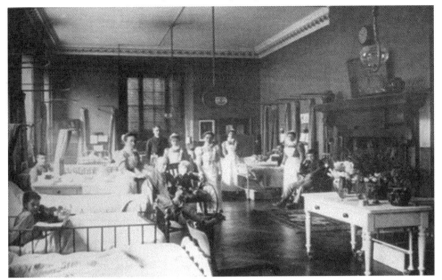

A Hospital ward at St. Thomas's under Florence Nightingale.

Notes on Nursing

The Florence Nightingale Museum records that she wrote 200 publications and 13,000 letters. Her most famous book: *"Notes on Nursing"* has been translated into many languages including German, Dutch, Danish, Swedish and Finnish. It remains a classic resource and textbook for nurses, managers and health planners to this day. It dealt with all aspects of health care, including hygiene, bedding and diet. It emphasised the two most important principles of nursing: observation (such as the pulse, appetite and breathing of a patient) and sensitivity to a patient's needs and comforts.

Spiritual Health

Florence incorporated Bible studies and prayer meetings as part of her trainee nurse's routines and appointed chaplains for the hospitals.

Worldwide Impact

Florence Nightingale's writings on hospital planning and organisation had a profound impact on health care worldwide. Her far-sighted

Florence Nightingale's writings and innovations had a profound impact on healthcare worldwide.

reforms saved innumerable lives and established nursing as a respectable profession.

A Most Productive Life

After a most productive life, at age 90, Florence Nightingale died on 13 August 1910. Over 1,000 nurses and many veterans of the Crimean War attended her funeral service at St. Paul's in London.

Lord Stanley delivered this eulogy: *"I know of no person besides Miss Nightingale who, within the past 100 years...has voluntarily encountered dangers so imminent, and undertaken offices so repulsive, working for a large and worthy object, in a pure spirit of duty towards God and compassion for man."*

"Then the King will say to those on His right hand, 'Come, you blessed of My Father, inherit the Kingdom prepared for you from the foundation of the world: for I was hungry and you gave Me food; I was thirsty and you gave Me drink; I was a stranger and you took Me in; I was naked and you clothed Me; I was sick and you visited Me; I was in prison and you came to Me.... Assuredly, I say to you, inasmuch as you did it to one of the least of these My brethren, you did it to Me.'" Matthew 25: 34-40

Chapter 31

CHARLES SPURGEON
The Puritan Prince of Preachers
(1834 - 1892)

In an age of great preachers the greatest was Charles Haddon Spurgeon. Both his father and his grandfather were independent congregational ministers. Charles was born in 1834 in Kelvedon, Essex, an area with a long tradition of Protestant resistance to Catholicism dating back to the persecutions of *"Bloody Mary"* in the 16th century.

A Son of the Manse

Charles was a *"son of the manse."* His earliest childhood memories were of listening to sermons, learning Hymns and looking at the pictures in *The Pilgrim's Progress* and *Foxe's Book of Martyrs.* Charles first read *The Pilgrim's Progress* at age six and went on to read it over 100 times. He regarded *Foxe's Book of Martyrs* as one of the most significant books he ever read. It vividly shaped his attitudes towards established religions, the tyranny of Rome and the glory of the Reformation. His childhood heroes were the brave Protestants who were burned at Smithsfield, and the valiant Puritans such as John Bunyan, who were jailed for their Faith.

A Prophetic Word

When Charles was only ten years old, a visiting missionary, Rev. Richard Knill, was struck by how young Charles read the Bible with such emphasis.

From age 16 Charles Spurgeon was proclaiming the Gospel, with power.

Richard Knill called the family together and said: *"I do not know how, but I feel a solemn presentiment that this child will preach the Gospel to thousands and God will bless him to many souls. So sure am I of this that when my little man preaches in Surrey Music Hall, as he will do one day, I should like him to promise me that he will give out the Hymn commencing 'God moves in a mysterious way, His wonders to perform.'"*

(This was fulfilled in 1856 when Charles was 21 years old.)

Converted to Christ

Charles' formal education was minimal. However, he devoured his grandfather's Puritan books and was well read. In 1849, when Charles was fifteen years old, under conviction of sin and anxious to know forgiveness, he was obliged to stop on the road due to a snow storm. He found himself in a Primitive Methodist chapel in Colchester.

The Primitive Methodist Chapel where Charles Spurgeon was converted.

As the service progressed it appeared that the minister would not arrive. At last a very thin deacon came into the pulpit, opened his Bible and read: *"Look unto Me, and be ye saved, all the ends of the earth."* Then, apparently looking straight at Charles Spurgeon, he declared: *"Young man, you are in trouble! You will never get out of it unless you look to Christ!"* He then lifted up his hands and exclaimed repeatedly: *"Look! Look! Look!"* Spurgeon later wrote: *"I had been waiting to do fifty things, but when I heard this word, 'Look' – what a charming word it seemed to me! Oh, I looked until I could almost have looked my eyes away, and in*

Heaven I will look on still in my joy unutterable."

Charles later wrote of the day of his conversion: *"And as the snow fell on the road home from the little House of Prayer, I thought that every snowflake talked with me and told me of the pardon I had found, for I was white as the driven snow through the grace of God."* Upon his return home, his appearance caused his mother to exclaim: *"Something wonderful has happened to you!"*

Believer's Baptism
For the next months Charles searched the Scriptures *"to know more fully the value of the jewel which God had given me...I found that believers ought to be baptized."* And so, four months after his conversion, he was baptized by immersion in the River Lark, May 1850. He vowed to spend his life *"in the extension of Christ's cause, in whatsoever way He pleases."*

His mother had often prayed: *"Oh that my son might live for Thee."* However, she was shocked when, in what appeared to be youthful rebellion, Charles broke with the congregational tradition of his family and was baptized by full immersion in the River Lark in May 1850, joining a Baptist Church. His mother exclaimed *"Charlie, I have often prayed that you might be saved, but never that you should become a Baptist."* To this Charles replied: *"God has answered your prayer, Mother, with His usual bounty, and has given me more than you asked."*

Called to Preach
Charles preached his first sermon at the age of sixteen before a small congregation of farm labourers and their wives in a thatched chapel in Teversham. Then, moving to a school in Cambridge, he joined St. Andrews Street Baptist Church and became a village preacher. Waterbeach Baptist Chapel invited Charles to become their pastor. His very young appearance was in startling contrast to the maturity of his sermons.

An Heir to the Puritans

All the great Puritan books that he had devoured in his grandfather's house came to the fore. He had a retentive memory, youthful energy and great oratorical skills. This made such an impact that people travelled to hear the *"boy preacher."* Within eighteen months his reputation had spread to London, and he was invited to preach at the historic New Park Street Chapel.

A Time of Crisis

Charles Spurgeon was 19 years old when he began his pastorate at the famous but rundown New Park Street Baptist Church in Southwark. It was March 1854 when Spurgeon begin his ministry in London. It was a time of tremendous economic and social upheaval. A plague of cholera hit London in 1854 and 20,000 people died in this epidemic. Also in that year the Crimean War broke out.

This was followed by the Indian Mutiny of 1857 which provoked such a tremendous outpouring of grief and rage leading to a national day of fasting and humiliation, during which Charles Spurgeon was invited to address the largest audience of his life: almost 24,000 people gathered in the Crystal Palace. The disruptions and economic hardships caused by the American Civil War in the 1860's also brought much suffering and economic ruin to many in London.

A Calvinist Evangelist

Very conscious of his youth and inexperience, Charles Spurgeon prayed that *"these may not hinder my usefulness."* Charles Spurgeon deliberately built upon the Calvinist teachings and Puritan Devotion of George Whitefield and he soon became the most popular preacher in London. When Spurgeon arrived at the New Park Street Baptist Church the congregation had 232 members. By the end of his pastorate, 38 years later, the membership had increased to 5,311. Altogether 14,460 people were added to the congregation during Spurgeon's tenure. He built New Park into the largest independent congregation in the world.

Charles Spurgeon preaching at Exeter Hall, 1855

Coinciding with such tumultuous international events and domestic distress in the greatest city in the world, his ministry immediately attracted huge excitement and attention. Soon it was necessary to extend the premises and for three months the church met at Exeter Hall in the Strand where crowds filled all 4,500 seats each Sunday. The meetings were switched to the Music Hall in Surrey Gardens while new church premises were built.

Innovative and Inspiring

Spurgeon was described as a compelling, charismatic speaker *"dramatic to his fingertips."* He frequently acted the parts in Biblical stories, pacing the platform and even running from side to side. His sermons were filled with heart-rending stories that ordinary people could relate to: Spurgeon's language was graphic, emotionally charged and compelling. The dramatic devices employed by Spurgeon have now become commonplace, but they were quite shocking for the mid-Victorian years. His many critics roundly condemned the young minister's style, manner and appearance. Many ministers were openly contemptuous of his *"sensationalism"*, although it was later pointed out that many of them came to copy his style and even appropriate his sermons.

"Prove Me Now"

On the evening of 19 October 1856, Charles Spurgeon was to commence weekly services at the Royal Surrey Gardens Music Hall. That morning he preached at New Park Street Chapel on Malachi 3:10 *"Prove Me now..."* He declared *"...I may be called to stand where the thunderclouds brew, where the lightnings play, and tempestuous winds are howling on the mountain top. Well then, I am born to prove the power and majesty of our God. Amidst dangers He will inspire me with courage; amidst toils He will make me strong...we shall be gathered together tonight where an unprecedented mass of people will assemble, perhaps from idle curiosity, to hear God's Word; and a voice cries in my ears, 'Prove Me now...'"*

Tragedy Strikes

That evening Surrey Hall, designed to hold up to 12,000, was overflowing with over 22,000 people. The service was underway when, during Spurgeon's prayer, several malicious individuals shouted: *"Fire! The galleries are giving way! Fire!"* In the ensuing panic seven people died and twenty eight were hospitalized from the stampede to evacuate the building.

This tragedy almost ended Spurgeon's ministry. He had to be carried from the pulpit to a friend's house where he remained for several days in deep, dark depression. He later remarked: *"Perhaps never a soul went so near the burning furnace of insanity, and yet came away unharmed."* Spurgeon later said that the panic at Surrey Gardens was *"sufficient to shatter my reason"* and *"silence my ministry forever."*

Charles Spurgeon preached face to face to over 10 million people in his lifetime.

The Metropolitan Tabernacle

At Spurgeon's request the new church was to be in the Greek style, for *"Greek is the sacred tongue"* in which the New Testament had been revealed. When the Metropolitan Tabernacle was opened in March 1861 it was the first mega-church, seating over 5,000 people. Every person who joined his huge congregation was personally interviewed by Spurgeon who wanted to ensure that each candidate's conversion was genuine.

Intense Opposition

During his early years in London, Spurgeon received intense slander and scorn. He wrote of a *"devastating bitterness of soul."* He wavered between rejoicing in the persecutions he received and *"being utterly crushed by it."* He wrote of being *"the laughing stock of fools and the song of the drunkard."*

The Greatest Preacher of his Age

During his lifetime Spurgeon is estimated to have preached to 10 million people, face-to-face. The theme for Spurgeon's Sunday morning sermon was usually not chosen until Saturday night, and the Sunday evening sermon was normally prepared on Sunday afternoon. He spoke at a rate of 140 words per minute for an average of 40 minutes. Including funerals, weddings, and other invitations, Spurgeon often preached ten times a week. Before he was 20 Charles had preached over 600 times. He typically read six books a week and could remember what he had read, and where, even years later. He built up an awesome personal library containing 12,000 volumes.

Spurgeon's Sunday sermons were delivered extemporaneously with seldom more than a one-page outline before him. These sermons were taken down in shorthand by a secretary appointed by the congregation, and revised by him on Monday mornings. These sermons were published every Thursday, translated into several languages, and even sold as far afield as Australia and America. In 1865 Spurgeon's sermons were selling 25,000 copies every week. They were translated into more than 20 languages. By 1917 over 100 million copies of Spurgeon's sermons had been sold.

The Most Prolific Christian Author of All Time

Throughout his ministry Spurgeon proved to be a prolific writer. He edited a monthly magazine *Sword and Trowel*, wrote several books and commentaries, and produced sermon notes and lecture notes for his students.

Charles Haddon Spurgeon is historically the most widely read preacher. Today there is more material available written by Charles Spurgeon than by any other Christian author.

Famous Contemporaries

Charles Spurgeon drew to his services the Prime Minister William Gladstone, reformer Lord Shaftesbury, members of the Royal Family, members of Parliament, Florence Nightingale, American evangelist D.L. Moody and missionary David Livingstone.

Charles Spurgeon

For almost 40 years Charles Spurgeon pastored the Metropolitan Tabernacle in London.

Hudson Taylor and George Müller
Spurgeon often met with China Inland Mission founder Hudson Taylor and the famous founder of orphanages, George Müller. Charles paid several visits to Ashley Down, Bristol, to talk with that *"heavenly-minded man"* George Müller. They often spent whole days together, stimulating one another's Faith by discussing the unfailing promises of God.

D.L. Moody
On arriving in England for the first time in 1867, American evangelist D.L. Moody made straight for the Tabernacle and sat in the gallery. When back home he was asked if he had seen various tourist sights or cathedrals, Moody responded: *"No, but I've heard Spurgeon!"* D.L. Moody wrote that: *"Heaven came down"* on his soul and he returned to America *"a better man."*

Pastor's College
Although Charles Spurgeon trained many pastors, he himself had received no Theological training, believing that God had spoken to him: *"Seekest thou great things for thyself? Seek them not!"*

Baptists had a long tradition of ordaining ministers, but Spurgeon managed to get his church to omit this step – he never was ordained.

He campaigned arduously to do without the customary title, *Reverend*, and he eventually succeeded in replacing it with *Pastor*.

To further the work of the Gospel, Spurgeon established a Pastor's College. He made himself responsible for a weekly lecture there and published his notes in *Lectures to My Students*, which remains a major textbook in Baptist colleges to this day. Nearly 900 students were trained at Spurgeon's college during his lifetime. Spurgeon's College continues to this day.

The Stockwell Orphanage
In 1866 a gift of £20,000 enabled him to found an orphanage at Stockwell, providing a home and education for 500 homeless boys and girls.

**The Stockwell Orphanage provided a home and a Christian education
for 500 homeless boys and girls.**

Bibles for Britain
In the same year Spurgeon formed the Colportage Association to give country people the opportunity to buy Christian books and Bibles at low cost. In one year alone his 96 colporteurs sold 23,000 Bibles. His Book Fund provided multitudes of pastors with resources for Biblical preaching.

A Centre of Controversy
Charles Spurgeon was a man of strong convictions and was often the centre of controversy. Although he was an eloquent and persuasive speaker, he was not a good debater and paid a heavy price, both emotionally and physically, for his involvement in theological and political controversies.

Theological Controversy
Spurgeon's opposition to liberalism split the Baptist Union. Many people had written to Spurgeon urging him to do something about the deteriorating situation in the Baptist Union with the spirit of modern Biblical criticism and liberalism undermining the authority of the Scriptures and denying the Deity of Christ. Spurgeon wrote articles in *The Sword and Trowel* defending the Puritan position and attacking the *"enemies of our Faith."* Spurgeon criticised those who were *"giving up the atoning sacrifice, denying the inspiration of Holy Scripture and casting slurs upon Justification by Faith."*

The Downgrade Controversy
The *"Downgrade Controversy"*, as it became known, pitted Baptist minister against Baptist minister and darkened Spurgeon's last years. The Baptist Union censured the most famous Baptist minister in the world. At the Baptist Union assembly in 1888 a large majority voted a censure against Charles Spurgeon. Some observers considered that the Baptist Union had condemned *"the greatest, noblest and grandest leader of the Faith."* However, Spurgeon rejected the suggestions that he form another denomination.

The Downgrade Controversy took its toll on Spurgeon's health. In his last years he suffered from a sense of isolation and declared: *"Scarcely a Baptist minister of standing will know me."* However, multitudes came to hear him preach.

Unsurpassed

Charles Spurgeon never claimed to be a Theologian. He was a Gospel preacher, and in that he was unsurpassed in his day and since. He combined old-fashioned Biblical doctrine and up-to-date preaching methods. He had an uncanny ability to sense the pulse of his times, and he knew how to reach out to ordinary and troubled people in a way that they could understand and respond to. He spoke the language of the market place, humorously, with common sense and compelling power.

A Man of God

Charles Spurgeon was a man of God, a man of prayer and a man of the Word. He studied diligently and read avidly. He broke with traditions and conventions, becoming the greatest communicator of his age. Devoted to the Scriptures, to disciplined prayer, and to godly living, Spurgeon exemplified Christian commitment when he stood in the pulpit. This gave power to his preaching.

The One Thing He Lacked

The one thing that Spurgeon lacked was good health. He constantly suffered from ailments and fell into serious depression at times. Yet he overcame physical limitations and relentless criticism to be established at the greatest preacher in an age of great preachers. Once while laid low by illness he declared: *"It is a great trial to be unable to preach in the pulpit, but it is no small comfort to be able to preach through the press."*

Spurgeon wrote: *"If ministers of the Gospel, instead of giving lectures, and devoting so much time to literary and political pursuits, would preach the Word of God, and preach it as if they were pleading for their own lives, ah, then, my brethren, we might expect better success."*

The Funeral procession of Charles Spurgeon.

Spurgeon's Theology

Spurgeon's Theology was radically Biblical. *"It has been my earnest endeavour ever since I've preached the Word, never to keep back a single doctrine which I have believed to be taught of God...if God teaches it, it is enough. If it is not in the Word, away with it!"*

It is well known that Charles Spurgeon was a Calvinist. He went against the contemporary trend of abandoning, and often denouncing, Calvinism. When the new Metropolitan Tabernacle was opened in 1861, his first series of sermons was on the Five Points of Calvinism.

The Puritan Hope
Charles Spurgeon shared the Puritans' Post-millennial eschatology of hope, that the Great Commission would be fulfilled before the return of Christ.

Mere Christianity
When people asked him concerning his theology he responded that he would like to think of himself as a *"mere Christian"*, but then he would add *"I'm never ashamed to avow myself a Calvinist. I do not hesitate to take the name of Baptist, but if I'm asked what my creed is, I reply, it is Jesus Christ!"*

The most prolific Christian author of all time.

Both of Charles Spurgeon's sons grew up to be preachers. Thomas succeeded his father as pastor of Metropolitan Tabernacle. Charles Jnr. took over the Stockwell Orphanage.

"I charge you therefore before God and the Lord Jesus Christ, who will judge the living and the dead at His appearing and His Kingdom: Preach the Word! Be ready in season and out of season. Convince, rebuke, exhort, with all longsuffering and teaching."　　2 Timothy 4: 1-2

Chapter 32
MARY SLESSOR
Missionary to Nigeria
(1848 - 1915)

Raised in Poverty

Mary Slessor was born, the second of seven children, into a poor and troubled home in Scotland. Although her mother was deeply religious, her father was a violent drunkard, who brought the family to abject poverty, fear and misery. Their one-roomed home had no water, lighting or toilet and hardly any furniture. Mary slept on the floor. Mary's older brother died, leaving her as the oldest surviving child. When her father died, the burden of supporting her family fell upon her young shoulders. At 10 Mary began work as a half-timer, spending half

her time at school and half her time at the mill. At 14 years Mary began working full time - a 58 hour week at the looms. However, her mother ensured that Mary went to Church every Sunday.

Conversion

Mary was frightened into the Kingdom of God by an old widow who warned her of the dangers of hell fire. Horror seized her and she could not sleep until she came to repentance and faith.

Called to Missions

Mary became a tireless Sunday school teacher, who gave herself

Fearless soul winner and pioneer missionary, Mary Slessor.

completely to working in a mission to the slums around the Church that she attended. Her mother's interest in missions, her memory of her older brother (who had often spoken of becoming a missionary) and the death of a younger brother (who also had been dedicated to becoming a missionary in Africa) led Mary to wonder if it was possible that she could take her brother's place! At that time single women in missions were unheard of. The news of the death of David Livingstone in 1874 settled the matter for her.

Training

In 1876, Mary left home in Dundee for missionary training in Edinburgh. The United Presbyterian Church appointed Mary as a missionary teacher and she was assigned to a mission station in Calabar (in present day Nigeria).

Mary boldly confronted witchdoctors and slave traders.

Evangelising Animists

The tribes amongst whom Mary was sent were animists who worshipped the sky, sun and rain, and the spirits of the rocks, rivers and trees. Enslaving people of other tribes was an accepted and entrenched practice.

Enthusiastic Soul Winner

Mary was enthusiastic and impatient, finding the progress of work at the established mission station far too slow. She ached for more demanding tasks, and was reputed to have climbed every tree in the region! Frequent illnesses and attacks of fever, which almost took her life on several occasions, did not seem to diminish her zeal for winning souls for Christ. Mary maintained a cheerful faith.

Missionary to Calabar

Mary was assigned to a mission station at the Old Town on the East bank of the Calabar River. The people in this area were utterly degraded. Amongst the many things which horrified Mary was the practice of killing twins: *"A woman who gave birth to twins was regarded with horror. The belief was that the father of one of the infants was an evil spirit, and that the mother had been guilty of a great sin to bear twins. At least one of the children was believed to be a*

A stained glass window of Mary Slessor caring for orphans in Nigeria.

monster, and so twins were seized, their backs were broken, they were crushed into a calabash or water pot and taken out – not by the doorway, but by a hole broken in the back wall, which was at once built up again, and thrown into the bush, where they were left to be eaten by insects and wild beasts!" Mary's fierce, red-headed passion raged against this massacre of innocents.

The Loss of Her Family
While Mary was desperately ill in 1883, a sister died in Scotland. Then Mary received news of her mother's death, soon followed by news of the death of another sister in Devon. These were dark and difficult days for Mary. *"Home"* no longer existed. She threw herself even more wholeheartedly into serving her new adopted family in Calabar.

A Simple Lifestyle
For practicality, she cut her hair short, abandoned all Western comforts and Western food (except for tea as her only *"luxury"*) and went about barefoot!

Ministering to Body, Mind and Spirit
Mary moved to Creek Town, where she began caring for the many abandoned children. She was constantly interrupted by people coming to her for help. The sick needing treatment, the hungry seeking food

and those with disputes seeking her counsel to bring about resolution. Mary set up schools in Ekenge and Ifako. Soon churches were built alongside the school houses. Amidst rampant witchcraft, drunkenness and immorality, Mary undertook much of the manual work of constructing the school and church buildings herself, as well as the daily tasks of education and evangelism. Mary served as a teacher and nurse, dispensing medicines and conducting four services each Sunday, walking many miles each day.

Healing Bodies and Saving Lives
Once when instructed to heal a dying chief, Mary knew that if she failed she would be blamed for his death. First she got rid of all the witchcraft charms and sacrificed chickens, then she prayed and gave the chief good medicine and nursed him back to health. His wives were particularly grateful as they would have otherwise been killed and buried with the chief. They were keen to learn about *"the Book"*.

The Harvest is Large and the Workers Few
A report of Mary's pioneer exploits in the Missionary Herald prompted a young Scottish carpenter, Charles Ovens, to come out to Africa to help her with the carpentry. His arrival was a great encouragement and practical help.

Missions above Marriage
In 1891, during her furlough in Scotland, Mary was courted by Charles Morrison and became engaged. However, when Mary realised that her marriage would mean settling in Scotland and not returning to Calabar, she broke off the engagement and returned to Africa.

Mother of all the People
At this point the British government recognised that Mary Slessor enjoyed an unparalleled trust from the local people who called her *Eko Kpukpro Owa* - Mother of All the People - and appointed her as a Consular Agent. Later she was promoted to being Vice-President of the

One of the Churches established by Mary Slessor in Nigeria.

Itu Native Court. All the public affairs of the Okoyong were conducted through her. She presided over court cases and ensured that justice was served.

Confronting Witchdoctors

On one occasion as a woman was spread-eagled on the ground to have boiling oil poured on her, Mary boldly intervened and physically prevented the witchdoctor from harming his victim. The people were astounded at her courage in confronting chiefs and witchdoctors - and that she survived! They concluded that it was the power of her God which protected her.

Consular Agent of the Crown

Mary was held in the highest respect by the local people, although the British government would not have approved if they had known of the extent to which she went in her court cases.

Mary never let legal technicalities get in the way of fairness. One plaintiff, while having his suit upheld against another, was punished for not treating his mother properly, failing to maintain adequate hygiene and for neglecting his farm!

Converting Cannibals

Mary was seldom free from illness. When the population moved, she moved with them. In 1903, Mary had the joy of seeing the first seven young Christians baptised, and the first Communion service held. Shortly afterwards she moved to the Itu, which was notorious as a market place for slavery, and where cannibalism was still practised. Soon she had gathered a congregation of 300 and established a school with 68 pupils.

Perseverance

Despite illness and discouragements, Mary was tireless in her hard work and pioneering of mission stations, schools and churches.

Mary Slessor pioneered missions to the Itu tribe.

Fever and sickness constantly afflicted her until in February 1915, at the age of 66, she went to be with the Lord.

A Legacy of Liberty

Because of her efforts, many schools and churches had been established, the killing of twins ceased, slave trading in Calabar was eradicated, drunkenness, killing and witchcraft diminished and most of the people of Calabar came to embrace the Gospel of Christ.

"Those who are wise shall shine like the brightness of the firmament, and those who turn many to righteousness like the stars forever and ever."
Daniel:12:3

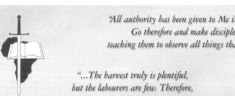

"All authority has been given to Me in Heaven and on earth.
Go therefore and make disciples of all nations...
teaching them to observe all things that I have commanded..."
Matthew 28:18-20

"...The harvest truly is plentiful,
but the labourers are few. Therefore,
pray the Lord of the harvest to send out
labourers into His harvest." Matthew 9:37-38

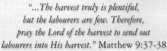

PRAY FOR AFRICA

"He shall have dominion also
from sea to sea, and from
the River to the ends
of the earth. Those who
dwell in the wilderness
will bow before Him,
and His enemies will
lick the dust."
Psalm 72:8-9

"Cush will submit to God."
Psalm 68:31

AFRICA FOR CHRIST

"From beyond the
rivers of Ethiopia, My
worshipers, the daughters
of My dispersed ones,
shall bring My offering."
Zephaniah 3:10

"That at the Name of Jesus every knee should bow, of those
in Heaven, and those on earth, and of those under the earth, and every
tongue should confess that Jesus Christ is Lord to the glory of God the Father."
Philippians 2:10-11

FRONTLINE FELLOWSHIP, PO BOX 74, NEWLANDS, 7725, CAPE TOWN, SOUTH AFRICA. Email: admin@frontline.org.za Web: www.frontline.org.za

Bibliography and Recommended Books

Alfred the Great by Jacob Abbott, 1849

George Whitefield Journals, Banner of Truth, 1960

Jonathan Edwards On Knowing Christ, Banner of Truth, 1990

The Ecclesiastical History of the English People by the Venerable Bede, 731

The Army of Gustavus Adolphus by Richard Brzezinski and Richard Hook, Osprey, 1991

Cromwell by John Buchan, Hodder and Stoughton, 1934

Reluctant Missionary by Edith Buxton, Lutterworth Press, London, 1968

Biblical Christianity by John Calvin, Grace Publications Trust, 1982

Calvin's Calvinism by John Calvin, Reformed Free Publishing Association (originally published at Geneva 1552, as *A Treatise on the Eternal Predestination of God*, translated into English, 1856)

Institutes of the Christian Religion by John Calvin, Westminster Press (originally Geneva, 1559)

Anne Askew: Brave Daughter of the English Reformation, Christian Family Publications, 1999

A History of the English Speaking People by Winston Churchill, 1956

George Whitefield: The Life and Times of the Great Evangelist of the Eighteenth Century Revival (2 volumes) by Arnold Dallimore– 1980

Gustavus Adolphus: A History of the Art of War, by Theodore Dodge, 1890, Boston and New York, Da Capo Press

Light for the City by Lester De Koster, Eerdmans, 2004

Heroes of the Faith by Gene Fedele, 2003

The Life of King Alfred by Dr. Giles

God of Grace and God of Glory: An Account of the Theology of Jonathan Edwards by Stephen Holmes, Eerdmans, 2001

The Life and Character of the Late Reverend Mr Jonathan Edwards by Samuel Hopkins, 1764

Bede: An Early Medieval Historian by Charles W. Jones, 1946

Gustavus Adolphus- A Hero of the Reformation by C A LaCroix, Grace & Truth Books, 2002

Alfred the Great: The Truth Teller, Maker of England by Beatrice Adelaide Lees, 1915

Gutenberg: How One Man Changed the World with Words by John Man, 2002

Jonathan Edwards: A Life by George Marsden, Yale University Press, 2003

A Life of John Calvin by Alister E. McGrath, Baker, 1990.

Jonathan Edwards: A New Biography by Iain Murray, Banner of Truth, 1987
Jonathan Edwards On Revival (including: *A Narrative of Surprising Conversions*, 1736, *Distinguishing Marks of a Work of the Spirit of God*, 1741
Jonathan Edwards Selected Works, edited by Iain Murray and published by Banner of Truth, 1958), Banner of Truth, 1965
Gutenberg and the Art of Printing by Emily Pearson, 1871
George Whitefield and the Great Awakening by John Pollock, 1973
Gustav Adolf the Great (translated by Michael Roberts), 1940, Princeton
Gustavus Adolphus, A History of Sweden 1611-1632, by Michael Roberts, 1958, London, Longmans
Gustavus Adolphus and the Rise of Sweden, by Michael Roberts, 1973, London, English Universities Press
Oliver Cromwell by Theodore Roosevelt, Charles Scribner's Sons, 1900
Johannes Gutenberg, the Inventor of Printing by Victor Scholder, 1963
The Great Christian Revolution by Otto Scott, Uncommon Books, 1994
Church History in Plain Language by Bruce L. Shelley, Word, 1982
Jonathan Edwards: Puritan, Preacher, Philosopher by John Smith, Notre Dame, 1992
The Hidden Dürer by Peter Streider, 1978
Dürer: His Life and Works by Moriz Thausing, 1882
Bede: His Life, Times and Works by A.H. Thompson, 1935
John Wesley: His life and Theology by R.G. Tuttle, Zondevan, Grand Rapids, 1978
This Was John Calvin by Thea Van Halsema, Baker, 1959
John Calvin – Father of Reformed Theology by Sam Wellman, Barbour, 2001
John Calvin by William Wileman, Gospel Mission Press, 1981
Jonathan Edwards: 1703-1758 by Ola Winslow, Macmillan, 1940
The Burning Heart, John Wesley, Evangelist by Skevington Wood, Eerdmans, Grand Rapids, 1967
Great Leaders of the Christian Church by John Woodbridge, Moody Press, 1988

Other Resources Available

Books
Answering Skeptics
Apostles Creed - Firm Foundations for Your Faith
Angola by the Back Door
Biblical Principles for Africa (Also available in Afrikaans and French)
Biblical Worldview Manual
Character Assassins - Dealing with Ecclesiastical Tyrants & Terrorists
David Livingstone - Man of Prayer and Action
Discipleship Handbook
Fantastic but True - A Manual for Working with Children's Ministries
Faith Under Fire in Sudan
Fight for Life - A Pro-Life Handbook for Southern Africa
Finding Freedom from the Pornography Plague (also in Afrikaans)
Going Through - Even if the Door is Closed
Great Commission Manual
Greatest Century of Missions
Greatest Century of Reformation
Holocaust in Rwanda (also available in French and Afrikaans)
In the Killing Fields of Mozambique
Make a Difference - A Christian Action Handbook for Southern Africa
Pink Agenda - Sexual Revolution and the Ruin of the Family
Practical Discipleship
Putting Feet to Your Faith
Reforming Our Families
Security and Survival in Unstable Times
Slavery, Terrorism and Islam - The Historical Roots & Contemporary Threat
South Africa - Renaissance or Reformation?
The Christian at War (also available in Afrikaans, German and Spanish)
The Ten Commandments - God's Perfect Law of Liberty
War Against God

DVDs
3 Days in Sudan (25min)
Sudan the Hidden Holocaust (55 min)
Terrorism and Persecution - Understanding Islamic Jihad (55 min)
Evangelisng in the War Zones (35 min)

AUDIO CDs, boxsets and MP3s
Answering Skeptics
Biblical Character Studies
Biblical Worldview Summit
Great Commission Course
Heroes of the Faith
Hunger for Revival
Muslim Evangelism Workshop
Soldiers for Christ
The Great Reformation

 Christian Liberty Books

P.O. Box 358 Howard Place 7450 Cape Town South Africa
Tel & Fax: (021) 689-7478
Email: admin@christianlibertybooks.co.za
Website: www.christianlibertybooks.co.za

Examples of Excellence

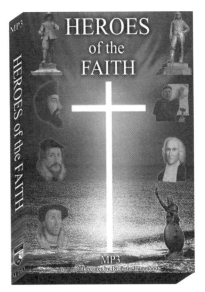

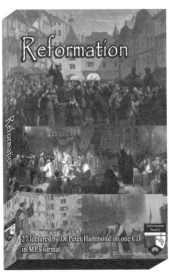

Christian Liberty Books

P.O. Box 358 Howard Place 7450 Cape Town South Africa
Tel & Fax: (021) 689-7478
Email: admin@christianlibertybooks.co.za
Website: www.christianlibertybooks.co.za

Do You Want to Change Your World?
Attend...

Put Feet to Your Faith!

The Great Commission Course

Is the Great Commission your supreme ambition?
Plan now to attend this uniquely practical missionary course.
Previous participants of the GCC have written:

"Outstanding. Completely amazing!"
"The lectures were incredible and inspiring!"
"Well organised and well thought through."
"Very practical"
"The best missions programme that I've ever seen."
"This is a turning point in my life'
"The best organised missions course I have ever known."
"Highly recommended"
"This is reality!"

For information or to register contact:
Frontline Fellowship
PO Box 74, Newlands, 7725,
Cape Town
Tel: (021) 689-4480
Email: admin@frontline.org.za
Web: www.frontline.org.za

About the Author

Peter Hammond is a missionary who has pioneered evangelistic outreaches in the war zones of Mozambique, Angola and Sudan. Since 1982, often travelling by off-road motorbike, Peter has travelled hundreds of thousands of miles to deliver Bibles to persecuted Christians in Africa and Eastern Europe. He has proclaimed the Gospel in 34 countries on four continents. In the course of his missionary activities Peter has been ambushed, come under aerial and artillery bombardments, been stabbed, shot at, beaten by mobs, arrested and imprisoned. On some mission trips he has flown far behind enemy lines to the beleaguered Nuba Mountains in Central Sudan with tonnes of Bibles, books and relief aid. He has then walked throughout the war devastated Nuba Mountains showing the *Jesus* film in Arabic, proclaiming the Gospel, training pastors and evading enemy patrols.

Dr. Peter Hammond is the Founder and Director of Frontline Fellowship, the Director of the Christian Action Network and the Chairman of The Reformation Society. He is the author of *Faith Under Fire in Sudan, Holocaust in Rwanda*, the *Great Commission Manual, Putting Feet to Your Faith, In the Killing Fields of Mozambique, The Greatest Century of Missions, Biblical Principles for Africa, The Discipleship Handbook, Slavery, Terrorism and Islam, The Greatest Century of Reformation, The Power of Prayer Handbook, Practical Discipleship* and *Answering Skeptics*. He has co-authored or contributed to: *Reforming Our Families, War Against God, Fight for Life, Make a Difference, The Pink Agenda, Character Assassins* and *South Africa - Renaissance or Reformation?* He is the Editor of both Frontline Fellowship News and the Christian Action magazine, as well as Contributing Editor of JOY! Magazine.

Peter was born in Cape Town (in 1960) and brought up in Bulawayo (in what was then war-torn Rhodesia - now Zimbabwe). He was converted to Christ in 1977, worked for Scripture Union and Hospital Christian Fellowship, served in the South African Defence Force and studied at Baptist Theological College, Cape Town. Peter is married to Lenora (whose missionary parents Rev. Bill and Harriett Bathman, have pioneered missionary work, mostly into Eastern Europe, for over 60 years). Peter and Lenora have been blessed with four children: Andrea, Daniela, Christopher and Calvin.